FACE YOUR SELF

Achieve Your True Potential

Pamela Laurence

Face Your Self®, Inc.
www.faceyourself.com

ISBN: 0615568793
ISBN-13: 9780615568799
Library of Congress Control Number: 2011944085
Face Your Self®, Colchester, VT

DEDICATION

To all those frequencies dancing in the four winds.
Unborn yet alive in Consciousness.

To all those frequencies that attract together through
Fire and ice birthing a new life
walking upon this Earth and breathing its air.

To all those frequencies that one-day unborn
Completing a cycle
Alive with That which is Love.

ACKNOWLEDGEMENTS

This book is a blend of many teachings and of my personal experiences. In my life I have had the honor and pleasure of many wonderful teachers: Swami Satchananda's Integral Yoga, Rammurti S. Mishra, M.D. of Ananda Ashram's meditation and self-analysis teachings, Osho's delightful way, Sharmaji's meditation and love. Rita Dombroff, my aunt who lived to 105 year, taught me to stay flexible and to be silly and laugh at myself, my Grandmother, Josie Marchesano, taught me unconditional love, Andre Enard showed me the way of the work of George Gurdjieff. I also have had the wonderful opportunity to study programs and receive certificates in the Science of Mind, Dr. Earnest Holmes teachings and was initiated in Feng Shui teachings according to Grandmaster Lin-Yun.

I thank my parents, Helen and John, for their major role of inspiration in my writing this book - My Mom taught me to see the beauty in Nature and my Dad taught me inner strength – a perfect yin/yang match. I thank my husband, Barry Dimson for his unconditional love, encouragement, and scrabble-playing eye as to the spelling and some edits of this book.

I thank my dear friend Briney Frange, who many times was like a second mother to me, for her constant love. I thank my friend Amy Mims for having me teach so many years at her school in CT and for her dear friendship. I thank Nancy Butler-Ross for her assistance in early editing of this manuscript.

I thank the stars above for my two children, Nicole Blythe, and Benjamin John, who both have given to me so much more than I could ever imagine. I love you both.

WELCOME TO FACE YOUR SELF

Face Your Self is a hands-on, multi-dimensional approach to wellness, offering you the foundational tools to transform and empower your mind, body and home to *achieve your true potential.* Face Your Self is based on the concept that YOU are a major part of the learning process. You must look within and without yourself to know whom you are to bring about the change you desire. You may need to dissolve, realign and soften old energy patterns that no longer serve you. This book is filled with ancient thoughts, exercises, explorations, practices, meditations, breathing and love. Through sincere self-talk and your quest for knowledge and personal growth, you will come to a place of self-awareness. You will come to a place of self-love, inner peace, power, beauty and joy. You will come to realize that we all - and that is everyone - are one.

Life is reflective as a mirror – a magic mirror. You can turn this mirror to face outside yourself and you can turn this mirror to face inside yourself - either way, you are facing your self: your brilliant, wonderful, powerful self. You can achieve what some would call magic when you become aware of this tool. This work is all about being responsible to yourself and others. It is about being in charge and mindful of your thoughts, motivations and actions.

MISSION STATEMENT FOR ONESELF

Wherever I look, I Face My Self. It takes work and constant reminders of what is real in my world. My true nature is happiness and this happiness is there always to see and feel once I understand and remove the obstacles and beliefs that I have attached to that are not for my highest good, which are blocking, tarnishing and manipulating my life.

Wherever I look, I Face My Self. If you are not doing
well than neither am I.
In reality, we are all one, breathing the same breath of life.
What I do to you,
I do to myself. Life is reflective as a mirror - what I see is what I get.

When I Face My Self, I am self-empowered with a light heart.
And it is good.

TABLE OF CONTENTS

INTRODUCTION

NATURE IS YOUR BEST TEACHER

Go with the flow,
Bend with the breeze,
Many of life's lessons are learned
From rivers and trees.

The Nature of the world does not change
- Zohar

Your true nature is happiness and you are perfect, whole and complete just as you are right this very moment. You are a natural being living in a universe of natural mathematical and spiritual laws. You are an energy being – living in the human body experience (imagine it something like coming from another place and putting on your human body spacesuit to communicate, live and breathe here on Earth). In reality, this life experience is not about money and power, fame and popularity. This life experience is the vibration of love.

In your spacesuit body experience, if you are not aware, you begin to attach to, identify and experience your body as yourself not just as your spacesuit. You attach to the senses, feelings and emotions that you experience through your body. You experience your thinking brain as your whole mind and attach to its countless thoughts and feelings that really are not part of your true nature.

Once you begin to understand the causes of your suffering you can do something about it. And once you relax and breathe, you can take some time to reflect and feel your soul nature. Through self-discipline and training in your mind, body and soul, you can step back from your day-to-day illusory self and life experiences, and learn tools which will enable you to end your tormented suffering. Life will go on (people will be born and they will die, careers will come and go, relationships will come and go) but you will live your life in natural harmony. You will see clearly through heightened awareness and your thoughts, speech and actions will change. Yes, you may experience sadness (we all do) but you will not become the sadness. You may express anger, but you will not become the anger. With mindfulness along with concentration and your will, you will create a life of happiness and beauty and live out your life as a natural *understanding being*.

After a storm and destruction, the sun comes out and flowers bloom as if the storm never happened. There is a part of you that is the same you as you were at five years of age and will be you at ninety-five years of age - that inner spirit of light and joy, who is creative, loving and expressive. In reality, you do not change just as the nature of the world does not change. What looks like change are actually the storms and stuff you have attached to that *shape-shifted* you into what you are today. Programming and life experiences that you have accepted, learned and processed into your mind, body and home - belief systems that cause you to miss seeing and knowing the true, beautiful, natural being that you are - this may be blocking you from your highest good.

To Face Your Self is an opportunity to renew, mend and restore your mind, your body and your spirit (which is reflected in your home and life). It is an opportunity to live your life going with the flow of your true nature and reflecting that into your life. This is a program of suggested small steps that will first help you to become aware of your attachments and beliefs and then to change the unwanted and unnatural programmed patterns of your mind, body, and home that no longer serve you. At that point you can look to manifest your dreams.

WHY FACE YOUR SELF WORKS

This is a guidebook back to your self. It works because the power is given to you – you are not looking outside yourself to others for the answers to your life. You are the master of your own life with compassion and wisdom for all. You will be given tools to find your own strength through self-examination and through mirrored reflections in your life. You will be supported and empowered and made to feel good about yourself if you don't already. It works because this "approach" wishes no harm on anyone – actually it wishes that everyone achieve his or her highest good. This is not a religion – though it touches on truths that weave throughout all religions. This guidebook is written to empower you. It is written with the intention to give and reinforce you with tools to be your own master and creator.

By removing your mind chaos, body anarchy and home clutter (which is an ongoing process), you will begin to see clearly. Only after you truly see clearly, will you recognize what is real and what is not real and understand what motivates you. You will be able to make unattached, lucid, powerful, focused decisions in designing your world into the world of your dreams and create not only for yourself but also for the highest good of all.

Everyone is affected by natural laws (or principals). We will be working with these principals throughout this book, weaving them into your daily understanding of how they operate. You cannot escape them. You will learn and understand methods of creating a *Magic Mirror* all around you, which will sustain your visions and support you throughout your life.

Science has proven that all gases, liquids, and solids vibrate at different rates; t*here is a **vibration** to everything*. Where you focus your attention and what you surround yourself with, affects and alters your personal vibration. You have an opportunity to learn how to intentionally choose, shift and change your choices and thus change your vibration to magnetically **attract** into your life your goals and to live a life of happiness even with your day-to-day issues of living right at this moment. You will learn how your breath can change your vibration. You will see how other people affect your vibration. You will learn tools to shift a sadness vibration to a vibration of happiness. You will learn tools and methods to shift fear into courage and insecurity into healthy self-esteem.

There is another principal, which has perhaps the most consequence to us all, and that is: *everything is a thought first.* Call this the principal of **mentality.** Everything is of the mind first, and that is a beautiful, wonderful and powerful thing (think of John Lennon's song, *Imagine*). Imagine it and it can happen. When you understand the power that your thinking, words and deeds have on you and the world around you along with the other principals, you will naturally and unsurprisingly want to live an honest life and think, speak and act for the highest good of all.

BREAKING LIFETIMES OF UNWANTED LEARNED THINKING AND BEHAVIORS

It is important to look at and question collective choices from groups such as media, religion, political parties and families and understand if such groups have programmed your beliefs and whether you are one of the sheep being herded here and there, or you are truly living with beliefs that are from a knowingness which comes from your own heart. Sometimes, some people can find it can be very difficult to even begin to question such beliefs if these beliefs have become so hardened and set in their life that one will not even be open to look at or listen to another perspective because of such things as fear, guilt, anger or hatred.

You are born into this world through your parents. They give you a name, country, religion, and standard of life to start you off. You learn lessons in schools and from your friends and neighbors. You grow up and listen to the news of the day, join clubs and groups, and buy into the mass-market advertising of that region of the world in which you live. This is all neither good nor bad – it just is. Your goal now is to see clearly – with no judgments and no delusions and illusions– to see just what is. In the Talmud there is a saying: *We do not see things as they are, we see them as we are.* Can you see things as they are?

There are no judgments of good or bad allowed of your self or toward anyone in working with Face Your Self and looking in the "Magic Mirror". This is your life and your life is that which it is because of time, space and circumstance. You can change those undesired grooved patterns with work by using the exercises provided in each chapter. Who are you? To get to the root of who you are, you must first strip yourself naked and see yourself with no attachments: no names, religions, political parties, and fancy clothes or cars to attach to. You must strip yourself of all upsets, money issues, illnesses, and unhealthy relationships. When you have truly done this you will begin to see that you are all and nothing at the same time. Working with the Face Your Self exercises in each chapter, you can observe with compassion and without judgment the patterns and beliefs that you own. Throughout this book, you will be guided in a multidimensional way to look at the "stuff " of your mind, body and home. Once you see clearly and are aware and present – then you will be able to manifest (create) that which is good for all – including you.

YOU ARE WHAT YOU THINK

Clutter, Litter, Disorder, Confusion, Things, Muddle, Stuff, Gobbledygook…

Most people have clutter in their home and their office. But, there is also a type of clutter that collects in your mind and body. There is clutter in your neighborhood, town, state and country. There are many types of clutter, which cloud, cover and hinder the true beauty and freedom of what and who you are – what we as a nation and as a world population would be if we were all aware, natural beings without need of fears, greed, hate, and power clutter. It is impossible to truly separate all the forms of clutter, yet in this book I will attempt to break clutter down into chaos of your mind, anarchy of your body and clutter in your home. I will use the examples of disorder in your work and confusion in the game of life as a means to give you a broader perspective.

When you Face Your Self, you must focus and have clear intention. By removing the chaos in your mind, healing your body anarchy and removing the clutter in your home (which I relate to your spirit), you will begin to see clearly, which will then empower you to come into alignment with your true self. This will then enable you to create and attract the life of your dreams without distortion.

Observe the strong thought patterns that appear when you least expect them or ones that crop up when you feel insecure or are feeling weakened. Do you ever get the feeling, "I'm not good enough?" Your thinking and feelings of this nature set up a strong energetic attraction around you, which looks like a beacon in a storm, to other similar like vibrations in thinking and feelings. Essentially your thinking can become so powerful, that you create this thought pattern into a reality. Your thinking also affects your feelings, breathing, speaking, acting, and responding. Your thinking creates who you are and attracts that life experience you think about. Your thinking and your life's experiences are mutually interdependent. Recurring thoughts and feelings create a magnetic attraction around your being. Essentially, you create these thought patterns into reality by attracting to you that which you think.

HOW TO USE THIS PERSONAL GUIDEBOOK

Each chapter is intentionally placed in the order in which it appears and intentionally filled with exercises and poetry as a form of thought for meditation. This poetry helps deliver you to your natural self. It is in the simple life that the grand is proclaimed. There is a **rhythm** to everything. It is in the heart of man that love begins and ends. It is in the simple action where greatness can be found.

It is suggested that this guidebook be read and worked from beginning to end. After that, you can pick it up and read any chapter independently as you wish. I do recommend you reread and rework this book at least every year as a check-up, such as you would go to the medical doctor or the dentist for a yearly checkup.

You will find that none of this work is linear – meaning that you cannot do one thing and then look to accomplish the next step. Everything taught is inter-related, is all woven together to create one basket of life - your life. The lessons will be presented in a somewhat linear form but remember this - everything you think, say and do effects everything you think, say and do.

Facing Your Self is about the interior design of your "Being" and the exterior reflections you see in the world around you and how each mirrors the other (**as within, so without**). In a sense you will be designing your life from the inside out and from the outside in. It is easy to be at peace and feel at one with the world on the top of a hillside, on a beautiful sunny day. Usually when people are in such a beautiful setting they exhale with a big sigh and release all pent-up tensions and thoughts for the moment. But life is always throwing something at us - it takes constant work and mindfulness to feel that peace in your day-to-day life in the center of your being. It can be done with practice, just like anything else - you must be taught how to do this.

I will show you how to break unwanted patterns of thinking that have been grooved into you for years and how to create fresh, new positive and healthy patterns so you can live an effortless life even under stress. The objective is for you to live a creative, healthy life of happiness, abundance and balance and to notice and be aware when something is not right (when you get a feeling of dis-ease or a bad habit) so you can address it, face it, massage it and understand where it comes from and then let it go. When you learn how to Face Your Self, you will learn how to live a life in harmony with nature: its seasons and elements, its time and place. Your nature - your true nature – your wealth, health and happiness is truly found by TRANSFORMING YOUR INNER SELF.

Sit quietly right now and exhale - imagine letting go of all toxic waste of your mind/ body and then inhale. Breathe in... and while you inhale - imagine and feel that you are perfect, whole and complete - imagine a whole new slate - a new chapter to your life. You are starting again. Each breath is like a new life.

Wherever you are, you are seeing you and living with yourself. So you may as well Face Your Self with joy, love, poise, and compassion. Get ready to become who you know in your heart that you truly are: a happy, prosperous, healthy, vital, fun-loving, joyous person with a peaceful, serene inner heart. Happiness is your true nature. *You can achieve your true potential!*

This is a personal guidebook. You can write in it or I suggest that you get a special notebook (I call it your Magic Notebook) that you can use for your exercises. The Face Your Self exercises encourage you to observe your life, thoughts, and actions throughout the day. You will learn how to observe your life and the interrelationship between your mind, body and home.

Happiness cannot be pursued. It is your birthright. You will learn how you can create a paradise right here on earth - right now - for yourself and those you love. When you do this program, you must recognize and be honest with yourself about what you experienced in your life that brought you to the present moment and look to the reality of your present experience. You must not lie to yourself (if you can't be honest with yourself, who can you be honest with?). You are required to look at the duality of yourself – your bright side and your dark side (in reality you are not either). What you think, what you do, what you eat, where you live, what household products you use, what you read, what music you listen to, who your friends are – all of this has a powerful effect and affect on your life. It also directly or indirectly affects your family, your neighborhood, and eventually the world in which you live. An added advantage of Facing Your Self is that Nature (and that includes all beings on earth) will also reap the benefit of your fresh natural thinking. Are you willing to drop all pretenses and give it a try? Are you ready for a transformation?

THERE ARE TWO ASPECTS (OR SIDES) TO FACE YOUR SELF.

One aspect of Facing Your Self (and a major focus of this book) is looking at your interior world - the importance of self-analysis - looking at the interior design of your mind/body/home connection – looking within. You learn from your own experiences, but you want to understand *why* you think, say and do the things that you do. There is an American Indian saying, "You can tell the child not to touch the campfire - that he will get burned. But, until that child touches the campfire and gets burned, he will not learn the lesson." Nothing teaches like personal experience, yet, I see many people speaking and doing the same thing over and over and wondering why their life is getting nowhere, their diet is not working, their relationships have the same situations time and again and life is an endless trap of dissatisfaction and unhappiness. What is that saying about insanity - "Insanity is doing the same thing twice and expecting different results."

The other aspect (side) of the Face Your Self is looking at your exterior world and observing what is reflected back to you. Your environment corresponds to who you are. On subtle levels and sometimes not so subtle, your environment mirrors who you are – Your environment (your home, your dorm room, that space you spend much of your time) is a reflection of your inner psyche – your spirit. In addition to your surroundings, other people and life experiences can be used as a very strong tool to knowing yourself. Ask yourself how something makes you feel. What does it make you think about? Sometimes what others say is not really about you – can you tell the difference? The patterns you have learned from your parents, families, teachers, society, and friends and at times from your children (for those of you who are old enough to have children) through the years shape you in mind, body, and emotions and weave what will become your spiritual breath. Sometimes you are reacting against something to rebel. Some of us have misaligned motivations. In reality, when you look outside yourself, you must look to yourself to see if you too have that which you accuse another of in your own personal "cupboard of clutter". If you see it and judge it, a good bet is that it is in you too. If you see it and have compassion, a good bet is that you understand and can relate either from your own personal experience or from your own wisdom and awareness to whatever is taking place. Where do you stand when you take action?

As within, so without – there is a **correspondence** between everything. With the Face Your Self program, you will become your own detective, looking without and within for bits and pieces to discover and understand the chaos, anarchy and clutter in your life. You will face the burdens that you carry around. You will understand the consequences of your choices and decisions (**cause and effect**). You will become not only the detective, but also the master of your own life.

If you are not aware, your exterior home will also affect and effect your "interior self" and cause you to absorb the unwanted vibrations and energy that surrounds you which may cause you unwanted thoughts or feelings such as unhappiness or feelings of lack. **As Within, So Without** works both ways. I once had a client who was having marital problems and self-worth issues. He had gained weight and found himself drinking more than he ever had. It turned out that he was surrounded in his home by hand-me-down furnishings from his mother-in-law who also belittled him at every chance. He never spoke up. He had given up control of his own inner home and his exterior home reflected that back to him. (Mind you, they could afford to purchase new furniture.) Once pointed out what was happening in his life, he made changes and took responsibility for his life and his own choices. The marriage became stronger, they bought new furniture and he started working out and felt much better about himself.

Your life naturally affects others as their life affects you. When you love yourself, when you are healthy and happy, your life will naturally affect those around you in a positive way and that happiness and positive energy will radiate around the world and be reflected back to you like a mirrored circle.

CHAPTER ONE

THE MAGIC MIRROR: THE SECRET TO A HAPPY LIFE

In the looking glass
What magic I see
When I look with clarity.

Do you want to be something that you are not?

With all honor, love and respect: imagine for one moment that there was no Buddha, Jesus, Moses, Mohammad or other spiritual teachers whose teachings you could follow. Imagine there were no sciences, no religions or councilors to fall back upon or to tell you what you should be thinking, feeling, experiencing or how to do something. Imagine yourself sitting in your world – observing and learning everything new for yourself for the first time. You would listen to the wind and observe the stars. You would experience the seasons and give fresh names to things according to your observations. Connected and part of the world around you, you would come to know yourself.

YOU ARE THE "ATTRACTOR" OF YOUR LIFE.

When you look into a mirror – do you feel ***Attractive***? That is, are you attracting to you, that which you see or that which you imagine you see?

In our current society, we have many choices, which may seem like a good thing on the surface. For example, if you watch TV or read magazines and newspapers, your attention is filled with advertisements for hundreds of diets, diet foods, diet pills, diet gurus, diet surgeries, and diet spas – still people are overweight. There is a plethora of priests, rabbis, monks and ministers, yet we still have a world without peace. Are we a society with too many choices where we find that we never can choose? There is a Zen proverb that states, "Too many options causes insanity".

Are we also a society with no time to relax for the multiple choices we have in malls, shopping networks, catalogs, magazines, and the internet that keep us on a wheel of searching for more, more, more – with the golden carrot always just out of reach. Do you feel that happiness is just out of your reach?

Are we also a society with too much time on our hands? We have the handiness of cell phones and internet connections, washing machines and laundry services, personal care services and commuter jet services, fast food delivery services and easy pill popping services to solve every imaginable physical and mental problem. Yet, have the computers, cell phones and the multiple personal services freed you up to become more creative, less anxiety ridden and intuitive? I notice people more stressed out and pressured for time than I ever noticed before. All of these services and choices have become a form of blockage if they keep you from living a life that is not in touch with your true nature. Happiness cannot be pursued. Happiness is there for you always when you stop gripping onto things and relax for a moment - let go.

The sun still rises and sets at the same speed it did back in early Egyptian days of the Kings. It takes a rose the same amount of time to bud and bloom as it did during Napoleon Bonaparte's crowning as Emperor of the French in 1804. You can eat faster and faster, but your digestive tract still needs the same amount of time to digest your food as in your great, great, grandparent's era. With the Face Your Self program, you will bring your attention back to natural laws and natural ways (still using current technology if you wish). You are a natural being. You are part of nature. There is no reason that you cannot come to the same realizations on your own that all the great spiritual leaders and teachers taught throughout time.

Wherever you go, whatever you do, you bring your interior home with you. This is your real home no matter where you are in life. If this personal interior home is blocked and not healthy, you will endure obstacles and restrict how much wealth you experience (and that does not translate into just money), how many opportunities you see, how many relationships have the possibility of entering into your life.

What is that saying, "Home is where your heart is?" Are you at home wherever you go and with whomever you meet?   You have the power and ability (unless you are very ill) to make and create your exterior home to reflect, mirror, and support you in keeping the vision of how you feel in your inner home – your heart – any time and any where you go. That means you can design your home, studio, dorm room to reflect (or reject) your hopes and wishes. If you travel, you can bring along a special pillow or stone to place in your hotel room to reflect to you the peace, comfort and security in your home away from home.

You carry all wealth, peace, health and happiness within you – it starts right there. Let that brilliance be reflected without in all aspects of your life no matter what your financial, career, or life situation is at the present moment.

WHAT IS YOUR MEASURE OF WEALTH AND HAPPINESS?

Our exterior wealth and happiness is different for each of us. What does Wealth and Happiness mean to you? Have you bought into the idea that you need a huge house with twenty high-priced cars in your garage along with designer products and private jets? My grandmother seemed happiest and felt extremely wealthy when she had the whole family over for dinner and she was spending the entire day in her kitchen cooking for us.

MINI EXERCISE

Ask yourself right now what is your motivation for wanting_____(you fill in the blank). Is it a want or a need?

The work outlined in Face Your Self is like the game of golf. In reality, you are playing only against yourself. You can lie about the lie of the ball and the number of strokes you took and maybe you will get away with it on the scorecard – but you know in your heart you cheated and you know when you really win. You truly win when you can look at yourself in the mirror of life and know that you are at one with yourself – you are not divided -you glow with a quiet joy.

HOW DO YOU MANIFEST YOUR DREAMS?

If you do not act presently but act from your past, your future is based on your past (since you are always bringing your past to the present). This is relevant since most people live as mechanical beings so you can easily predict the future for them. It is mathematical: this thought plus that feeling = that future. Most people repeat their past, many even until the day they die. It is like a wheel that keeps turning where you cannot bring in anything new. You cannot have a breakthrough because you may have a breakdown.

How do you get off a wheel that is turning? You sit in its center. You let it all turn around you but you are not turning with it. You must learn to sit in your center. It is the only place where you are alert and awake. It is here that you manifest your dreams with clear, mindful work and intention. When you are in your center, you are aware of those thoughts and patterns of behavior that no longer serve you or your life. You begin to see clearly without ulterior motives and intentions blurring and distorting your vision. You will function naturally with the time, space and circumstance of your life. You will keep a clear vision, and that will be a magnet for your future.

A THOUGHT TO REMEMBER:

Be Careful What You Wish For

While doing the Face Your Self exercises be careful and very specific of what you wish for. Sometimes what you think you want is not what you really want in your heart. You must be very clear and always ask for that which you wish or better (this way you do not attach to your wish and open opportunities that you may not even have imagined to come your way). If you had three wishes what would they be? See your wish as already being a reality and try it on for size. For example, the thought of having a baby right now seems cute and wonderful. But, the reality, even if I could have a baby at my age, would be different on a day-to-day living experience for me.

The unseen world is much larger than the seen world. What that means is that the unseen world (the world that holds all the yet-to-be-manifested creations of your intentions) is like a vast "genie cookie jar" just waiting for you to put your request in so you can take a delicious bite.

I often say, "The proof is in the pudding no matter how long it takes the pudding to cook." What this means to me is, once you know, feel, and declare something, it <u>is</u> such. When you focus clearly on a destination and you walk toward it, a type of magic happens; (I write more about this in the Appendix, About the Author) your goal begins to come to you with very little effort. This is a very powerful law: that of **attraction**. For example, let us say that you are in your 40's and you would like to become a doctor. If this is truly your heart's desire, there is nothing to stop you, except your own fears or doubts, which deplete your energy for your desire. Yes, you may have to take undergraduate biology and chemistry classes. Yes, you may get frustrated from time to time. Yes, you may have to realign your whole life. It may be years before you actually get into medical school and then graduate – but you can do it if it is what you <u>really, really</u> want. Creation is at the thought point when you combine it with your will and clear intention. That point creates the opportunity for an explosion of a new life current. Then you have to embrace it and work it! Time is not of the essence when it comes to creation (you can't force a rose to open). Time is only a mental thing of the past and the future – Reality is here now!

A THOUGHT TO REMEMBER

Always Work for the Highest Good of All

In the Face Your Self practice of self-analysis, you are always working for the highest good of all. It is important to state and intend that all of your wishes and desires be always for the utmost good of all. You wish no harm on anyone. If there are people you do not care for, it is best to bless them and energetically release them. Allow them to live their own life. There's no need to keep anger and hatred inside of you. Let them go. This work is for the supreme good of all. It works with the laws of nature and those laws affect us all.

RECOGNIZING UNIVERSAL PRINCIPLES

By understanding universal principals, you will become aware of Divine energy flowing in and through all living things. Divine energy is sometimes called Tao, Father, Mother or Great One, or, God. This energy flows in and through every living thing and moves with universal principles. It is flowing in and through you now.

MINI EXERCISE

Hold your hands up in front of you and feel the pulsation radiating out from your palms. You are alive with this spiritual, divine energy. There is one Life. There is one Breath and It is flowing in and through you right now. Perhaps you can even hear it ringing an OM sound in your ears right now. You are a part of It. It is a Creative Life Force that you can clearly connect to when you are not muddled. You are not separate from it.

Unlike man-made laws or dogma, Universal principles found in the Kaballion (in the Appendix of this book) of: correspondence, vibration, polarity, rhythm, causation, gender, and mentality are multinational because they are Universal. They are basic principles, recognized tens of centuries ago, which are the basis for many esoteric and present day teachings. They deal in the mastery of your own mind force. You will learn how to change one kind of mental vibration (what I call mind chaos) into healthy mental vibrations to focus and attract the life you want. You will become aware that you live each day, hour and minute with these forces or principles of nature just as you live with Divine Life energy flowing in and through you. You will learn to work and live beneficially with these principles for the highest good of all, which includes your own good. You cannot pay off someone to avoid punishment or run and hide from these laws. Universal Laws are realities in the purest, most truthful sense. They affect everyone everywhere – the good, the bad, the ugly and the beautiful people ... no one can escape, nor would you want to, if you live your life honestly and naturally. By working from this universal perspective in a healthy way, all of your actions will benefit mankind and the nature spirits of our environment.

Where your mind goes... your energy will follow.

Where your mind goes...your body will follow.

Where your mind goes... your home will follow.

MINI EXERCISE:

I recommend that you get a "magic" notebook (you can call it magic) to keep by your side (you will need it for further exercises throughout this book). Jot down (for just one day – do not get obsessed with this task) all of the things that come across your path, which in turn attracts your attention. I suggest that you only jot down those things that ring a bell with you. For example, you may hear a commercial jingle on the radio about life insurance – you do not need life insurance, however, you notice that when you watched the commercial you begin to think about your parents and their health, which leads you to start to worry about what you are going to do with them, which leads you to search your purse or glove compartment for a snack because eating has become a grooved pattern of survival under stress. The point of this exercise is to notice how your mind, body and home are interrelated, and how this realization will help you to start becoming aware and responsible for your life and your life choices. Another example: You bump your toe (a simple act that can happen to anyone), then all of a sudden you feel anger, the next thing you notice is you are cursing about your neighbor and then you feel overwhelmed and tired. The toe bumping had nothing to do with your neighbor but in your mind and body, there was an energetic connection. Here is another example: You walk into your home and see a broken faucet. Drip, drip, drip, you wanted to workout but now you feel stagnant and toxic – you start getting a headache – you run to take some drug... You will be able to become more aware of the connection between your mind, body and home as you practice with the help of additional exercises throughout the book.

In reality, all you have is yourself. If you live in a one-room walk up or live in a 50-room mansion, you still are you and your breath - your sense of self will reflect that. Life changes. Sometimes we move from a big house to a small house. Sometimes we move from a small house to a big house. Do not let the circumstance of your life disturb you – you are still you no matter where you live. For example, I have known people who became very wealthy and got so impressed with their self-importance that they lost everything they had. I have known others who lost everything they had and still projected wealth and prosperity. We all have seen a poor area where there is one house or window with geraniums and pretty curtains in the window, or a wealthy neighborhood where there is a home that looks unhealthy or not cared for. The same with people – you can read their life force, their energy, their posture. What is it that keeps some people positive no matter what happens in their life, and some people negative no matter what happens in their life? Why do some people keep on going and some people give up? Could it be that those who always seem happy know a secret? They go with the flow of life and live life with ease, despite the hardships.

A THOUGHT TO REMEMBER

We Are All One

Two sides of Face Your Self are: looking within and looking without. Wherever you look, wherever you go, you face your self. When I look at you I see myself. We are all one, breathing one breath. We are one network of life force flowing in and through us all. We are all connected (and not just by cellular telephones, the internet, twitter and goodness knows what else in the future).

LIFE AFFECTS US ALL

We are all responsible for our own lives. This may sound hard to believe and harder to stomach but it is true. Life affects us all and there are certainly times that you are going to feel unhappy, sad or blue. There will be times that you feel unworthy and unjustified. There will be times when you are angry or fearful. This is normal and human. There are times when we need to lean on a friend or family member for support. But remember, it is not natural when unhappiness, depression, unworthiness, or anger takes on a life of its own, where day after day, week after week, year after year all of your actions come from this adopted (grooved) belief system at your root being. We want to learn to use the anger, sadness, or whatever you may be feeling but not to become it. Observe yourself. I once had a teacher who said, "Create the illusion – don't become it."

It is not your circumstance, which makes you sad or blue. It is the way you think about your circumstance. This thinking is a learned process and it takes deep work to change your thinking patterns. You learn and assimilate into your core systems your thinking and emotional responses from your early childhood family and school interactions – from events in your life that may have been traumatic and stressful. These patterns will most likely be with you for your lifetime, but they do not have to rule your life. Embracing the Face Your Self principles will empower you to become aware of your root feelings and thinking patterns. They will help you look to see if there is, or is not, a reality any more to your thoughts. Then you can address them.

The Face Your Self approach is a simple multi-dimensional systematic way of:

- Understanding that life is life and things happen.
- Understanding your true nature.
- Recognizing the types of mind chaos, body anarchy and home clutter that you do not want to own. This includes Post Traumatic Stress Situations.
- Self-examination, through numerous exercises, to change old grooved unwanted patterns of thinking and behavior.
- Understanding the Mind/Body/Home Connection
- Understanding how your home reflects and affects your life

- Removing the stuff (including people) from your life that no longer serve you.
- Making new natural choices for yourself with tools and exercises to allow you to stay on course and attract your wishes into reality.
- Working with universal principles to magically live your life in a natural way.
- Putting it all together to create a world of peace, harmony, and joy.

Face Your Self works by simply having you become aware and responsible for your own life: your thinking, feelings and actions. You cannot hide behind your possessions, body, career, friends or mate. You cannot live on other people's experiences. You cannot feel with others' responses. There are well-meaning parents, teachers, clergy, family and friends who may have your best interests in mind and/or imposed their truth and thinking on you. Ultimately, you come of age and you must look at your own life and own your own life. You must Face Your Self to be true to yourself.

This does not mean you would negate everything that your parents, teachers and friends have said, or avoid them altogether. They all can serve as the magic mirror for you - they love you and want the best for you - they are doing the best that they can, given their life's experiences.

I have had many wonderful, inspirational teachers who have taught and shown me wonderful ways to see and live life and that it is good. I welcome new teachers to come into my life, for life is ever expanding. My aunt Rita always taught me to laugh at myself and keep a flexible spine. She would say, "A flexible spine is the key to youthfulness." One day when Rita was about 102 she said to me laughingly, " Can you believe that I am back in diapers!!" One of my dad's favorite expressions when I was growing up and needing to make a decision or when I was feeling blue was "Let the world turn for a day." Or, "Whatever floats your boat, when I was interested in something. My grandmother Josie taught me unconditional love. My mom taught me to look at the trees and see beauty in nature. Yet, I have also had teachers who have not been so wonderful, and I absorbed feelings of lack, insecurity and fear from them. But know, that we are all teachers and students at the same time – all is in its right order.

When the proverbial shit hits the fan, it comes right down to how well I am able to apply, from a place of knowing within myself, the tools to think and act. Unfortunately, there is no time to stop and reread a book on right thinking or to take a quick one-minute class on behavioral response when you are in the middle of an immediate life crisis or at an irritating luncheon. When you Face Your Self, to paraphrase a proverb, "You are not given the fish – you are taught how to fish."

CRUTCHES CAN BE HELPFUL FOR AWHILE

Sometimes you need crutches to get over a certain situation. For example, you may need to take an aspirin to get over a headache or you may need some extra hugs or a little ice cream to get over a disappointment. You may need to talk to a therapist or a friend about some stress that you are experiencing. These crutches are all fine and dandy, natural and normal if you do not abuse or continue day after day, month after month, year after year to use the same crutch for the same disappointment which happened years ago without ever healing the real, core situation. In the Face Your Self program, you will face your pain and learn to ask yourself, "Why do I have a headache, or why am I disappointed to begin with? "

If you had a pair of crutches to help you heal a broken leg, that would be a good thing, right? The crutches would help you to gain your strength and help you to walk when you could not walk on your own. However, if you never let go of the crutches and forever depended upon them, your walk would stay limited and your leg would never get strong. You would forever be carrying the extra crutch, the extra weight that would burden your life - it would limit your movement, your life, even though you could go on living your lifetime with crutches.

Many of us continue to live our lifetimes with metaphoric crutches and blind ourselves to experiencing our true nature and feeling true happiness and joy. Do you have any crutches in your life? Be honest with your self for you will need to face them in this book, and that is good.

YOU ARE IN THE DRIVER'S SEAT

Have you ever observed successful people who always seem to know what to do in any given situation?

Quick test: When I said successful people, what was the image that came to mind? Rich or Poor? What do you base success on? This is the type of important self-observation you will need to do to learn about yourself.

Are you in the backseat or are you in the driver's seat of your life? Sometimes when I speak with a certain relative who still exhibits unhappiness and poverty thinking, it can be like a magnetic pull back to a world of suffocation in my youth where I felt that I was not heard. I do not want to go to that place. I need to do everything in my power (eat, drink, yell into a pillow, hang up, breathe, go for a walk, shower or call a friend) to fortify myself sometimes to not get pulled to the backseat of the car and let this person effect and affect me and, in a sense, rule my life. Sometimes this person makes me feel angry, frustrated, upset, and deflated to know that they still do not hear me and can affect me the way they do. I am working on this relationship. But through the work of Face Your Self, I look at this situation to see what it is in <u>me</u> that makes <u>me</u> feel that way. What is my part in this situation? I ask my self:

- Why do I react that way?
- Why can't I be detached enough to see this person (or situation) clearly to let them have no effect on me?
- Why can't I see that this person may never change because of their own "grooved" thinking and behavior patterns?
- Can I have compassion and non-judgment toward this person?
- Do I still feel unheard? Why? What core issue is not speaking?
- Do I still feel unworthy? Why? When did that begin?
- Do I still have spaces in me where I feel I am not good enough?
- Why am I upset and frustrated?
- What is really going on here with this situation?

Face Your Self works because it will make you ask questions like these, which help you begin to see yourself clearly so you can be truthful to yourself even if you cannot be truthful to others at this moment. You need to go there now if you truly want transformation in your life. These questions allow you to be honest with yourself. Then you can be honest with other people. It is only then that you can get on with your life and say, Yes, I know that about myself but I am working on it. To make the intentions of your heart truly come to pass it takes constant awareness and work because life is always throwing new things at you (and many people you meet have not faced themselves).

OWN YOUR OWN FEELINGS

If a friend or family member told you that you had purple hair, you would look at them and not be bothered by their remark, for you know that you do not have purple hair (though in today's world purple hair is becoming more common!). But, if that same person told you that you looked fat or that you were stupid would you be bothered? You could acknowledge that you were fat or stupid and laugh with them about the situation. Or you can notice if you are bothered by the remark and put the anger you feel toward them (which, in reality is anger you feel toward yourself because you do feel fat or stupid on a subconscious level.) I invite you to Face Your Self and ask yourself if you do have feelings of fatness or stupidity somewhere deeper in your being that you have attached to, and identify with, which make you sensitive to that remark. If you can acknowledge and own these feelings and address the core part of them then you are on your way to Facing Your Self and living a natural, truthful life (more of this in Chapter Four, Mirror Images: What You Think, Is What You Get). Once you are truthful to your self you can observe your mind chaos and change your thinking if you choose. Then, like magic, you can freely attract to you the life of your dreams. But, if you block the reality of your feelings and blame the other person, you are not truthful to yourself and will not be able to ever fully open the pathways for happiness and success (whatever that may be to you) to come into your life.

Here is another example. When you see two people holding hands walking down the street are you happy for them and love the thought of love, or are you jealous or angry and spiteful, remembering your last breakup? Is it a lack of love in you that makes you feel that way? Do you love yourself even with all your quirks? When you own and look to the core reasons for your feelings, you are taking the first steps in Facing Your Self.

If you do not ask these questions when you get irritated, frustrated, angry, or upset, the subconscious thoughts and feelings you have will forever rule and sabotage your life and block your own wishes. Be truthful and own what is your part in all relationship issues. As you become more aware and loving, you will see that most issues are not about you. Often, it is the other person not owning their own stuff and they are trying to put it on you.

TIME SPACE AND CIRCUMSTANCE

Life can turn on a dime. Life is life and things happen. People are born and people pass on. Careers come and careers go. Relationships come and go. Illnesses of the body and mind happen. The sun rises and sets. The tides come in and out. There is a **rhythm to everything**. Life can seem very difficult at times. (I suggest reading *Candide,* written by Voltaire in 1759. This is a brilliant work of tough times leading to a better place.) Yet, with all the hard times, many people learn from their difficult life experiences and grow. Often, a difficult situation actually leads to a better space. Life can be filled with disappointments but good often comes from what at first seems like a bad thing. My mother-in-law used to say, "What doesn't kill you strengthens you." All of your life is affected by: Time, Space and Circumstance.

You came into this world with nothing and will leave with nothing except the vibration of your life spirit. Think how wonderful it would be if you could look at the life you have and see everything in it as a gift: your friends, your family, your home, your career, your clothes and jewelry, your toys and cars. Think how wonderful you would feel if you viewed each as a gift and did not feel like you needed to grip on to your girlfriend or boyfriend, marriage or career. Non-gripping is a *secret key* to releasing and allowing your happiness and joy to express and manifest itself. Imagine how free you could feel if you did not attach to anything and enjoyed everything. Non-gripping allows you to move freely and comfortably with the changes in your life, with less pain, and with a positive outlook for the future. Like everything worthwhile, learning to not attach to things, feelings, illness or ideas takes work, which is enhanced by practicing and working with the Face Your Self exercises. But, I promise that even a little of this understanding will go a long way in helping you get control of many unwanted situations in your life.

Even when you are feeling fat, bored, lonely, tired, angry or disappointed, these feelings have developed because of something you have attached to. It might even be the weather or something you ate. These feelings may be because of poor diet and exercise or because you allow other things or people around you to control or influence your life. These feelings can create an unwanted reality if you are not aware of the root cause and you allow them to infiltrate and rule your life, affecting your thinking and behavior. Sometimes these feelings come up because it is time for a change and you have been resisting what you know in your heart you must do.

Even with time, space and circumstance, think how wonderful it would be if you could live your life knowing that life is abundant. That your every need would be answered. Remember the Universe is always in the right order. What you think may be bad may actually be leading you to a better place or having you learn a needed lesson. There is cause and effect to everything. When you understand this *secret,* you will be more responsible for your actions. There is no need to hoard and be greedy because excess would only make you sick (like eating and eating and never going to the bathroom to release what you do not need).

LOOK AT YOUR LIFE RIGHT NOW

Take a look at your life right now. Is there someplace where that flow of your life force is blocked or hindered like a twisted or stuffed up garden hose? Is there something you are holding onto which you could or should let go of to allow new good things to come your way?

How are (is) your:

- Relationships?
- Career?
- Your Past?
- Your Future?
- Your sense of self?
- Your sense of worth?
- Money?
- Father issues?
- Mother issues?
- Sister? Brother?
- Children? Friends?
- Health?

By using the simple Face Your Self exercises and meditations as you read through the chapters, you'll be able to explore these areas in depth and determine what is working in your life and what is not. You'll learn how to live with those unpleasant situations of the past that will always be a part of you, like a scar that heals but can be used to remind you of your human compassion to yourself and others.

A THOUGHT TO REMEMBER

Count Your Blessings

It is important that we realize that sometimes we do not know what is really good for us and that sometimes we limit our good. The Universe always has more abundance in mind for us if only we allow it into our life. Count your blessings.

When you are present and aware of your blessings you feel grounded and good. Take inventory. Sometimes your good is right in front of you, or it is showing up in an unplanned way that you are missing. Be aware, you may miss it if you are looking one way or at one particular thing that you believe your good should come to you from. When you make a wish, always ask for that wish or better, and let it go. Trust. But you have to work it! (More on that in Chapter Eight: You Have to Polish your Mirror: You Have to Work It.)

DO OVER

I remember when I was a child playing a game with my friends when all of a sudden someone would yell, "Do over! " Everyone would respond, "Okay." My point, and the premise of Face Your Self, is that you can learn from your experiences and do it differently the next time. You can do it differently this time by cleaning up your mind, body and home to get clarity for what you want to attract. We cannot relive the past, but we can use the past as a footing to spring forward. (Remember my mother-in-law's words, "Whatever doesn't kill you, strengthens you."). Each breath is a new breath. You may have had some horrible experiences in your life. But, you can learn to put your life into a different perspective. If you keep dwelling on the past, you bring that past always into your present life experience, which shapes your future. Scientists say that every seven years you are a new person on a cellular level. When you work with the Face Your Self program, you can look seven years down the road and begin to shape yourself to be that which you imagine now for the future. A whole new you!

You Can Change Your Ways. You do not have to hold on to the old ways you have always done things. You have permission to change your ways. You do not have to keep eating the same foods or taking the same way to work each day. You do not have to live in the same neighborhood or state or country for that matter. You do not have to keep that ugly lamp you hate or the collection of elephants you had since you were nine. You can start over. You do not have to talk badly about your ex-lover. You do not have to think badly about yourself. You do not have to do what everybody else is doing.

THERE IS NO RACE TO THE FINISH LINE

In this book you will learn to take one thing at a time and focus on the aspects of your life that need cleaning up. You do not want to overwhelm yourself. Rome was not built in a day (but Rome collapsed from its chaos, greed and disorder). You can start simply: choose one thing and make a positive change. Another secret: there is no race to the finish line in life – that is the big fallacy that so many live by. Life is not a race. Life is an experience and you will experience life more fully and richly when you are not bogged down with mental and emotional worries or disorders. Remember it takes work – your work.

Make a commitment to yourself. It is one thing to keep saying, I know, I know, I should do _____ (you fill in the blank). It is another thing to make a commitment.

MINI EXERCISE

Where your mind goes…your energy will follow.

This is the law of attraction. What do you think about most of the time? Some clues come from listening to the words that come out of your mouth. What do you find yourself talking about with your closest friends? Two questions that will help you to identify your current primary thoughts are:

What is the last thing on your mind when you go to sleep?

What is on you mind when you wake up?

A THOUGHT TO REMEMBER

Sometimes it is Not about You

There are times when you will be speaking from your heart with no motivation other than to express your feelings or how you see something simple and direct. There may be times when others are hard, closed and attack you. If you are doing the work, you will see that it is not about you. Do not take it personally. Many are dealing with personal issues and blocks and many are not brave enough to really own their own stuff. Be honest with yourself about your part and then bless and release the others to their highest good with compassion. Harbor no feelings that you are better or more aware, for it only shows that your ego has gotten the better of you.

YOU ARE NOT ALONE

Remember, you are not alone. Every breathing person on this planet wants the same thing: to live a life of joy, peace, health, self-expression, prosperity and happiness. We all want to be loved and to love. We all want to be heard and honored. We all want to be understood. We all need a pat on the back and a hug from time to time. We all need each other.

- It is confusion that makes some want to kill for power.
- It is a disorder that makes some feel needy and abuse substances.
- It is dis-ease that makes 90% of all illness in man.
- It is uncertainty and fear that blocks the good of our nations.
- It is litter, which is growing at an alarming rate that is suffocating our planet and the people who live upon it.
- It is selfishness, which causes people to be rude.

GETTING STARTED

A man or woman is not fully developed until he or she has found their own way – their own expression. Like any art, learning to Face Your Self and taking responsibility for creating your life takes practice; a lifetime practice for it is the art of living. There are many lessons in one's lifetime. As a beginning painter, you learn methods to approach a canvas. Once you have mastered them you let them go and paint in your own style. As a new chef, you learn the use of tools and measurements to bake a cake. Once you have mastered them, you can then let them go and create your own cake sensation. As a budding writer, you learn certain styles of the written word. Once mastered, you create your own style. I once had a teacher who said to me, "Pamela, just start – everything else will fall into place."

A THOUGHT TO REMEMBER

Don't Judge.

What is Good and What is Bad? Sometimes what seems good to you is actually a bad thing, like eating a large hot fudge sundae, which can wind up giving you a stomachache - or a relationship that looks too good to be true that winds up in divorce. Or sometimes what looks like a bad thing, like a marriage winding up in a divorce, is actually a good thing because each person moves on, meets someone new and lives happily ever after.

Is there good and is there bad in the universal scheme of things? No there is not. There just is what is. The label of good and bad is from a perspective that has attachments. Know that your life is always moving forward to a higher good. The Indians and Tibetans have a god called Ganesh. He is a favorite of mine, too. He is a god who will remove obstacles in your way and he will also put obstacles in your way if he feels that you are not on your right path. All in all, Ganesh guides you and keeps you on your right path in life. Look at life's experiences from that perspective.

AUTHOR'S PROMISE TO THE READER

The reality is that we come into this life with nothing and we leave without anything except the nature of who we are - love and happiness. Remember, you are not your body, your thoughts or your possessions. The secret of living a joyous life is to develop a way of being present. Life can turn on a dime and the playing field may change. I promise you, when you let go of your fears, anxieties, old burdens, anger, and emotional blocks and stand free, you will enjoy your life and the gifts that it has to offer you each moment. There is much wonder in the world. You will open the energy pathways to your door for good things to come and your world will reflect peace, happiness, cheerfulness, abundance, health, good friends and freedom. When you Face Your Self, you will come into direct contact with divinity.

You are the creator of your life.
Your Life Mirrors What You Create.

I Am That I Am
So here I sit.
So here I breathe.
So here is now I do believe.
This is it I say
I have today.

CHAPTER ONE
FACE YOUR SELF EXERCISES

EXERCISE #1:

IT'S MY TIME NOW

This is an exercise to have you create your own time, space and circumstance – letting go of all worries, body illness, or personal issues for the moment - allowing you to be in a state of non-gripping – to be present. (Think of it as a present to yourself).

OBJECTIVE:

➢ To be able to live each moment in a state of joy and non-attachment.

➢ To be able to clearly see what is real and what is not real in your life experiences.

WHAT YOU WILL NEED:

➢ Time: 15-20 minutes (remember, this is a gift to yourself; you deserve 15-20 minutes to yourself).

➢ A private space with no distractions (roommates, children, pets, telephones).

➢ A peaceful view, art scene, flowers, or candle to rest your eyes upon.

➢ Pen or pencil and your Magic notebook (not a computer or anything electronic).

EXERCISE:

- Find a comfortable chair, mat or cushion (not lying down on a bed or couch for you may want to fall asleep). Keep your pad and pen next to you for easy reach.
- Declare to your self: " I am taking this time, in this space, to reflect upon my circumstance at this moment in my life. I do this with a light and joyful heart. I am a wonderful being." Pat yourself on the back and give yourself a hug.
- Inhale slowly and exhale slowly. Do it again now relaxing your shoulders. Again, relaxing your face , neck and arm muscles.
- Close your eyes for two minutes (doesn't have to be exact) and be aware of your breath as it comes in and out. With each exhale, imagine letting go of all bad, toxic things and with each inhale, imagine breathing in all good, clean, refreshing things.
- When you feel ready or motivated to write, pick up your pen and divide your paper into two columns. On the left side list all the things that are on your mind: exams, reports, taxes, neighbor's bothering dog, dinner party next Friday, your last check-up at the doctor, the doughnut you ate after lunch. Don't hold back or edit yourself. Write whatever comes to the front of your mind. Do this for about five minutes. Do not push your self to have to think of things.
- Now the biggie: Spend the next five to ten minutes not writing but mentally letting go of all that is on your mind. Now all your issues are down on paper, they will not go anywhere. Watch your thoughts "go by" as you would watch a movie and try to detach yourself from them to the point where you can imagine seeing yourself sitting in your room just as if you are part of the furniture. See if you can pretend to be observing yourself sitting there as if you are another person looking at yourself and seeing the beauty of you sitting in the room. One advanced technique is to imagine yourself not even there – just observe your space as if you are dead or not there. Then think on the following:

You are here now. This is your time. The things you have written will all be waiting for you to address or deal with when you get up and leave the room but right now you are free of them. You are free of it all. No wealth can change this moment, for even if you were the richest or poorest person on the planet doing this exercise here you would be with yourself. No friends or family can change this moment for even if you had the nuttiest friends or most loving family or no friends or family at all that would not change this moment, for here you would be with yourself. Let go of all the things on your paper in your notebook - none of it matters at this very moment. Give your mind a spa treatment. Feel yourself perfect, whole and complete. Breathe in and breathe out slowly. Release the tension in your neck and face. If a thought of your life comes to your mind – let it go or if you must, write it down. Use this time to just be - sitting in the air, in the room, with the flowers you chose or with the other items in the room at this time – feel yourself present in this moment. You are perfect, whole and complete and in alignment with life.

- Take the last five minutes to write on the right side of the paper all the good things in your life.
- Smile and give yourself a little hug and promise that you will give-gift yourself this mind spa treatment – daily/weekly/monthly. You choose what will work for you. But I will tell you that the more you practice this little exercise, the more potent it will become and the easier it will become for you to detach from identifying with dis-ease.

The more often you do this the easier it will be to let go and to be present. It is essential to shut out the rest of the world and take time out for yourself. If you are not strong and healthy for yourself you cannot even begin to be strong for others.

Here are two additional exercises you can add into your life to accelerate your transformation:

NIGHTLY EVALUATION

I recommend you let go of the day before you jump into bed each night. When you rest your head upon your pillow, do not take all the stuff of your day and life to bed with you. Before you close your eyes make a mental list of things on your mind and declare; " Now I am going to sleep to nourish my mind, body and soul. All of these things can wait until tomorrow. They are just things of life and are really not a part of me. I am free of all concerns when I sleep."

One thing I like to do each evening is to wash the day away when I shower. I use my shower time for meditation as well as cleansing.

MORNING SALUTATION

Upon waking, washing and relieving yourself, face toward the sun, bow and give thanks with joy for the new day. You do not need to be outside but it is nice. Stand straight and hold your hands up toward the sun. Imagine the sun's rays entering through your palms and your forehead. Feel the sun's heat and healing powers. Allow this sun energy to renew you with a strong life force to face the day.

PLAY ACT-DRESS UP-CHANGE YOUR NAME
STRIKE A POSE

This is an exercise where you create a personality of the ideal person you would like to see yourself become when you: *Achieve Your True Potential.*

> Before you do this exercise, know that you are in the right place at the right time and that you are where you are for a specific purpose in life. We are all teachers and students at the same time. For example, your suffering may be giving the opportunity for others around you to learn more compassion and understanding. Your suffering and pain may be an opportunity for you to grow and make changes in your life. Play-acting is a tool to feel what it would be like to experience the life you want.

OBJECTIVE:

> You will begin to experience and know how it feels to be the type of person you want to be. You want to think in general terms, for example, a writer, an actor, a chef, a spokesperson, a politician, a social worker, a teacher, a ski instructor, a banker, a farmer...
>
> You will act as if you are this person at all times. This acting is actually an accepting on your part.
>
> You will develop the mental skill of bringing your dreams and reality together.

WHAT YOU WILL NEED:

➤ Time to play

➤ Wardrobe: You make it up: perhaps a scarf, jacket, hat

➤ Props: You decide: perhaps a briefcase, paintbrush, pen

➤ Mirror

➤ Good friends to play with (not necessary but fun)

EXERCISE:

When you were a child, did you play dress up? This exercise encourages you to act, speak, dress, and think like the person you would like to become. It allows you to use all of your senses to feel and accept the future right now. This exercise helps you to better focus on your intention by becoming it, feeling it and thus, attracting what you want.

➤ Do you want to be a writer? Well then, write. When you sit down at your computer, wear a scarf that you only wear when you write. Claim that scarf your "Writer's Scarf." You may also want to wear it out to lunch or to a party to keep that feeling as a reminder that you are a writer.

➤ You want to be a successful businessperson but you have no business plan and little money. Strike the pose. Act as if you are the successful entrepreneur you would like to become. Look into the mirror and see yourself as a successful businessperson. When you sign your name to a check use a special pen. Even if you are working at a low paying job keep your inner poise as that of a successful businessperson - think, say and do in alignment.

➤ I have friends in Key West who give everyone new names at parties. It is great, harmless fun. There is a good lesson here which allows you to let go and try on another hat - another personality. It may be a hat you might like to wear or you may discover something about yourself.

By doing this exercise you will begin to assimilate into your being the type of person you want to become. When your heart works in alignment with your thinking, your speech and your body actions follow. This will activate the Universal Creative Mind to work using your direction.

Mind, body and speech working together are a secret of creation. Put your intention in alignment together with your actions and your speech and watch what happens.

CHAPTER TWO

REFLECTIONS ON YOUR TRUE NATURE: JOY

New Beginnings

Sitting at the water's edge
A darkened sky did glow
The earth had turned another day
Which turned into a show.

The sky lit up the pinkest pink
The water it did sparkle.
When suddenly a golden orb rose
Right before my eyes!

It lit a day of new beginnings
For the birds, flowers and trees.
For me my breath released
To the new day with ease.

I thought, how easy to begin again
If I let go
Of controlling the rotations of life
And live naturally with the flow

"We are here to laugh and celebrate our life in spite of everything. If we wait for good times, they will never come. When the good times do come, there will be something there to bother you." Sharmaji

WHAT MAKES YOU JOYFUL?

This chapter deals with what I call Mystical Joy: A profound, instinctive, essential joy that is not dependent on others or upon addictive substances. This type of joy doesn't require you to abandon yourself or give away your power to others, and it isn't dependent on your wealth or physical possessions either. It is connected to your personal center – that part of you that is, always was and always will be: joyful.

What makes you joyful? When I ask this question of my clients many of them say, "To get away from it all!" Or, it makes them squirm and feel uncomfortable; for they feel that joy is a concept somewhere out there in fairy tale land. Some are embarrassed or feel guilty because they have learned to not be joyful because so many others suffer. Others answer that their friends, spouse, children or grandchildren give them joy, which is wonderful since we all are a reflection of each other, but in reality (when you think about it) puts their joy into other people's hands.

Often, between thinking about past upsetting experiences, daily tasks for school, taking care of: parents, children, work, social obligations, meetings, answering e-mails, texting, paying bills and grocery shopping just to name a few - there is little time to think about joy.

Actually, in reality, you do not even have to think about joy – it is your nature. Joy is a natural state of mankind. You miss this awareness because of all humbugs (nonsenses, hooeys, rubbishes, hog washes). Such things as: limitations, evil, sufferings and uncertainty fill our lives. Many people actually believe that these hard-core "things" are a solid reality. It is said that the older you get the wiser and more content you will become because you will begin to let go of insignificant, petty stuff; realizing that is just part of our life experience - understanding what is real and important. Yet, some never learn and go to the grave missing life's joy.

To uncover your joy, it may help to pretend and daydream about being a child again. Not a selfish child who demands and cries when he does not get what he wants, or a child who must obey every command of their parents and teachers, but the innocence of a child who goes outside and plays. Imagine getting caught up in the wonder, amazement and fun of splashing, climbing, or building with stones without a care in the world or any thought or plan. This is when your greatest insights come to your mind and it is when you experience pure joy. When you are mindlessly *not gripping* onto any experience, person, place, thing, or outcome. You and your attention are one. There is no separate ego talking to you or separating yourself from your reasoning and actions. Some could say that you are mindless.

You cannot change your past, but you can understand. With the knowledge you gain, you can shape a joyful future. Perhaps you have experienced anger, greed, delusion and ill will from others. Perhaps you have been bullied. Perhaps you have seen awful things happen to others or even yourself. It hurts your heart. Perhaps, you may have made mistakes and blunders yourself. The past you lived has created you in your present day (cause and effect) and that is good because here you sit. Now is now and then was then. You can be the architect of your future. You can start first by imagining (like you did in the last chapter: Strike a Pose exercise). Once you have imagined how you see your future then you might draw up your plans and take action. Start with the beginning and build the foundation, the walls, the floors, the roof and you will begin to see the pathways to the rest of your life. Of course you will need to deal with plumbing and electrical issues and other mundane tasks as to where to put the garbage can – but that is part of being the architect in life. Where do you put your attention? A joyful person is not affected by praise or blame.

TYPES OF JOY

When you use drugs and alcohol they may give you the fantasy of being happy and joyous for a while and you may even feel free and expansive. You may feel connected to the world, insightful and very powerful. In reality, this is a delusional-transitory state, which usually ends with the opposite feeling of being let down, empty, tired and depressed.

Or perhaps you tend to be happy and joyous when you get a new car, or new pair of shoes, or when you are involved with a new love relationship. You tend to be joyous when you get a promotion at work or win an award or get an A on an exam or ace out your buddy in tennis. But, like alcohol and drugs, wealth and power, these things do not bring lasting happiness. Eventually the newness wears off and you are searching for something new or bigger or better to fill your void.

MINI EXERCISE:

Have you ever wondered why you are never really satisfied or happy or content?

Answer in your Magic Notebook: What is this void? Where is this void located in your body? What does it feel like? Why is it empty? What would fill it?

With Mystical Joy, no matter what is happening in your life, your world is joyous and good because you feel good. And you feel good because you have detached yourself from identifying with outcomes, weather patterns, or day-to-day ups and downs. You feel grounded and good because you are living from your center - balanced and at peace with a private knowingness. This does not mean that you do not care about others, your grades, new things in your life or your environment – you actually care more completely and compassionately. This does not mean that you do not feel sadness when you lose a good friend or family member, or feel total "jumping up and down happiness" when you see a loved one after a long period of time. It does not mean that you will not feel pain from an illness. It does mean that you will see that the illness is not affecting that part of you (your center). It does mean that you know deep in your heart and soul - know beyond a shadow of a doubt - that you are a light, harmonic sound. You are as beautiful as a scent of a flower. You are a joyous being blessed to be present here and now and thankful always for the gifts right in front of you. This part of you does not change, just like the nature of the world does not change.

There is a principle in Nature: **Cause and Effect,** which states: Every cause has its effect and every effect has its cause. You are born with your body, which has a brain and mind (consciousness). As you grow, you begin to sense things. You learn (and are taught) desires and attachments to things and ideas, which determine your actions, which determine your life. Unless you Face Your Self, you can actually become the pawn in your own game (more on this in Chapter Six, Achieving Your Personal Best in the Game of Life) for these desires can be a source of humbug, which blocks your Mystical Joy.

De-cluttering your mind, body and home is a beginning point for uncovering your Mystical Joy. Once you have done this, clarity and light will enter into your life. You will feel lighter and not so pressured and stressed. You may find that you sing songs and dance around your home or yard. When you simplify your life, you are beginning to open the doors to experience Mystical Joy.

There is another principle in Nature: **Correspondence**, which states simply: As within, so without. This law works both ways; As without, so within. (As above so below; as below, so above). As you become more aware of this principle, you can use it as a tool to look at your life and adjust what may be blocking your joy.

Look at your present life experiences (call it your without). Can you see any correlation to what is happening in your thoughts (your within) with that on the outside? If you make changes or adjustments to one, you actually affect changes and adjustments to the other. Ask yourself right now how perhaps the humbug or clutter in your home (dorm room, office) might be affecting the amount of joy you feel in your mind, body and life? For example, are you tripping over a pair of skates in your hallway that you haven't used - feeling guilty on a subtle level each time that you pass them that you are not skating as you had promised yourself – thus feeling overweight and then not liking yourself, which causes you to get angry at your love relationship... Notice the ripple effect: you feel overweight and then do not really like yourself...Get rid of the skates, move them or skate!

Ask yourself other questions: Are there any unwanted present situations in your life regarding relationships or money issues or unfriendly neighbors? Ask yourself: Could this situation, which is manifesting on the outside of you, be from some form of humbug on the inside of you? For example, suppose you feel you did not have enough money in your life - you did not feel prosperous (everyone I have met always feels that they could use just a little bit more money). Could this manifested situation of not feeling prosperous actually stem from you not feeling deserving or loved? Could this manifested situation stem from you not feeling good about yourself? When you look in the mirror do you see a strong, healthy, prosperous person or do you see a person who is weak, poor or unworthy? In your home, do you live with old, worn-out, broken items next to your bed and where you spend much of your time? Begin to make some adjustments in your home, such as bringing something new with a wealthy feeling into your space, it does not have to be expensive. Get your hair done. Begin to bring the *feeling* of wealth and prosperity into your home and life as a *reflection*. The more you feel it within and reflect it without, the more you will develop a sense of prosperity and the more you will attract prosperity to you (And remember, wealth and prosperity comes in many ways, it is not just about money).

MINI EXERCISE:

Answer in your Magic Notebook: Name 10 ways that you are wealthy and prosperous right this very moment. Look at what is positive in your life.

I had a client who called me into her home because she was having many arguments with her husband. Right next to her bedside was a beautiful, silver framed photograph of the both of them in formal attire. They were smiling and he had his arm around her. But something told me to ask her about that picture next to her bed. She looked at it and in a split second she said, "You know, we had the biggest fight of our life that night! " That photo reminded that couple, on a subtle level, of an argument every night before they climbed into bed creating tension and setting up a situation that was not loving: As without, so within.

I had another client who had just been laid off from his work. He felt unworthy and always undermined by his mother-in -law. These feelings came across in his speech and body language as well. I asked him where his favorite place was to hang out and just relax in his home. He brought me into the den where there was an old couch. I asked him about that couch. Where did it come from? What did it mean to him? He told me it was a hand-me-down from his mother-in– law when they moved into their new home. The couch supported his feelings of being undermined by his mother-in-law, even when he relaxed; he needed to be supported by her: As without, so within.

Know this: If there is clutter in your life it is affecting your health. Most importantly, it is affecting and blocking the relationship you have with your true joyous self.

THE JOY OF SELF-AMUSEMENT AND SELF-EXPRESSION

It is very important that you have a creative outlet. It doesn't matter if you are good or not. Paint! Write! Cook! Act! Sing! Garden! Create a business! You know what an apple looks like – draw it – feel it – make it a color you might never see in the food store. So what. Find your passion and expression. You can do this by exploring different avenues: sign up for cooking classes, go to the bookstore and wander through the shelves in sections you never even looked at before until you find something that piques your interest, go to lectures or gallery openings, take a vacation and see what and where you are drawn.

I have had many clients and students who say to me, "But I am not creative." Well, that is not true. We all have a gem and sparkle of something that is creative - something that excites us. I have worked with CEOs and presidents of companies who love what they are doing. They have poured their creativity into creating a company – a business and they do it with love and with a great creative spark. Many started out in their garages or basements doing a little side thing that they enjoyed and it grew into a large corporation. I encourage you to explore your joy. You have many talents.

I was playing tennis one day with some friends and one lady said to me, "Pamela, you are so talented, you write and paint. All I do is childcare. " It takes quite a talent and creative expression to take care of children. Part of the burden that blocks people's inner joy is that they miss identifying their own creative self-expression. Do not care what others think about your creative work. I suggest that you do not even call it work - call it play.

When you express from your heart, with no expectations of income or praise, and you create just for your self, you create work/play, which is Heaven sent. Have no preconceived ideas of what your art should be, no preconceived ideas of how your dress should look, no preconceived ideas of what your music should sound like. Just play. Explore. Try on different hats and take things to the limits. Give yourself space to feel the materials, the words, and the notes. Become that which you are expressing. Get lost in that which you are creating. The arts are meant to inspire – write a poem, a song, do a dance of joy. Be mindless.

You will be lifted to a different dimension. When this happens, to me this is true art - I feel the Divine expressing through my hands. This, to me, is true freedom. This, to me, is the wealthiest, most wonderful, powerful place to be. Immersed in your Divine self-expression. Not judging your self – not even knowing yourself is there - just creating with pure freedom- guided by a higher power from within and without. I suggest that you fuel up that inner fire and burn up any inner blockages that hinder and cloud your self-expression -your creativity. Dance.

How do you do this, you may ask? By being yourself (simple, right?) By acting with your own style. By never losing sight of who you are. A secret I have learned: joy is in the mundane course of your daily work, your daily life. I once saw a cartoon years ago that has stuck with me where a man was lying on his deathbed surrounded by his family – he was propped up with pillows and he had his hands opened wide to the heavens – the caption said: "This is it?" Many may say, "Don't let life pass you by." But I say, "Don't let yourself pass life by." Life remains. It is us who come and go. You do not need to take time off to experience your time of joy (though naps and vacations are fun and joyful). Developing your own creativity is a tool to help you learn about yourself and begin to like yourself. When you have success in your own fame (you like your self), your own work and your creative expression will feel joyous. No one will ever be able to take that sense of self away from you. This is a key to being joyful.

MINI EXERCISE:

"I Am Here Now." Take this thought and express it in as many creative forms listed below (not listed in any form of preference) as you can. Remember, have fun. Call your work "Expressions From My Heart". Let no one judge your efforts, and only you will know if you've sparked an ember of joy in your heart.

Poetry
Singing
Dancing
Cooking
Starting a Business
Writing
Boating
Kite Flying
Painting
Gardening
Sculpting
Movie making

BAGGAGE

I have a client who once told me, "I don't have baggage, I'm carrying freight!! "Unfortunately, this is the case for many of us. You are born into this world with no material things, no worries, no deadlines, no commitments, and no hurts. As I stated earlier, your family, your friends, your home, your experiences, your clothes, your jewelry, your cars, your cell phones, your computers, your money, and toys all are gifts to enjoy while you are alive (good, bad or indifferent). Yet, all of these things can put pressure upon you and if you let the pressures add up they will block your joy. Staying on top of your excess baggage is a constant battle, which is a recurring theme in this book.

You can carry emotional/inner baggage for a lifetime, unless you Face Your Self and look truthfully in your own Magic Mirror at your life. Perhaps it is something from your childhood that you never got over, or a fear, maybe a death of a loved one, or the shock of an illness or an accident; something that happened to you that makes you act the way you do. Little babies who are one with the world are given a name that has a special meaning to the parents. Along with a surname from your family, you are assigned a religion, a nationality and a social status. You may have experienced hurts and injustice in your early life or in your later life. This is the beginning of your baggage, which blocks who you are: a natural joyous, light, human being. As your baggage increases, you slowly lose sight of your true nature: joy. Your life becomes overwhelming and stressful and you may feel lost.

An important key for living a joyous life is to learn to let go of your baggage. You may say, "Oh, how do I do that?" Well, you pack up all your cares and woes - here you go... Logical reasoning may tell you to keep your baggage neatly packed. But then your baggage may explode and spill out all over the sidewalk and spill into your current life with unpleasant results.

You will have to face your baggage sooner or later so you may as well take a look at it now. You can always choose to put it back in your suitcase and carry it around with you later if you want – the choice is always yours.

Your intention is to get to the root cause of why you carry your baggage (this is where the exercises in this book, a good confidant friend or therapist may assist you if you choose). Once you face it, inventory it and air it out, you will clearly see where and what your baggage weight is in the first place. Then, through a systematic process of reflecting and reasoning, you can begin the process of realizing that this *Baggage* holds no *real* hold over your present life other than what you give power to it in your mind or unless you for some other intentional/motivational reason continue to allow it to be a part of your life. Picture your worries, issues and hurtful experiences as types of clothing or cosmetics that you wear every day. For example, you wake up and choose to put on the dress of *Oh how will I pay the electric bill?* Which actually means, *I have never been responsible with money.* Try on the jacket of, I *need to get a better job,* which maybe means, *I will never amount to anything.*

How will I ever meet that deadline? What will my family think about my decision to move? My boyfriend or girlfriend is a cheat. All the above appear on your face like a mask of make-up and all have a deeper root, which causes your unhappiness which will then, if they persist, grow somewhere in your body as an illness. Perhaps you have been carrying the same baggage around with you daily for ten, twenty, thirty or forty years: you vacation with your baggage, bathe with it, make love with it, eat with it and sleep with it. Many people have hurts from their childhood years. They have many issues with their parents. It is helpful to realize, once you look at your parents' lives, that your parents did the best that they could given their own lives and personal circumstances. It may not be the way that you would have done things, it may not be the way that you do things, but it was the best that they could do. IT IS VERY RARE THAT A PARENT WENT OUT OF THEIR WAY TO INTENTIONALLY HURT THEIR CHILD. I recommend that you bless them and release the pain (your baggage) for your own good and joy. Has your baggage become even more closely protected than the family jewels? Face your baggage, see it clearly for what it is and put it down for a rest.

Staying on top of emotional baggage is a constant battle, but you can use every event and obstacle as a source of self-understanding and self-advancement. Make it a game. You can use all events and activities of your life as investigative tools to find out more about your self while you uncover the true joyous you. It takes constant work to clear and to stay on top of all your stuff before it compounds into situations that you do not want; like illness. Everyday new circumstances happen – some may be life changing. Give thanks.

This poem is about letting go of your baggage.

Letting Go
As I travel the conflicting paths of life
Of good and evil
I come to the river's edge.
Here I leave my baggage and strip myself of clothes.
No mask
I sail to the other side
Once there
I leave even the boat aside and let it float away.
Ecstasy of nothingness
And of All.
Joy
Om Shanti

NOT FORCING JOY

You do not need to compel things to happen. If you force something, you run the risk of it breaking (my dad always would tell me. "Don't force the window open - it may break - if it is stuck it is for a reason"). If you try to force someone to love you, they usually turn and run away. If you try to force singing a song, you usually hurt your vocal cords. If you try to force yourself just to make money, you usually do not have pleasure and ultimately fail. If you try to force yourself to be on a diet, you usually are not happy and fail. Relationships, singing, earning money, and diets all require attention but, when you lighten up and approach them without pushing and squinting your eyes and putting pressure on yourself or others to make it happen - all will happen with ease if it is in the right order of things. When you approach anything with a light heart, things will happen quicker and with more permanent benefits. The same is true of making room for joy in your life.

The Egyptians would measure a heart on a scale against a feather. Would your heart, metaphorically, weigh more or less than a feather?

MINI EXERCISE:

Here is a "Joy" questionnaire for you. Take time to consider your answers:

- Do you take time to play?
- Is your play your work? Is your work play?
- What have you learned from serious challenges you have had?
- Do you take time to be in Nature?
- How often do you wake up naturally without an alarm clock?
- Are you aware of your unique creative expression?
- What was the name of the last good book you read just for fun and relaxation?
- How often do you listen to music?
- Do you engage in any physical exercise or play sports?
- How many times a day do you smile and laugh?
- If you were a rabbit would you be a silly rabbit?!
- When was the last time you sang in the shower?
- When was the last time you took a day off just for you?

When you realize that there is nothing in you, which denies that which you truly desire, you can get on with the active part of living your life. In this work, it is not enough for you to just imagine your life the way you want it (you cannot, for example sit back and eat potato chips on your couch and expect the world to come to you). Thought sets forces in motion, and you must then actively do your part. Struggling and forcing things or people to get what you want will not work in the long run. You want to work with the flow of natural rhythms and forces. This will bring you joy. The following pages have suggestions to gently open the door to remembering your joy.

PLAY

I suggest that you get a bell: a tiny, light, happy, little bell with a happy sound. Use this bell as a tool to break up your fears, worries and baggage. Ring it whenever you feel that old heavy baggage weight coming on or when you feel unhappy. Keep it near you and ring it so that its vibrations will break up what appears to be dense, heavy thought patterns.

Daydreaming is good and healthy from time to time. People do not do enough daydreaming any more. With daydreaming you can visualize and imagine situations as a reality. When you daydream, you muse about things and take them into your system to try them on. You feel them to be a reality. While daydreaming, you imagine a situation, such as a love relationship or living in a seaside resort or being the president of a company, as a reality. Daydreaming is actually a practical method to help you create the visions of your ideal life and situations you would like to experience. The more you visualize and feel your daydream as an imagined reality, the more you are moving energies around you which will magnetically and magically attract that which you dream into a reality (Remember: time is not a factor - life will unfold naturally for you in right order).

MINI EXERCISE:

<u>Paper Dolls</u>
What you will need;
      Cardboard
      Paper
      Scissors
      Crayons/colored markers

1. Draw an image of yourself in a comfortable standing pose on a piece of cardboard. Color it in with eyes, nose, lips, ears, and hair (you can even paint your toenails if you want!). Cut it out and put it aside.

2. Think about all of the "hats" you wear – the different roles you play in life, or the different "yous" that there are.

    1. Brother/sister
    2. Mother/father
    3. Student
    4. Nurse/fireman/teacher/businessperson/ policeman
    5. Lover/friend
    6. Adventurous flyer/earthbound gardener/ soldier
    7. The out on the town you/the stay at home be comfortable you

3. Draw outfits and hats that express each of the different "yous" that will fit on your paper doll.

4. Play. Let them talk. Let them act out. (You may want to even frame them and display them in a personal space of your home.)

What if there were:
 No threat of bio attacks?
 No threat of nuclear attacks?
 No threat of war?
 No need for personal drugs?
 Pure tap water?
 Enough water for everyone?
 Clean air?
 Healthy food?
 Enough food for everyone?
 Money was a means – not an end?
 No fear of old age?
 No fear of dis-ease?
 No fears in young age?

What if all:
 Children loved their parents?
 Parents loved their children?
 People loved each other?
 People drove the speed limit and used signals?
 People said thank you and please?
 People honored Nature?

What if:
 We all had time to play and rest?
 We had no need for wars?
 We all understood?

How would you feel if you had no fear?
 Feel like that.
How would you behave toward other people if you realized that they could not hurt you?
 Behave like that.
How would you react to so-called misfortune if you saw its inability to bother you?
 React that way.
How would you think toward yourself if you knew you were perfect, whole and complete?
 Think like that.

Joy depends upon the way you react to life. Make time for joy in your life. Allow joy in your life; do not cover it up with materialistic things. The more time you make for joy, the more joyous your life will become. The more joyous your life becomes, the more joyous your life will be. Soon your life will be joy. You will be one with Mystical Joy and this joy will affect all those around you radiating out into the world.

No matter how old you are, you're never too old to:

1. Play like a dog and be silly.
2. Build a tent under a table and crawl in and eat some cookies and read a storybook.
3. Give your imagination space to speak, drop water on a plate and move it around and let the drops come together and make patterns.
4. Enjoy mindless work. This is the best work for creative development and getting out of your own way, rake leaves, vacuum, clean a closet, weed…
5. Watch the clouds and see if you can make them move. What stories can you make up from the cloud pictures you see?

DURING YOUR LIFETIME HAVE YOU MADE TROUBLE FOR YOURSELF?

To understand what impacts your life, it is important to Face Your Self honestly. You may have people in your family who have been unfaithful to you. You may have had friends in your life who have been inconsiderate. You may have people in your workplace who do not appreciate you. You may ask, "How can I change them?" The answer is to change your self. Live your life honestly and mindfully. Everyone is ultimately responsible for their own self unless they are a young child or a person with a severe illness. Sometimes you may even find that you need to bless and release a person from your life. We are all faced with pain, temptation and confusion. Most people create their destructive self-deception. Many people get comfortable with their misery and are too lazy to change even though they say that they want to. Can you recognize your own self-deception and excuses and stop it? Do you live under hypnosis of denial? Do you live under a spell, which keeps you living a life of delusion when you look in the mirror? Well, you can begin to break the spell now if you want.

When you identify either mentally or emotionally with something inside or outside of yourself, you become absorbed and captivated by that. You may attach to these things in hope that you will be secure or happy. These things (people, careers, money, jewelry, religions, cars, etc.) seem like they are real and secure and permanent but you know that they are not – life changes. They are not security. You could lose it all tomorrow. It is lovely and wonderful to have nice things in your life and loving people in your life. It is good to have a career and a home to go home to, and it is fine to have a religious family you share spiritual time with. But all of these things are not part of your true essential self: the "you" who was you at birth and will be you when you are ninety-five. You can never lose your Natural - Divine - Self. When you have nothing, you still have everything. There is always love and joy.

Joy

No voice can sing, nor artist paint
The lightness of the dancing bliss
My heart does take
When nature's kiss upon my lips,
Circles time.

CHAPTER TWO
FACE YOUR SELF EXERCISES

EXERCISE #1:

LOOKING AT THE LIFE YOU HAVE

With this exercise, you will take a serious look at the reality of the life that you currently are experiencing. You will look at your finances, relationships, family, career, neighbors, your spiritual practices, your joy and creativity…

It is important for you to be truthful and honest with yourself, for only then will you be able to make adjustments in your life.

OBJECTIVE:

To be able to identify your baggage clearly and truthfully as it now appears in your life.

WHAT YOU WILL NEED:

Notebook (Make it your Magic one.) (I would rather you use an actual notebook, not an e-pad or some other electronic means. There is an honoring and a personal, private connection with pen to pad.)
Pen or Pencil

EXERCISE:

➢ If you can, take a walk beforehand in the park, woods or along a beach or riverfront. It is good to clear your head and aura in the environs of Nature. (It is always good practice to start any exercise such as these with an honoring and cleansing of the heart in nature, but it is not imperative for the exercise to be effective.)

➤ It is important to find a quiet, comfortable, safe place to do this exercise. Pick a time when pets, friends, children or visitors will not disturb you and a time when you have no pressing engagements. Turn off your cell phone, radio, stereo, television and all electronics.

➤ Open your windows for fresh air, if possible. I like to also have a vase of fresh cut flowers in view and to burn a natural scented candle or incense. All of this preparation aids in creating your sacred space and special time.

➤ Once settled down, breathe deeply in and out a few times and roll your head and neck gently back and forth to remove any extra tension. Sit quietly for a while, at least five minutes, and feel the beauty of the moment. Peace with no agenda. There is nowhere to go, no appointment to make. Just be with yourself in the silence of the space you created. Allow the weight of your shoulders to lift and any heaviness in your heart to melt. Do not be afraid to let go and just be, for this too is a beginning of developing your psychic energies. See your thoughts as if you were watching a movie or the television, but let them pass. This will help you in detaching from your thoughts. It is important to ground yourself with the knowledge that you are safe here and now and realize at this moment in time the you, you were at five and will be at ninety-five- are healthy and happy (even if this is not necessarily the you of your present state of body or mind).

➤ When you are poised, relaxed and have a clear mind for concentration answer the following questions and write down your answers. Do not just answer yes or no – answer why or why not or explain what you are feeling. Be open, truthful and sincere. You will immediately begin to clear your mind, body and home and open the pathways to a more powerful and happy life.

- Do you feel prosperous?
- Do you share your wealth?
- Do you like yourself? (why or why not?)
- Do you have many friends?
- Do you feel like you are on the right path in life?
- Do you like what you do as a career?
- Do you have someone you can call on in the middle of the night if you need help?

- Are you in love?
- What fears do you have? Do you get anxious? Where?
- Do you have a spiritual practice? What do you know versus believe?
- What are your family relationships like? List your important living family members and those who have passed on and write a word or two about your relationship with them. Include children, parents, grandparents, aunts and uncles and those friends who may be like family members.
- Are you creative? (Why or Why not?)
- What gives you joy?
- Do you care about what people think of you?
- Have you traveled outside of your country, state, town within the past year? Where?
- Do you know your neighbors?

- Do you procrastinate?

Is there anything in addition to the above that is on your mind or in your life right now, which you want to write down? If so, add it to the list.

- Keep this writing (list) in a private place. Eventually you may want to dispose of this writing, (perhaps in a month or two or when you have finished reading this book). You can create a special, private ritual: start with prayers or sayings to your own liking and then, to liberate yourself of this list, you can either burn it, toss it into a moving body of water, bury it in the ground, or toss it in ripped up little pieces into the wind. This will allow the elements of fire, water, earth, or air to absorb it without harm to anyone or the planet. (Note: these are our burial choices too.)

- You can congratulate yourself, for you are uncovering and identifying areas where you may have some hidden issues that are keeping you from experiencing joy.

  Take some time to ponder your answers. The objective in this exercise was only to identify how you perceive your current life. As you read on you will learn more ways to focus on the life you want. You can, of course, start right now in making positive changes in your life. Call an old family member or friend, help out a neighbor, sign up for a class in painting, plan a trip, start making plans to move to a new city...

EXERCISE # 2:

VISUALIZATION OF THE LIFE OF JOY YOU WANT:

This exercise is for you to learn to get clarity about your desires and be able to focus with intention to create the life that you want to experience. This is not a make-believe exercise.

I recommend that you be wise about who you share your hopes and dreams with and do not share your hopes or dreams with too many people, for they may "poo poo" you and take your excitement and drive away from you - in a sense deplete the energy and vision (seeing clearly) of what you want.

OBJECTIVE:

You will be able to state clearly and see in your mind's eye the joyous life that you want to experience.

WHAT YOU WILL NEED:

A Magic Notebook (declare it as such)
Pen or Pencil

EXERCISE:

➢ Make a list of all that you are thankful for right now. Write it down. This links you with the collective or universal consciousness. It is also a way to open your heart and allow more good (how do you like that English!?) to enter your world.

➢ Say a prayer of thanks in your own words.

Think of an offering of thanks that you can make to Nature and the Universe. This offering can be some apples tossed in the woods for the deer or birdseed tossed to the four corners of direction and toward heaven and earth, for the birds. It can be flowers at your grandmother's grave or bread baked for a neighbor. There are no right or wrong offerings, but these steps are important for you to remain grounded, real and to open your heart.

Once you have completed the above, answer the following question:

IF YOU HAD THREE WISHES WHAT WOULD THEY BE?

MAKE YOUR THREE WISHES AND WRITE THEM DOWN NOW.

Do not limit yourself to specific names, places, or exact objects or ambitions. Allow your visualization no limitations. Write down your wish but add, "or better" next to each specific wish or ambition. It is also important to note that when you make a wish, you wish no harm to anyone or anything and to note that we do not wish to control anyone or thing. Everything that you wish for is always for the highest good of all.

Based upon your three wishes coming true, answer these questions projecting:

In 1 year: In 5 years: In 10 years:

Where do you see yourself getting up in the morning? Would you be:
    Listening to birds or city traffic?
    In the woods?

By the water?
Both?
In what country?
In what state?
Describe it as fully as possible.

What colors would you surround yourself with?
What color are your sheets?
Your towels?
Your robe?
Your dishes?
What color would your bedroom be?
Your living room?

What music would be playing in the background of your life?
Rock and Roll?
Classical?
Country?
Jazz?
Blues?

How would you start your day? Would you be:
Sleeping in?
With Yoga?
Meditation?
Reading a newspaper?
Kissing someone?
Exercising?

What foods would you eat?
Write out what a day's menu might be.

What work would you be doing that day?
Write a paragraph on how and what you see yourself doing for work.
Write a paragraph on how you are expressing your creativity.
Write a paragraph on how you are socializing.
What friends would you have in your new life?
What would be their interests?
How would you spend your leisure time?
What classes would you be taking, if any?
What clothes would be in your closet?

How would you dress for work?
How would you dress for fun?
What would you wear around the house?
How often would you see your family?
What charity would you support, if any?
What would your finances look like?
What would be your three wishes at the end of 10 years?
Once you have completed your questions…

<u>Now begin to live your life as if it is the life you envision.</u>

<u>NOW begin to live your life as if it is the life you envision.</u>

<u>Now begin to LIVE your life as if it is the life you envision.</u>

The seed is sown

Be patient

It may take days or it may take years but it is done and will

be done.

CHAPTER THREE

WHO IS THAT IN YOUR MIRROR?

Two questions to ask.

Do you love it? Or do you use it?

If your answer is no - then why is it part of

your mask?

There is a Zen proverb that states:

Too many options cause insanity

Perhaps a new proverb for the 21ˢᵗ Century could be:

Too many options causes: Anxiety, stress and unhappiness.

WHAT IS HUMBUG?

In the last chapter we mentioned humbug.
Humbug is:

- Anything that no longer is useful – but is still in your life.
- Anything that you do not like or love – but is still in your life.
- Anything that hinders your functioning – but is still in your life.
- Anything that blocks your joy – but is still in your life.

Humbug comes in many forms – some external forms are obvious, such as huge stacks of papers and junk mail on your dining room table. Internal humbug is more subtle, such as a repressed fear or hurt. Humbug can be having too many things in a small space or it can be having too many thoughts flying through your mind in a short time. Humbug can be ingesting drugs or eating overly processed foods. Humbug can be anything that blocks and affects your good.

Humbug is universal. From wealthy to poor, male or female, young or old, humbug is one of the main reasons across the globe for unhappiness, anxiety, and stress. Humbug crosses all religions and nationalities. It can be absorbed from your parents, teachers, business associates and friends. You absorb it from the newspapers and television shows that you watch and the advertising that you see. It is absorbed from religious dogmatic beliefs and political party thinking.

Humbug is everywhere: in our towns and villages, in our national budgets and on the once beautiful pathways throughout our country and planet. It is in all of our homes, it runs through our bodies and minds. You carry it around with you wherever you go, and wherever you go, there is humbug. Many people go to therapists and psychologists to clear out their mind humbug. Other people go to gyms, healers or involve themselves in fad diets to try and clear out their body humbug. Many people have garage sales or give items to their local church or temple to clear up their home humbug. Our society is filled with humbug on many levels.

WHY IT IS IMPORTANT TO ADDRESS & REMOVE HUMBUG?

Your humbug – or lack of it – is a reflection of who you are and where you are in your life. Your internal and external humbug creates who you are.

Personal humbug situations can begin at a very young age- before we are even able to speak our own mind and make our own personal choices. We can absorb other people's humbug once we are born, for as a young child we learn by what we see and hear. We all get programmed like a human robot (that seems like an oxymoron but it is not) or a personal computer before we have any say about what programs we want installed.

You are taught what to eat and how much you need to eat. You are programmed with certain religious and political beliefs and ways. You may be programmed with respect and love of others, or with disregard and abuse to those who do not think like you. As a baby, you can hear arguments and absorb that energy. You can feel love and absorb that energy. Your voice and actions are shaped to fit the parenting situation you were brought up with.

As you grow up, you continue to live as if all of your early childhood humbug is natural, real and the way it is. Of course you think it is your truth, for that is the only reality that you have ever been made aware of and you see the whole world from that false reality (another oxymoron). You make your choices based upon this. You think, act, speak, eat, love, purchase and breathe from this learned perspective. Sometimes, even wars are started from a humbugged base belief. People begin to reflect their humbug. If you are not aware of it, year after year of living with your internal humbug, it will be reflected in your speech, your walk, and your dress. It will show up in how you dance (or do not dance) and how you play or do not play. It will show up in your body (your posture, health and disease patterns, such as eating disorders). It will show up in your thinking (as depressions and anxieties or as feelings of superiority). It will show up in your work. It will show up in your face. It will show up in whatever you do.

Eventually, you grow older and you begin to see others living, eating, and acting differently. One day, you may become aware that you are not happy and you may try to blame others. Once you realize that your life is not working for you, which is a good thing, it is time to Face Your Self. You are now responsible to be your own explorer: de-programming and de-humbugging your own life. You are on your way to becoming responsible for your own life.

Mind Chaos (humbug) is important to remove because it opens your mind to new possibilities and allows you to see clearly. Mind humbug affects your body's health and your life's beauty.

Body Anarchy is important to remove because you will be healthier and less of a burden on your family, your society, and yourself. Body disorders also affect your mind and may create chaotic thinking.

Home Clutter is important to remove because your home, which I see as a reflection of your spirit, reflects and affects your thinking, health and life path (the as Without affecting as Within). Your home can be a beautiful mirror to see into your life.

10 WAYS THAT HUMBUG AFFECTS YOU

If you are not aware, your internal and external humbug will take over your life. You may even begin to look like your humbug – just like people begin to look like their dogs (dogs are much cuter than humbug) or the people they hang out with.

1. Humbug depletes your energy and makes you feel tired.

   You don't focus on the projects you want to accomplish.

2. Humbug keeps you out of the present moment and blocks your future happiness.

   Humbug keeps you living in the past because it is from the past.

3. Humbug affects your weight.

    It weighs you down and keeps you physically and emotionally heavy.

4. Humbug dulls your sensitivity and capacity for passion and understanding.

    You sex life is dull. You find that you just do not care anymore.

5. Humbug confuses you and you can't find a clear focus in life.

    You become distracted by too many options; fears, frustrations and you are unable to prioritize.

6. Humbug costs you financially.

    You spend your resources on an alarm system to protect all of your stuff, or costly diets and therapy sessions, or you miss out on that great job or relationship because of humbugged thinking.

7. Humbug is distracting.

    You spend time dealing with your mind, body or home humbug instead of the important things you want to do.

8. Humbug owns you.

    You are a slave to your humbug, which is reflected in your emotions, fears, habits and physical humbug.

9. Humbug affects your health.

    You have back pain, poor eating and exercise habits. You do not feel good.

10. Humbug triggers negative emotions.

    You become angry, jealous, anxious, depressed, tired and cranky.

HUMBUG CLOUDS YOUR MIRROR:

IT SHOWS UP IN YOUR THINKING

IT SHOWS UP IN YOUR FEELINGS

IT SHOWS UP IN YOUR WALKING

IT SHOWS UP IN YOUR TALKING

IT SHOWS UP WITH EACH BREATH

IT SHOWS UP IN HOW YOU LIVE

IS YOUR HUMBUG RULING AND DIRECTING YOU OR ARE YOU RULING AND DIRECTING YOUR HUMBUG?

Have you ever experienced any of these things?
- Feeling like you're not on your true career path?
- Your relationships always seem to fail?
- Feeling that you never have enough money?
- Trying every diet and can't ever seem to let go of the weight that you want?
- Starting projects and never finishing them?
- Feeling that you just can't get beyond your past?

All of the above situations at their root are what I call humbug situations.

Almost any troublesome situation can be traced to its root by having humbug somewhere in your life – somewhere in your mind – somewhere in your body.

What you think is a problem is simply a situation in your life. You can deal with it. One way is to look deeply to find the root cause of the situation. Each manifested situation (such as lack of relationship or lack of money, or feeling pain either physical or mental) can be traced to its root cause. If you can identify that cause: massage it, remove it, change it or make it not have power over you any longer, you will clear energy pathways and all of the gunk of humbug will begin to: move, dissipate, and/or dissolve. Life will begin to manifest an optimistic situation.

For example, let us say that you always seem to fail for one reason or another at your relationships. They can be your friendships, family, work or romance relationships. After doing some deep personal investigation, you will find that the problem is not the other person at all (for they are who they are and have their own situations).

Some questions you may want to ask yourself are:

- Why are you even trying to be in a relationship with someone who has even more personal problems than yourself?
- Can you love this person unconditionally? Why or Why not?
- Are you trying to change this person? Why?
- What in you makes you attracted to a person who acts like they do?
- Could it be that you do not have a loving, respectful relationship with your self?
- What are you trying to prove? To them? To yourself? To others? Why?
- What is your true motivation to want to be in this relationship?

Your lack of love of yourself is filled with internal humbug which, when addressed, will give you the permission and freedom to love and be loved for who you are. When you Face Your Self and do the exercises at the end of each chapter you will open doors to see the humbug that you carry.

Once you see the humbug, it will melt away like magic. You will realize that it has no power over you. You will realize that your lack of love in reality has no solid basis – it is like smoke blurring your vision. Once you are honest with yourself, the stumbling blocks will be removed and your choices of a mate will come into alignment with a person who will respect and love you for whom you are. You, too, will love them because you will see them clearly for who and what they are. And, most importantly, you will love your self.

WHY YOU COLLECT AND CREATE HUMBUG

People often purchase things to feed an inner desire and rarely actually need the items that are being purchased. They revert to old behavior and thinking patterns, i.e. internal humbug. People often eat and drink foods that feed an emotional need and not a physical need. Here are 10 of the most prevalent reasons why many people collect and create internal and external humbug.

Connection:
You have a connection with the past: through ideas, memories, photos, and vacation travel reminiscences.

Status:
You use material things, or outdated thoughts to hide a poor self-image.

Security:
You feel safe with the things around you, the thoughts, and the foods.

Fear:
Poverty consciousness reflects a feeling that you may need it someday when you may not be able to afford it. Fear of the unknown.

Inheritance:
You can't let it go because it was in your family for many years. You feel powerless to change. Guilt.

Laziness:
You do not want to take responsibility for your own life.

Programming:
You believe you are, and always will be, unhappy. You will always eat and live that way because that is the way you are.

Money:
You paid money for it. Money is always on your mind, regardless if you have too much or too little money.

Boredom:
You have too much time on your hands and have nothing to do but shop, eat, drink, think and gossip.

Illness:
Illness of the mind, body and home influence your health, actions, thinking and home space. Help is needed to answer an inner need that the dis-ease highlights.

HUMBUG EXCUSES THAT PEOPLE HAVE TO KEEP HUMBUG IN THEIR LIFE TO AVOID CLEANING UP THEIR ACTS

To de-humbug first takes <u>awareness</u>, then a <u>desire</u> to clean up your humbug, and then it takes <u>work</u>. In our society we are programmed to have the American Dream, and to believe that owning multiple possessions, believing radical ideas from movies and video games, eating and drinking new foods and drinks displayed on the grocery shelves, purchasing money markets, and behaving as our peers, parents and personal teachers will satisfy our inner self and needs and bring us happiness. The pushers of humbug have large advertising budgets:

- Buy this and you will be a champion.
- Purchase that and you will get the man or woman of your dreams.
- Drink this and you will be in the in crowd.
- Own this and you will be king of the road.
- Take this drug and you can dance in a field of flowers.

… the list goes on and on. Unfortunately, this marketing is a smoke screen for big business and political control.

Awareness:

With all our freedoms, with all our technology, with all the scientific new wonder drugs on the market we are becoming a society of depressed, obese, needy, rude, and anxiety-ridden people. What is wrong with this picture?

Have you bought into this Misrepresented Dream? Think of what you purchased during the previous week. How much were you influenced by the advertising surrounding each product?

Desire/Procrastination:

To help you identify your fear of change that may be keeping you in a state of procrastination, see if any of these excuses sound familiar to you for why you do not clean up your act.

I'm too busy. I can change any time I want.
It's too stressful.
I'm too overwhelmed – I don't know how.
It's not that important – this is how I am.
I feel safer with all this stuff around me.
I'll let my kids, friends or parents worry about it.

It's a beautiful day – I want to be outside.
It's a rainy day; I just want to cozy up with a book.
I'll do it tomorrow, next week, next vacation, next lifetime…
I can't make a decision right now.
Everybody else is doing it, buying it, eating it...
Everybody else is messed up so it's ok to be like that.
Everybody else is always late so why should I be on time?
It is not my fault that I am like this.
I am fine - it is everybody else who has the problem.
I can do it any time I want – I am not just ready yet.
It's the way of the world– we are the land of plenty.   (Plenty of what? Fears? Weight? Anxiety? Pressure?)

Once you've identified your resistance, it's easy to get to work creating the life of your dreams.

CLEANING YOUR MAGIC MIRROR

Here are a few suggestions or thoughts to keep in mind while you read this book and deal with your internal and external humbug.

Only you know if you are humbugged or not. You must be true to yourself – you can only be true to yourself. But, sometimes it is helpful to get an opinion from someone you trust, for everyone has personal blind spots.

What may be humbug for one person may not be humbug for another. No judgments are allowed, for judgment is a form of humbug.

You can become too humbug free. You want to live your life in balance. Do not become machine-like and find yourself rigid and calculating every word you say or every purchase you make to a heightened degree. Trying to be a perfectionist becomes a form of humbug if and when humbug thoughts are always in your mind. A little humbug is natural. Just be aware of it and laugh with yourself and take notice of yourself with daily practice or meditation.

To De-humbug your life takes work and constant awareness.

Humbug stuff is coming into your life each day. A telephone call may make you feel angry or depressed. An unpleasant situation may cause you to want to eat or drink more than you would normally. Getting ready for finals and end-term papers may cause you stress. Be aware of your feelings.

LIVING WITH A HUMBUG PERSON

This book is about your inner work in dealing with and releasing your personal humbug situations to create a life of grace, ease and happiness. There are many people who do not recognize their own humbug issues or may value their humbug situations differently than you do. Some people may never want to face themselves for whatever reasons they may have. Sometimes we need to live with humbugged people, who often do affect the happiness and events of a home and family. Separating your self from an overly humbugged person, such as an abuser of drugs or alcohol, can be a difficult thing to do if they are related to you or are a good friend. Keep a personal space (in your home and heart) – a place where no one else can go, even if it is only a closet or a drawer or dresser top and a silly little string that you wear on your finger to remind you of your center. Positive changes will occur on all fronts for you when you no longer absorb the humbug from another person and can own what is yours.

You can give a copy of this book lovingly to your humbugged loved one in hopes that they too will take a look at the humbug in themselves and tell them that you would be willing to talk with them after they read the book. But you can't force anyone else to face themselves. All you can be is your loving, giving, compassionate self; doing your own self work. Keep a vision that your clearness will shine a light on the world you live in such that others around you will be reflected in that light (that mirror) and see themselves. Allow them to naturally make changes on their own. Sometimes you may find that you need to bless and release a person from your life - wishing they achieve their highest good.

CREATE THE LIFE OF YOUR DREAMS

All chapters in this book will support, empower and encourage you to recognize and become aware of your personal humbug, to manage or rid yourself of it, and to live a happy life. It takes work and constant (daily) reminders. It does become easier with practice.

Your true nature is happiness and this happiness is always there for you to see and feel.

What is Your Label Please?

Where do you work? What do you do?
Who are you?

What do you own? Where is your home?
What car do you drive?
What! Are you deprived?
Who did you say you were?

Where were you born? How do you play?
How do you pay?
Who did you say you were?

CHAPTER THREE
FACE YOUR SELF EXERCISES

EXERCISE # 1:
WHO AM I? AN EXPLORATION OF SELF

This exercise will take you back to your birth. You will look at all the possible labels (see # 3 below) you were given or gave yourself, which are potent forms of humbug that you have accumulated during your lifetime.

OBJECTIVE:

By peeling away the layers of labels, you will be able to begin to see yourself clearly. From this point of view you will become lighter of heart and better able to focus on the choices you want to make for the rest of your life. You will develop more compassion for others and your psychic abilities will sharpen.

WHAT YOU WILL NEED:

A pad or notebook (make it the Magic one)
A pen or pencil
Optional: Old photo albums, yearbooks, holiday cards, family movies

EXERCISE:

1. Find a comfortable, quiet, personal space where you will not have distractions (avoid cell or land telephones, have pets and children tucked away).

2. Fold a piece of paper into two columns.

3. In the left column, starting with your birth and continuing to present day, begin listing as many labels you can think of that have been given to you or those that you give yourself. (You may want to flip through old photo albums to let the images trigger other labels you may have forgotten).

> For example:
> Boy/Girl, name, family name (were you named after a relative, dead or alive?), religion, nationality, cute, the quiet one, the wild one, smart, stupid, lazy, a homemaker, a home-wrecker, a student, President or CEO of the XYZ Company, High School Prom Queen, Drag Queen, mother, daughter, sister, aunt, friend, father, son, brother, uncle, Brownie Scout leader, pain in the butt, Civic Council President, Fireman, Nurse, the wealthy uncle, US citizen, political party, etc.

4. In the right column, next to each label, write one to three words (no more) about how you feel about each label. Be truthful. No one will see this list unless you want them to.

5. On a new sheet of paper you will play pretend. Give yourself some new labels. Use these new labels as a means of getting to know yourself better and how you might like to have people know you.

> If you were to pick a new name – what would it be?
> If you were to pick a hometown – where would it be?

6. Imagine what it would be like to live your life, label free.

7. When you look at others, notice how people communicate by using labels. Labels are a big part of advertising and marketing – people often purchase because of the label. Watches, pocketbooks, sneakers ... label you in the in crowd.

8. Live your life (now that you have recognized that these labels are not really about the real you). You can act as a label free person even if you choose items with labels. You can make choices that reflect who you truly are.

EXERCISE # 2:

LETTING GO AND BREAKING OUTDATED HABITS

Without thinking, you carry on certain habits. Some people twirl their hair, some people smoke or drink diet soda. Some people shake their leg or foot while they talk on the telephone or with friends at the local diner. If we do not know that we are doing them, habits take energy away from us that we can use elsewhere. Collecting humbug, both internal and external, is habit forming. This exercise makes you aware of how you have attached to simple habits and allows you to change some routine habits.

OBJECTIVE:

You will be able to recognize some of your habits and change them so that they do not become ingrained in you.

WHAT YOU WILL NEED:

Your watch
Your coffee cups and water glasses that are in your kitchen cabinets
A car, bus or taxi

EXERCISE:

1. Put your watch on your other wrist for three days. Watch (no pun intended) yourself – see how many times you look at your old/

former wrist before you adjust to the new wrist. After three days put it back on your regular wrist. Do this every three or four months. It is a good tool to keep you alert.

2. Move your coffee cups to another cupboard or another place in your kitchen. See how many mornings it takes you to remember that you moved them. After you have adjusted to the cups in their new spot for three days, put them back to where you originally had them. Do this exercise twice a year just to keep you alert.

3. When you are at a stop sign or red traffic light, STOP in your thinking, too. Observe what is on your mind – what is your thinking pattern? What were you just thinking about? What is your body language (posture)? This will help you become aware of some of your mind habits.

When I was an elementary school teacher I would play this game with my students. I found that after their lunch period they would come back to class all wired from the sugar that they had eaten. Arms and legs would be moving in all directions and they had a hard time sitting still in their seats. I would be in the middle of a lesson and all of a sudden yell, STOP. The children knew that they had to freeze just as they were and look at themselves to see what their bodies were doing. They all loved this little game for it was not only fun, but taught them to become more aware and in control of their bodies.

In the next chapter you will let go of even more old humbug patterns that have kept you from your true nature: Joy.

CHAPTER FOUR

MIRROR IMAGES: WHAT YOU THINK, IS WHAT YOU GET

Mind Chaos

Chaos, clutters your mind

It blocks your thinking

It sends you off sinking

It watches you wallow in a pool of sorrow

You trip, you fall, you stall.

Weighted down

You become your own clown.

Why do you keep it?

Lord only knows

It may be of use in one of your shows!

When you are filled with fear, gripped by depression
and dissociated from reality,
That is an unhealthy consciousness.

When you are evading, torn by conflict and divided
against yourself,
That is a blocked consciousness.

When you have an integrated, unobstructed, open
mind, thinking for the highest good of all,
That is a healthy consciousness.

YOUR MIND AS A TRANSMISSION STATION

Your mind filled with your thoughts is like a radio station that sends out messages. Your mind, unlike your body, which has physical limitations, is like a science fiction character or superhero that can penetrate walls, leap over tall buildings and has no limitations of time or place. Your mind is unlimited, and can reach and touch people, places or things in your life and afar. If you have a healthy mind, your life and home will be a reflection of that health. If your mind is filled with negative, unhealthy thoughts, your home, body and relationships will reflect that back to you too. These messages (your mind's thoughts) are also magnetic in nature and attract to you what your mind energy continually, frequently and persistently puts out.

- Have you ever walked into a room right after an argument and felt the tension in the air?
- Have you ever thought lovingly about a person and then they called or showed up at your door?

- Have you ever sensed an unhealthy situation where you felt that you were not safe?
- Have you ever thought about something happy happening and then it happened?
- Have you ever gotten caught up in the excitement of a situation?
- Have you ever thought that when people say they love you – that they are lying?
- Have you ever changed the stations on a radio and listened to entirely different programming?

Mind chaos is the number one reason we experience stress and depression. It is even the number one reason we experience hate and guilt. Many fears also would disappear if we looked at our mind chaos. Mind chaos is also the primary cause of most unhappiness. It can add weight to your body and activate illness, tighten muscles, and limit movement in your life.

Looking at your mind chaos can tend to get heavy and wearisome, which is why most people tend to ignore facing their own self. So I am suggesting that you approach this chapter on your mind chaos with fun and a light spirit. Approach your mind chaos like a game - a game that you can only win. You are the explorer of your own self. If at any time you find yourself getting saddened or overwhelmed, I suggest you take a walk in Nature, take a break, talk with a trusted friend and re-read chapter two; Reflections on Your True Nature -Joy.

Mind chaos comes in many forms: thoughts set up by belief systems, emotions attached to past experiences, fears and doubts. All of this mind stuff can show up in many ways in your life. It can show up as aches, pains and dis-ease in your body. It can show up in your life with circumstances that you do not want. If not kept in check, day after day, week after week, year after year, your mind chaos, i.e. your persistent thoughts and emotions, lay down a pattern, which triggers and creates an emotional *grooved* field, which surrounds you. This field, if it is allowed to continue, eventually affects your body's health and the health of your life.

No emotion (except perhaps guilt) is unhealthy in minor amounts. Your emotions flow in and through your body - carried by your breath and blood. Imagine a heavy, sad heart pumping away, or your veins squeezed with anger or your breath paralyzed by fear. But, when emotions such as worry, fear, guilt, sadness, anger, anxiety [yes, I am naming that as an emotion – mixed with fear and worry] become a major part of your living;

this will affect your physical body by creating dis-ease. Healthy emotions (such as love, trust and joy) affect your body by creating a sense of ease and well-being – an openness. Your emotions control (drive) you in how you act and speak, which then affects: how you create your home's interior design, your family relationships, your friends, your work, and your life. If you follow this line of thinking, your emotions affect the whole state of your world.

MINI EXERCISE:

Sit in a quiet space and see if you can detect an emotion that you have at the moment. If you can't find one – make one up for this exercise. Feel it. Feel it totally. See if you can locate where in your body the emotion is located. Breathe into the emotion. Explore it – how does it feel? How does it move? What other sensation or thoughts come up for you? Make notes in your Magic Notebook.

KARMA

Your mental nature not only affects you, but also those who live with you. Even your dog and cat will become unhealthy and unhappy if that is the mind energy in your home. The pillows on your couch will look dirty and the windows in your home cloudy. There will be chaos reflected in your home to mirror the chaos of your mind. If you are unhealthy, plants and flowers will not thrive and the air in your home will become stagnant.

The principle of cause and effect (some call it Karma) is circular in nature. This means your mind chaos affects you in very real ways. Sometimes, for example, there may people in your life that operate from a base of greed. These people will do everything to try to put onto you, that you are the greedy one and twist things so much so that others, who may not be aware, believe what they say and find fault with you too. This can hurt your heart and your being. When you are so grossly misunderstood, you of course as a Face Your Self explorer, need to look at your own part in the whole situation. In the long run, if indeed you know that it was not about you, it is not healthy for you to *have to go out of your way* to prove them wrong. If they will not hear because of their own personal blocks in their life; a good action for you, is to bless and release these people (and situation) from your life to their (its) highest good and allow karmic laws to take care of all. Let it go.

There is an ancient Chinese proverb, which says:

You think your mind is as quiet and deep as a bottomless abyss, but your thoughts are as loud as thunder.

If you are constantly unhappy, angry, or upset about something, the people close to you will receive that subtle message even if you say you are happy and fine. Much of what you communicate is in your tone and in your body language. As you continue to do this work, you will become more sensitive and pick up subtle energies of people. There may be times when you feel "out of tune." You may not understand why you are feeling something icky or unhappy and you may blame yourself. But it may not be about you. You could be picking up a negative thought pattern from someone near you. A large portion of how we all communicate is in the consciousness behind our words and actions. Some call this the sub consciousness. This consciousness is a very strong sender of messages (frequencies). It also has a magnetic attraction as well. It is this deep-rooted consciousness, which you as an explorer, want to discover, de-chaos and uproot. It is this deep emotional self that you want to become aware of so that you know from where you operate.

If you are feeling down and you surround yourself with people who also have feelings of negativity and dis-ease, they will gladly tune in to your sad sack radio station. Like attracts like and the mind chaos cycle will spiral onward with each person fulfilling the other's mind experience and life experience.

> ## MINI EXERCISE:
>
> Families and friends support each other's belief systems – this is neither good nor bad (no judgments). Can you name 10 beliefs that you have that are supported by either your family or friends?

Mind chaos can be sent through generations of children. Make a conscious effort to stop bequeathing your mind chaos. Chaos of the mind, body and home can get passed down through the generations and lead to constant chaos in the world. If you do not see clearly, identify, and take charge of your own mind chaos – future generations will suffer.

RECEIVING MESSAGES

The opposite of being able to send out messages from your mind's radio station is that you can also receive other people's messages and thoughts (as others can receive yours). If you are not aware, you may be tuning into and absorbing messages that you really do not want - such as poverty thinking, feelings of ill health or feelings of (ego) and misplaced grandeur and power. For example, if I do not like the waiter in a restaurant – I will not eat the food. Usually the wait staff is a reflection of the kitchen staff, which touches and prepares the food. I do not want that energy in me. Food becomes a part of you (more on that in Chapter Five, Reflections In the Mirror: Body Anarchy). Conversely, food made with love and caring (like my grandmother's cooking) always tastes wonderful, nurtures and feeds my mind and body.

If you meet someone who expresses anger or unhappiness and you <u>do not</u> have those thoughts or feelings and you <u>do not</u> want those thoughts or feelings – <u>do not</u> tune in to them. You need not receive their radio program. You do not have to listen to negative conversation. You do not have to accept other people's mind chaos. You do not have to believe that what someone tells you about another is truth.

How do you do this you ask? Sometimes it's simple: you can walk away or change the channel to a different topic. Other times you may find yourself in a situation with a friend or family member where it is not possible to change the channel or the topic of conversation, or to walk away. Lend a sympathetic ear and listen as a compassionate friend. Unless you are asked, do not offer advice or get caught up in telling your own disaster stories, which will pull you into your mind chaos along with theirs. If you find that it may be beneficial, tell your disaster stories without personal attached emotion. When offering advice, make it constructive and positive.

Bright colors often give you a more positive, cheery attitude; consider wearing something that makes you feel positive and healthy of mind when you know you'll be in a potentially *hazardous situation,* such as a family gathering or other sticky situations where all types of mind chaos from others may be going on. You can also intentionally put positive energy into a special piece of jewelry, which when you touch it, reminds you and gives you some extra inner strength and peace of mind to carry you through. (Remember: This is only a reflective tool for your mind that you have declared. The object itself has no power other than what you give to it).

I like to keep a little glass vile in my purse of jasmine or lemon grass oil that I can dab on my wrists, chest or right under my nose to make me feel good if I am in a difficult, toxic circumstance. I also like to wash the day away at the end of each day. It is my special time of day when I shower off all of the day's energy that I do not want to take to bed with me. I send it down the drain. It is an intentional ritual. I light candles in my bathing room and use the fire energy to burn away all unwanted thoughts, attachments or events. In this way I purify my mind and body from any of the day's events or negative energies I may have picked up that day.

MINI EXERCISE:

The first step for getting a grip on your mind chaos is to become aware that your mind can send and receive messages.

1. Make a list right now of the messages you are sending out of hate, selfishness, ego related issues, boastfulness... Be truthful – you must be truthful to yourself – Face Your Self.
2. Make a conscious list right now of the messages you want to send and those you want to receive. Have no limitations.

Are your lists similar? There is a circle in life. What we put out we get back. Save this list; you'll use it for review at the end of the chapter.

A THOUGHT TO REMEMBER

Lighten Up! Make this a game. You want to: Achieve your TRUE Potential. Face Your Self in your Magic Mirror and remember; you really are not your thoughts (they change). You are perfect, whole and complete right here and now. This is a chance for you to align yourself with that goodness, love and abundance. The laws of cause and effect are working with you right here and now.

Set your mind radio for victory, health, wellness and enjoying your day. When you wake up say out loud or to your self, "I am planning on having a good day!" or "I can enjoy this day even with obstacles." Set your receiver to accept only positive thoughts. Say to yourself, "I am getting better and better and releasing my mind chaos and accept a healthy, happy life." Make an intentional effort to not personally leave chaos in your own wake, as that of a boat as it moves on through the water. Be mindful of how you live your life as you sail on through this life.

RESTLESS MIND SYNDROME

In the course of your daily life you have normal things on your mind: the grocery list, the tennis match, the dinner party, where your next meal will come from, the important business meeting, the school project, the children's birthday, your partner's clothes to be picked up at the cleaners, house construction, paying the bills... the list goes on and on. In the course of your daily life you need to figure out things like: whether to take the medicine your doctor recommended or how to get your next business contract, or how you will survive without employment. This is not mind chaos or restless mind syndrome. Restless Mind Syndrome is that deep-rooted thought which pops up and comes back time and again and undermines your life. It can show up at family gatherings, it can show up at a fashion show, it can show up while you are reading a magazine it can show up when you are looking for a job. The next step is to recognize what mind chaos is blocking your good and making your mind restless.

Mind Chaos is any thought that triggers a feeling of anxiety, hate, fear, depression, depletion, envy, superiority, prejudice, trouble, immorality, lack, unhappiness, jealousy, anger, shame, insecurity … If your mind chatters on in a negative way, this chaos of your mind can and will, rob you every day of a happy life.

Do you find yourself wanting to apply for a job that you know you would be great for, yet the thought, I'm not good enough." grips you? – This is mind chaos.

Do you ever find yourself looking through a fashion magazine and thinking how fat and out of shape you are and then you get depressed and go eat something because you feel that you are inferior? – This is mind chaos.

Do you ever find yourself at a family gathering suddenly feeling uncomfortable and wanting to leave because you feel depleted? – This is mind chaos.

Do you ever call a friend and if they don't return your call you begin to think that you did something to offend them or feel guilty of something? – This is mind chaos.

Do you ever find yourself not happy with what you have – looking at a neighbor, family member, or others' possessions with envy? - This is mind chaos. (By the way, my Dad would often tell me, Pamela, someone always has a bigger boat. Meaning that you can spend your life trying to feed your ego with bigger and better or you can be happy with the "boat" that you have.)

Do you ever have an idea and think about it often, but never get it off the ground - but regret about not getting it off the ground? - This is mind chaos.

Do you ever think you are better and know more than everyone else? - This is mind chaos.

Why do you always react in a certain way in certain situations?

Why do you always avoid new experiences?

Why do you shrink to the background when you are faced with certain issues?

Why do you get dizzy and can't breathe when you face certain things in your life?

Why do you always loose your temper and yell when presented with a challenge?

Why do you always see everything that someone says as a challenge?

Look to the root cause of these things - for these are reflections to your mind chaos.

Finding the Root Cause of your behavior takes serious self-observation – you must face your demons and Face Your Self. When you recognize your mind chaos, you can do something about it and that is a good thing. The following mind chaos situations are listed in a mindless order of significance. They are listed for your benefit so you will be able to begin to recognize mind chaos situations. There are exponential multiple combinations of mind chaos that create a restless mind.

Make a little check or note in the margin if anything rings a bell. You can add more to the list if you want. Face Your Self suggested solutions are in italics.

Grudges of any kind
Forgiveness is a very important aspect of releasing mind chaos and will let you get on with your life.

Worries
Keep your thoughts in the present moment.

Procrastination
Get organized and take action.

Pressures
Work, family, financial, legal, health …Stop. Let the world turn. Take time out for yourself. Then you can face your priorities clearly again.

Religious beliefs
Spend time in Nature and find your own truth.

People who bring you down or make you feel bad about yourself.
Ask yourself why these people are in your life? Can you bless them and let them go? If they are family members decide when and how you will interact with them.

Old boyfriends or girlfriends
Watch for energy leaks in your current relationship. Assess how serious you are with your current relationship.

Addictions of any kind - Obsession
The reality is that there is no such thing as a good addiction. An addiction rules you versus you ruling the addiction. Before you reach for that drink, cigarette, or telephone… touch your nose for a slow count to five.

News and bad stories or movies
Turn off the TV and be selective of the books and movies you choose.

Fear
Love and fear are primary motivators: choose love:
Go for that audition.
Enter that contest.
Write that book.
Ask that woman or man out on a date.

Low Self-Esteem
Look in the mirror and into your eyes and see the prize.

Envy
Remember: the universe is abundant – there is enough for everyone.

Criticism
When a child does something wrong do not criticize – teach with understanding and compassion
Self-analysis and change is good. Do not listen to mean-spirited criticism by others or yourself.

Other people's wishes that are not your own
Only do things that you really want to do. Trust your heart. Do not allow yourself to be hypnotized.

Assumptions of others
You do not need to prove anything to anyone. Always speak the truth.

Taking care of others (children, parents, spouses)
Take some time out for yourself and put yourself first –this is not being selfish. If you are not good you will not be good for any one else.

Correspondence (telephone calls or emails)
Simplify, prioritize and organize your life.

Old patterns and habits
Declare that you are changing old, outdated patterns that no longer serve you. Make a commitment.

Perfection
Strive to be the best you can.

Hanging out with people who you really do not like
Bring people more aligned with your thinking into your life.

Mistrust
You can only know yourself and your own motivations. Trust must start somewhere – make it start with you. That doesn't mean to be stupid or to put your self in danger.

Past life experiences and your ancestors
Honor your past – visit the gravesite of your family members or make a donation in their name to a charity. Feed the birds in their honor. You can change past patterns that may be imprinted on your palms or soul. Shift your

vibrations, for when you die you take that which is on your mind and in your heart with you.

Desires and anticipations

It is good to visualize your dreams, but keep your reality in the present, and your visualizations and desires in check.

Facing reality

Turn off the television and telephones for a day. Spend the day in a natural setting alone with yourself to determine what in your life is genuine and what is not.

Old hurts

Do not take everything personally – sometimes (most times) it is not about you.

Looking backwards

Remembering the past is good as your foundation to spring forth from, unless it keeps you from living in the present.

Success

There is more prosperity in virtue than money in the bank. Count the blessings you have now.

Anger

Find a way to release it. Prolonged anger is only hurting you and your health.

Embarrassments/Shame

Get on with life and laugh it off. We all make a fool of ourselves at some time. Find empowerment and beauty in yourself.

Gossiping or passing rumors

Focus your energy on remembering your own self: not the misfortunes of others.

Regrets

Make amends if you can – then get on with your life. You cannot change others. Find clarity and teach what you have learned – if even to just one person.

Ethics

Live your life as if we're all one – be mindful what you do to others.

Hate

Get it out of your system (Shout into a pillow). Let the hated party go and live their life – life takes care of all.

Prejudices

Stop and observe. Look to understanding hurts or fears which cause you to have a closed-mind.

Arrogance

Ask yourself where your feelings of arrogance come from? Be thankful and compassionate - life touches us all.

Impolite Manners/Disrespect

Come back to your senses – you only hurt yourself. Be kind and thoughtful.

Doubt

Discover and live your own truths. Keep open to the world, but at the same time, return to yourself. Taoist proverb.

Guilt vs. Pride

Feel good when you have succeeded or achieved your goal. Do not be ashamed. Those who succeed with real love will never have false pride.

Failure

Use failures as a way to learn and gain inner strength (failures are actually steps on the ladder of success). There is no failure unless you give up on yourself.

Struggle

Pick your battles; you do not have to overachieve.

Money worries

Feed the birds and allow your prosperity to multiply. Trust the abundance of the universe – connect with your spiritual abundance. If you spend less than your income, you are wealthy. Wealth is not just about money. Count your blessings.

Shame

You are beautiful.

FACING DEPRESSION

Happiness is not something that is reserved for special times. It is something you choose to experience wherever you are and whenever you want. This can be easier said than done. When your relationship falls apart or you lose the love of your life or you just got fired from your job, or you fail a class, or someone close to you dies in body; it is *normal* to feel heartbroken, lonely, sad, scared and blue. We all need time to heal. Some life situations take longer than others. Do not judge yourself as to how long you may need. Face Your Self. What feels healthy to you? As time goes on what do you do after a day or two? A week? A month? A year? Five years? Ten years? Do you find yourself going deeper and deeper into a space of confusion, sadness and discord? Do you let the world turn, breathe, and realign yourself with your greater good? You must realign yourself with goodness, love and abundance. You must regroup and count your current blessings – taking account of what good your life held in the past and now currently. Life's, heartbreaks, and ups and downs happen to everyone – you are not alone in your experience of life. And I send you love and Light. Find a friend to talk with – one who has perhaps experienced what you experienced. Be mindful of your diet (more on that in Chapter Five: Reflection in the Mirror: Body Anarchy) for what you eat affects your thinking and feelings as your thinking and feelings affect what you eat.

MINI EXERCISE:

Write down every positive thing in your life that you can think of right now. Align yourself with these things, using these good things as your footing and your foundation. When you recognize your good it is easier to move on, step by step.

Life affects us all. No one escapes from experiencing life. Life can be difficult and dark at times. It is in the difficult times – the so called hard times – that Facing Your Self separates the men from the boys and the women from the girls. It is at times of stress and sadness when it takes the most concentrated mind and body effort to remember who you truly are and what is real in life - despite the hardship you are experiencing. It is important to give yourself a hug and be good to yourself. It is easy to feel good on a mountain top on a sunny day with the breeze gently blowing in your face - but we all have a life to live - even on top of a mountain things happen. Remind yourself that actually all we have in life is a gift to us – we can't and don't take any of it with us. What looks like a bad thing can actually be a good thing – somehow you must know in your heart; from a Universal Perspective, that everything is in its right order. What you can do is to keep counting your blessings in life and know that the current situation can lead you to a whole new experience, which you would never know about had the so called bad thing not happened.

There may be times that you may feel depressed for no apparent cause. This might be a wake-up call from your spirit - your soul. This might be your mind and body's way of pushing you forward to make needed changes in your life – changes which you may have been avoiding.

> # MINI EXERCISE:
>
> Are you avoiding making some needed changes in your life? Take a moment and think if there is something in your life you would like to see change. Is there something that you do not like.

The next time you are sad and depressed observe your self. Many aspects of your sadness are probably related to some aspect of your past and/or your diet/ and/or your surroundings. Sometimes depression may be a repressed anger or sadness (mind chaos) that you have been carrying around for a long time and have not addressed. Or, you may be remembering and comparing your present situation with something that was more romantic, more rewarding, friendlier, more wonderful in the past than it is now. Perhaps you are comparing yourself to others or another time. In this case, this feeling of sadness or depression is really only related to nostalgic memory (mind chaos). All things change – you know this. The only thing that does not change is at your center: love. You let your memory have control over you. Try removing any pictures and photographs from your home (for a time being), which may make you sad. If you sit on your special chair and look out into the room that you spend most of your time in, what do you see? Do you see things which have memories of days gone by? Bring something new into your home to spark you up (to light your fire). You do not need to throw out all of your old things; ask your family or friends if they would like some of the special (but making you sad) things which you do not need in your life any longer. Sharing is good for the soul.

I once had a client who was still very sad years after her mother died. Her family called me into her home to work with her. There was a cute little dog that was running around. I talked for a little while with the client and then we walked around her home. In the dining room, which was in the center of the home and a room which she had to pass through several times each day, there was a large, beautifully framed oil painting of a woman sitting in a chair with her head down petting her dog. I asked the client to tell me about the painting. She started by explaining that she had bought her dog right after her mother died in hopes of having a friend. She continued to tell me that she saw this painting and it reminded her of herself right after her mother died. While she was talking to me she was getting sadder and sadder. All of a sudden she looked at me and smiled and said, "You know that painting makes me sad – it reminds me of when my mom died." We agreed that the painting should be removed from the dining room and sold. Her family reported that after my visit they removed the painting, and their mother and wife was expressing more joy and looking forward to the future.

When you can get to the root cause of your depression you will then be able to make adjustments in your life. Finding the root cause can be like peeling an onion. There are many layers, and each layer may make you cry before you get to the center. Crying is a good release if you are not saying, "Oh poor me, I suffer so." If you do say that, then ask deeper questions of yourself – why do you feel like poor me? It is good to look at your sadness. Remember to look at this as if it's a game of detective work. Do not be afraid to go back in time and face old hurts and bad times. They can't hurt you any longer unless you let them. Remember, that then was then and now is now. You are strong of spirit. If you feel the need, do not hesitate to get a professional psychologist or therapist to assist you with this process.

A THOUGHT TO REMEMBER:

Do not attach mentally and emotionally to your thoughts while you are the detective asking the questions. Keep asking questions. Why do I feel like this? What is bothering me? …Yes, I do not like this, but what about it is annoying me? Why?…

I want to acknowledge that there are many horrible things that happen to men, women, children and families in this world. There are places on the planet where kidnappings, murders, death and explosions are part of the daily experience. There are places where food and clean water are very scarce. There are children who grow up after experiencing family members killed and are injured and orphaned. There are sexual hurts and abuses. There are places where there is no social or family stability. Children grow up with paranoia and fear and are persistently insecure and depressed. Children are resilient –yet these experiences can cause a life of distress and depression if not addressed. Have you experienced a life-altering situation, which causes you stress and depression?

POST-TRAUMATIC STRESS DISORDER

Post– Traumatic Stress Disorder (PSTD) can make certain "trigger" experiences feel like the original traumatic experience. It takes a lot of love, understanding and awareness to recognize that you are safe and not in that past situation any longer. It takes a lot on your part to give your self *permission* to live your life in joy. Your body and mind are connected - each has natural built-in protective mechanisms (which were good at the original time of the event), which trigger your body and mind into action. Your breath may shorten, your heart rate go up, tension in your body may tighten your muscles, your body chemistry may trigger certain chemicals, which put you in active mode to protect yourself. All of this is real and real for you.

I once went through a very stressful time in my life where I felt that my life was threatened. After about 15 years, an event happened that brought me right back to the terror I experienced years earlier. I received a telephone call. I had to consciously sit, literally talk to myself and walk myself through each breath I took and remind myself that I was safe and what happened in my past was not real for my life any longer. I had to remind myself that I was safe. It took work and love and understanding, not only of my husband, but of myself to get me through.

I have a girlfriend who has gone through many hardships in life. One of her favorite quotes is, "Then was then and now is now." which helps her see clearly her life as it is today. She is laughing and loving, not bitter, scared or angry. Sometimes your mind chaos gets so ingrained into your system – your very being - that you find yourself stressed out, fearful, or depressed and you personally can't get to the root cause or cannot face it alone. There are social and psychological programs in many towns and cities if you need assistance working out a stressful life situation and I sincerely recommend that you seek them out if you find you need help with this. Help is good - we are all in this thing called life together and we each should not ever feel ashamed or embarrassed to seek and ask for help.

YOU AND YOUR SEASONS

Here is another thought for you to consider: You are a natural being. You have your own personal flows of high tide and low tide. You actually have your own personal seasons of summer and winter. Sometimes you may be experiencing a growth period like springtime flowers and the buds of leaves on the trees, while at other times in your life you may be going through a dormant winter period where you need to cocoon, withdraw, and think about what you want to grow next. Both are normal, natural, and good. You must know your own rhythms and they may not always match those of your friends.

You also live under the influence of stars and planets, which rotate around you. There is no reason to think that the gravitational pulls of the planets and moon should not affect the waters of your soul and your nervous system as they do the waters on our planet. After all, you spend your first nine months floating in a sac of water, and 68% of your body is water, which hydrates all of your cells. Rather than running to take pills, looking for experiences that will bring you an upper, or worrying that you have a severe problem, remember: sometimes it is good to let the world turn and know that your sadness or low energy is in the natural flow of things. There are earthly seasons and each of us experiences our own life seasons. I know that in my life, there are times where I need to let three or four months go by before I start again. And, when you think of the earthly seasons – each season is about three months long. Live naturally with the seasons of your own body and life. All things have their highs and lows (ups and downs). All things also have their cycles. It is natural and it is good.

THE MIND, BODY, HOME CONNECTION

The work you are doing with Face Your Self is about de-cluttering and re-designing your true home – you. People affect your life balance - so be mindful of whom you surround yourself with. You are responsible for your own life (your mind and your body) first and foremost, and it is important to cultivate healthy living choices to keep your interior design in tip-top shape. However, your home (dorm room, apartment) day after day, week after week, year after year is a major supporter or "depleter" of your life.

Your mind, body and home all inter-relate and affect each other. They weave your life into a beautiful woven basket or tapestry – called your life. Or, they weave into a knot of tangled, discordant fibers (energy cords, if I may) – called your life. The good thing is, if you are in distress in one area (mind, body or home) you can use the other two, to enhance, adjust, or cure the depletion of the other area with the intention of balancing your life working with the law of **correspondence.**

When you do this work, it is important to have a clear intention and always do it for the highest good of all. The following are a few home and body suggestions to adjust and cure certain mind chaos situations:

If you have a heavy heart, feel depressed, or feel sluggish and can't seem to get things started:

Bring in light by making sure all your light fixtures work.

Buy some bright colored dishes, pillows or towels.

Adopt a dog (animals are great mood adjusters).

Eat sprouts and light foods, apples and fruits that grow on trees to get the high prana energy from these foods.

Sleep in a light material such as a silk.

If you do not feel grounded:

Bring a heavy weight into your space, such as a statue or a large stone or rock that you happen to find appealing.

Use dark colors of the earth (browns, deep golden) on a wall or on your place-mats and seat cushions.

Eat earth food, such as rice or 7-grain breads.

Sleep in a heavy material, such as terry cloth.

If you feel sad:

Bring in some happy plants like ferns and flowering jasmine.

Bring in bright flowers.

Use sunny colors, such as yellows or pinks or light greens in your kitchen and bedroom.

Eat happy foods such as bananas or cereal with fresh blueberries.

Sleep in the color orange (maybe polka dots or a color that reflects joy to you).

HOW DESIRE CONFUSES YOUR MIND

There is a poem, Richard Cory, written by Edward Arlington Robinson, about a man who seemed to have everything anyone could want in life: money, position, success, and many worldly possessions. However, Richard Cory, despite having it all, self-destructed.

Desire can be a good thing if it leads you to aspire for a higher purpose or healthier lifestyle – this can be viewed as an inner calling. However, desire, when it becomes a craving, a wishing and wanting which develops into coveting and yearning for something that in reality will never satisfy you, is a form of mind chaos. Do you want more and more; only to find that all you desire does not bring you real happiness? Sooner or later you must Face Your Self and find your true identity. By finding your true identity, through your own self-discovery, you can get out of the shadows of falsely assuming that things, money, power, and compulsive desires will bring you happiness. What do you truly want?

- Never permit the desires or behavior of other people, to influence what you want or how you should feel or live your life. Any friendship based upon keeping up with the neighbors or friends is not worth your time and energy. If you fail to be one of the gang and friends disappear because of this - was there a real friendship to begin with?
- You can never be hurt or deceived if you are free of all unnecessary desires or expectations toward other people. If you expect nothing, you get everything.
- Do not mistake desire for love. Desire is filled with self-gratification and constant searching for that higher and higher sensation of passion. Love is at home with itself. You do not have to prove anything. It is as comfortable as an old pair of slippers. It is as easy as a walk in the park. It is as magnificent as a sunrise and sunset. It is as strong as the strongest magnetic attraction.
- Nervousness is a symptom of desire. It is a fear of nothing happening or happening as fast as you desire. It is a desire to constantly fill space and time. It is like a mind wandering and jumping like a monkey from tree to tree. It is a symptom of not being present and not wanting or respecting with whom or where you are. Are you a control freak? Do you always desire to be doing something? Do you ever observe your foot tapping without you knowing it? Your eye twitching? Twirling your hair?
- If you do not identify your desires with being young – you will enjoy your whole life in years and feel, look and act youthful.
- If you do not identify your desires with food – food will have no power over you and you will remain your correct body mass. Allow food to fill your true physical hunger, not the hunger of your mind and lack in your life (Avoid unnatural foods which can cause cravings).

BE AWARE – BEWARE: MIND CHAOS TRIGGERS!

No matter how hard you try, you will find yourself from time to time smack in the middle of a mind chaos trigger situation. Most triggers involve interactions with others (I believe that only flowers and trees are always loving and understanding and bend with the breeze). If you were raised on a negative life perspective or you have developed negative thinking you will need to retrain your self to be positive and not fall victim to old mind fields of mind chaos. The Face Your Self exercises are designed to gently, yet powerfully, release old patterns.

With practice and awareness, it will get easier and actually become fun. Before you know it, you will find that even the most stressful situation will not affect your inner happiness and balance and you may actually enjoy the challenge to test how your are actually doing in this game of Facing Your Self. Good luck, and remember to laugh at yourself when you see a personal mind field or a chaos situation developing in you.

The following categories are a few examples that are notorious for triggering most people down a path to a less than healthy place full of mind chaos. Tools for survival are listed below. See if you can add more to each list.

Places:
Doctors' Offices
Beach Clubs
Fancy Restaurants
A Church, Temple, Mosque
Your Parents' House
The Principle's office

Events:
Birthdays
Deaths
Bankruptcy
Weddings
Births
Surgery/Medical events
Mondays

Things:
Sounds or music
Scents of cooking, cut grass, perfume

Money
Photos
Jewelry
Bills
Rejection Notices

Words:
You are ugly
Fat
Diet
Young
Aging
I need it now
How about a drink?

Activities:
Football games
School Social
Vacations
Your child's soccer game
Your tennis game
Family Bar-b-que
Telephone calls
Job interviews
Watching skinny people on television or in the movies
Reading about successful people

People:
Your ex-spouse or current spouse
Your mother
Your father
Your friends
Your boss
Your co-worker
Your neighbor
Your priest, rabbi, monk, or shaman
Your children
An annoying or rude person
Your sister
Your brother
Your in-laws

SURVIVAL TOOLS:

- STOP. When you find yourself in a mind chaos situation and notice that your personal mind chaos has been activated. Do not blame others, the situation or activity. Give yourself a little laugh and pat on the back for recognizing your attachment to the situation and then breathe and center yourself. Start asking yourself questions like: Why am I feeling angry, upset, bored, lonely, and insecure…? What in me is making me respond this way? Is it something from my past? What is it? Is it me? Is it the other person who has his or her own mind chaos? What is the best way to proceed?

- You may need to utilize an external tool as mentioned before, such as a piece of jewelry or a stone in your pocket to hold for inner strength to deflect the situation and enhance your positive reflection.

- Repeat a comforting phrase to your self silently, such as, " I am healthy, whole and complete." or, "When my mind is at peace, I am at peace and can then remain healthy and virtuous." Or, "This is my mind chaos, but I am not my mind chaos, I look forward to working through this."

- Music is one of the best influences you can employ when you are feeling you are in a mind chaos trigger. Allow the music to massage the chaos away.

- Wear red underwear (or some powerful color), which you can infuse with mind protective powers using your intention. You can re-mind (reprogram) yourself.

- Keep a beautiful, calming scent in your pocketbook, pocket, book bag or glove compartment of your car. Dot it on your forehead, your chest, and each shoulder and wrist with the intention of giving yourself a protective, loving shield (you may even want to dot it on your belly button).

- Take some orange peels from a fresh orange (I like to cut out small quarter size round circles with my thumb nail). Keep about nine or ten in your pocket. Allow the orange peels to absorb any negative influences. You can also take one of the peels out of your pocket and bend it in half to release a spray of orange scent into the air. The scent of orange is a happy, refreshing scent. At the end of the day, throw them out.

- Keep a picture of someone or something that inspires you in your pocket (a natural mountain stream, Albert Einstein). You can excuse yourself and go to the bathroom and look at the picture for a moment to refresh your being.

- If it is an option, excuse yourself and leave a stressful mind chaos trigger totally. Especially if you find that more harm and hurt will be experienced than good.

WORDS TO LOOK OUT FOR

When you speak, listen to what words come out of your mouth. The following are types of words and phrases to observe and eventually avoid, for these phrases and others like them can entangle you in mind chaos. When you find yourself walking or jogging down an old mind chaos path, such as gossip or feeling sorry for yourself, stop. If you do not, before you know it, you will be emotionally and physically entangled and wonder why you are so frustrated, unhappy, depleted, angry, frightened, or feeling ill.

Misery loves company (so does anger and hatred) – so if you find yourself around perpetually miserable, angry, hateful people, do not get caught into their web. You do not have to be food for other people not facing their own self. Listen with compassion, make recommendations if asked for and let it be.

MINI EXERCISE:

Play a game: When you catch yourself speaking any of the phrases below in a negative and draining way, you get one point. If you catch yourself before you speak, give yourself five points. However many points you accumulate – you're a winner!

Did you hear about...who did...???

I can quit any time I want, so I will just have this....

I'm not good enough/ I'm better than them.

I'm so ugly/ I'm so good looking.

Remember when...???

I can't stand it when...

I am so angry right now at... I could...

That's the way it always has been done.

I hate her, him, it.

I am really tired right now.

I can't breathe.

You selfish person.

Nobody uses their blinker any more in their car.

You never cared about me.

I am all alone.

Enough – I don't want to hear any more.

What's wrong with you? Me?

I can't.

I'll do it tomorrow. I'll start tomorrow.

I bought this because everyone has one.

Everyone is in debt.

What are your own mind chaos words or phrases? Make a list

One should examine one's mind and mental phenomena constantly, as a physician examines a patient. As a physician gains experience and insight into the problems of his patient and cures the patient of the disease, so one should gain insight into one's own mind and mental problems, and should work out solutions.
Ramamurti S. Mishra, MD
Self-Analysis and Self Knowledge

WAYS TO LET GO OF MIND CHAOS

There are many ways to release your mind chaos. I have listed my favorite "Top 10" ways below. There is an additional 26 ways included in the appendix of this book.

Give thanks for what is good in your life and count your blessings.

Breathe – Take a deep breath; exhale a sigh intentionally pushing out any frustration, anger, and jealousy. Offer it up to the gods to massage it away. (Then give thanks.)

Shout – I like to scream into a pillow as loud and as long as I can after I speak to a person who goes unnamed. This gets their sad, negative energy out of me. The pillow is used not to disturb the neighbors or family dog.

Travel and get out of your routine life. Sometimes just getting away can change the way you think. Go on vacation – a change of scenery is a good thing – even if it is only for a day – or take a drive for a few hours to a scenic area – the sea, a park, the hills, mountains, a horse farm, a nursery, or just look out your window at the flowers, grass and clouds.

Think about it tomorrow - sometimes you just need to let the world turn a couple of days.

Read a good book to get your mind off of things.

Clean out a closet or some drawers.

Play a game or sport – tennis, golf, softball – this makes you give your attention to other things like balls.

Make love – always a good mind and body lifter when you are in love.

Call a friend and talk about what is bothering you, thank them and than let it go.

CHAPTER FOUR
FACE YOUR SELF EXERCISES

EXERCISE # 1:

RELAXING POSE

Your mind is separate from your thoughts, which are in your brain – you are separate from your thoughts. You really are not your thoughts – though at times (most times) you attach to them and think that they are you. You are not your feelings either – though at times you attach to them and identify with them. These simple exercises will help you to become a witness to your thoughts and feelings and aid you back to connecting to your divine self.

OBJECTIVE:

To be able to watch your thoughts and not be attached or personally identify with them. This exercise will also relieve stress and develop a sense of clarity and vision.

WHAT YOU WILL NEED:

➢ One large beach or bath towel, or a yoga mat

➢ Loose, comfortable clothes.

EXERCISE:

• Lie on your back on your mat on a flat floor. Have your arms about six inches away from your sides and your feet about a foot or two apart. Breathe deeply in and out three times to relax your mind and body.

- Raise your right arm about a foot off the floor. Begin to squeeze your fist. Tighter and tighter until you can squeeze it no more – then hold it for another two seconds and drop it. Let it fall where it may. Gently rock your arm back and forth and then forget about it – it is no longer a part of you – it no longer exists.
- Continue to do this same thing to your left arm and then each leg. Each time squeezing so tightly that you no longer can squeeze any more. Then let them drop and gently rock them back and forth and then forget about them – they no longer exist.
- Next, squeeze your buttocks and groin up and together – tighter and tighter and hold a few seconds – now drop! Forget about them – they no longer exist.
- Move your attention to your abdomen and squeeze everything toward your belly button – tighter and tighter (you should not be using your buttocks or groin muscles or your arms or legs for they no longer exist) – hold it – now drop it – release it and forget about it – your abdomen is no longer a part of you right now.
- Move your attention to your shoulders and upper chest (do not move your arms, remember, they no longer exist) and squeeze. Tighter and tighter – hold it and then drop it. They no longer exist.
- Move your attention to your face, your mouth, eyes and ears. Squeeze them all real tight. Tighter, tighter... now drop them – they no longer exist.
- Next move to the tip of your nose. Do not move anything on your face for it no longer exists. Squeeze tight. Tighter and tighter... hold and drop – it no longer exists.
- At this point, do not move any part of your body – for it no longer exists. If you feel any stress or discomfort in any part of your body mentally go into that area and mentally massage it away. Take this time to realize that you are not your body (don't worry – it is not going to go anywhere). With each breath let your body fall deeper and deeper into the mat.
- Next, move your attention to your mind – you are not your thoughts – begin to detach from your thoughts and watch them like you would a movie on a screen – just watch your thoughts – do not attach to them – if you find yourself attaching and following a thought – gently let go and go back to watching. Soon, with practice, you will become the observer of your thoughts. Ask yourself at this time (when you are the observer), who is the one who is thinking

these thoughts? Who is the one who is watching these thoughts? Eventually, you will find yourself in a space, which no words can express - you will be one with your self. You may be in this awareness for just a moment but you will know. The more you practice, the longer the state of awareness will be and the easier it will become to attain.

- When you are ready to stop this exercise, do not just jump up. Gently bring your awareness back to where you are. Gently rock your head, arms, legs and body, which will allow you to rejoin with your body. Then slowly sit up – keeping your eyes closed. Sit for a minute or two and when you are ready, slowly open your eyes looking at your hands. When you are ready, look at your room and connect with your day – you will experience a general glow and feel a peace and happiness.

EXERCISE # 2:

RENEW YOUR MIND

A key to discovering your mind chaos is self-observation. This 4-part exercise gives you ways to watch what is going on both inside of you and outside of you. Do not personalize, get upset, or angry with any of your observations. Do not judge if something is good or bad. Simply watch and observe as you would a television program.

It is a truly remarkable experience to watch a fear or a depression or passion pass through you without personally attaching to it. Self-observation is not thinking about yourself - it is watching yourself. This act of self-observation will enable you to see yourself as you really are, not as you imagine yourself to be. It is from this point that you will then be able to build a new self. When your mind thinking is different, your life will be different. But first you must Face Your Self and observe.

OBJECTIVE:

You will be able to refresh your thinking, Face Your Self and become your personal best at all times.

WHAT YOU WILL NEED:

➢ Paper (Your Magic Notebook) and Pencil

EXERCISE:

A. Take a moment right now and write down all of the things and feelings that are on your mind at this exact moment. Be honest – no one has to see this list. If you are not honest with yourself, you cannot be honest with anyone else and you will only hurt yourself.

B. Ask yourself: Of the things that you believed as a child, what beliefs are now not productive in your life? For example, were you led to believe:

> You are the little princess.
> You never will amount to anything.
> You are God's gift to the world and can do no wrong.
> You are a selfish child.

C. Review your lists from the beginning of Chapter 4, the messages you want to send and those messages you want to receive. Are your lists similar? Do they correspond? Remember, this work is circular - call it Karma – call it the Principle of Cause and Effect.

D. Metaphysical solution. Do this even if your lists have positive thoughts. After you have written all of your mind trouble and your nonproductive childhood beliefs on a paper, bury it in the ground, burn it, tear it up and toss it to the wind, or let it go into moving water such as a river or the ocean. You can use this process as a clearing process for any of the Face Your Self exercises.

Or

Keep your lists in a private, accessible place for you to review on a weekly basis. This will aid you in keeping your mind chaos in check and to see your progress (Just do not get caught up in your lists of the past and find yourself being dragged down by all this old stuff that you have released.).

Sometimes it is not easy to recognize your mind chaos, for you may have a blind spot about it. These blind spots affect your life. The more you do the lists, the more you will find your blind spots. But sometimes a blind spot is a blind spot. When this happens, it can also be helpful to ask for an outside opinion from a respected friend, family member, or from a professional therapist. Watch your reaction when they tell you what they see about you. Do you get angry, agree and laugh, or feel hurt? Then ask, "What is that about?"

A little story about a blind spot: I once was feeling achy and rusty. I had been practicing feng shui and had looked around my home for things that may be reflecting that energy pattern in my home. I was sculpting back then with rusty nuts and bolts and pieces of rusty metals that I would bind together with rattan. I loved the natural colors of the rust and the odd shapes I would find at the junkyard. I had a collection of a few of my favorite shapes on my windowsill right above my kitchen sink. I loved to wash dishes by hand and look out my kitchen window at my garden. One day, it was like a lightning bolt went off in my head – I saw the rusty pieces in front of my face and made the connection! Of course I removed them and actually stopped working with rusty, old pieces of metal and moved onto weaving baskets with gemstones and feathers.

CHAPTER FIVE

REFLECTIONS IN THE MIRROR: BODY ANARCHY

My Body

My body is a reflecting pond.
Looking into mirrored waters
I see a face.

Beyond its eyes are stories of lives gone
past and those yet to come.
Its ears hear truths through silent channels
and echo sounds to distant planets.
Each wrinkle and line, each beauty mark
and scar, mirror a map of heavenly stars.

What nimble fingers weave my basket of life?
What footprints walk it's path?
What lips shape words into realities of the future's
past beyond the present of all time?

It is not the color of my skin, which seizes the day.
It is the love in my heart, which shows me the way.
It is my nose that knows the secret sent to all life
The essence of oneself
The scent of a flower
A wisp of smoke.

Of all the riches in the world, there is none
so golden as good health.

WHAT IS BODY ANARCHY?

There are many forms of body anarchy. Tensions mount up in your stomach and affect your digestion and heart rate. You gain weight and it becomes a layer of fat around your waist, wrist, arms, ankles, thighs, chest, and buttocks. You live in an area where there are high occurrences of cancer or brain tumors. Your nose keeps running whether you're indoors or outdoors. You are losing your eyesight, hearing, or hair. It is not so easy to bend over and tie your shoes. Walking up a flight of stairs causes you to stop to catch your breath. You can't go out to walk your dog without all of your jewelry and designer clothes as armor on your body. If you do not dress like your friends, they will ignore you.

A THOUGHT TO REMEMBER

Cell phones, electro-magnetic waves, unnatural traffic sounds, airplane noise pollution, environmental toxins, smelly indoor cleaning products, processed foods, unbalanced diets, upsetting daily news and media shows, lack of exercise, unfiltered air in hotels and airplanes, unnatural beauty products, over cleanliness, alcohol, drugs and massive prescription pills, heavy backpacks and handbags, lack of sleep, stress, fat, fatigue, disease, aches and pains…

These all add to and create body anarchy.

Body anarchy is anything that interferes and alters the natural balance of your body and mind challenging its natural design. A lot of people look for a quick fix, such as a pill, to get instant health and healing. Health is not about a quick pill fix. Health is a conscious lifestyle, which includes personal choices. The choice is yours.

LOVE YOUR BODY

Your body – do you love it? It is important for you to love your body – and that includes all parts – even the old, broken and not working too well parts. How you feel about your body affects the way you think and behave and actually affects the health of your body. If you do not like your body, chances are you are in a vicious cycle of creating more body disorder, which then, makes you hate yourself even more. Though you are not your body (you could cut off your arms and legs and still be you), your body and mind are closely connected, and your life; as you know it, is connected to how you feel and think about your body. If you are sick, you do not feel good, and if you do not feel good, you are sick. It is important that you make peace with your body and love it, even with all of its quirky aspects because it is the only one you will have during this lifetime. Of course there is plastic surgery, skin treatments and transplants – but do these because you choose to, not because you feel that you have to.

Your body was born and your body will die, this is a fact of life (even if you freeze dry, or alcohol preserve your body). My son once told me, "No one gets out of here alive." He is right. We die and let go of our bodies – these spacesuits we use to communicate with each other. In the meantime while we are alive, we all would like to live in a healthy body. Your body is a tool and a wonderful gift for you to express yourself through. With your body, you can communicate with others and dance. Your body holds your head (which holds your brain – which controls your thinking). With your body you are able to hug one another and make new bodies with minds and bodies of their own. Your body serves you, and you in turn want to serve your body and take care of it.

I once read a card, which had a picture of a very old person leaning on a cane on the cover. When you opened the card up, it said, "If I knew that I would live so long I would have taken better care of myself."

Are you taking care of yourself? I see so many young people still smoking. With all the clear information about how cigarettes harm you - why do some still smoke? Is it a thought that they will never die? Never get ill? Or are they so weak as to not be able to think for themselves and get caught up with the crowd?

MINI EXERCISE:

What do you eat and drink each day? Write it down

What would you change about your daily eating and drinking habits?

It is very easy to gain weight. It is harder to lose weight than to gain weight. It is harder to get back to health than to stay healthy. It is harder to come back and gain a person's confidence after they lose faith in you because of lies, cheating, or poor behavior. If you can prevent developing a body disorder situation in the first place, such as added weight gain or ill health, you will not have the added distress of trying to get rid of it later.

MINI EXERCISE:

It is important for you to know your own body. Take a good look at your physical self in the mirror without clothes, jewelry or hairpieces. Look at your posture, the condition of your skin, and the lines on your face. Study your hands and feet. Look at the curves of your arms, belly and those of your buttocks. While you are looking at your body, what are you thinking? What are you feeling? What do you love about yourself? What do you dislike? Can you change what you do not like with diet or cosmetic surgery? Can you live with what you see? I hope so, for your body is your vehicle to work through, and affects your mind's health, which oversees and is interrelated to all of your body systems – another circle in life.

Your body is your real house. Wherever you go in life, wherever you live, you take this house with you. As you grow up there will be many hats you will wear, many places you will go, and many people you will meet, and your exterior homes will change. But you will always live in your body house until the day that you let it go.

This is your life. How you choose to live, whom you choose to play with, and what you choose to eat are only a few of the many personal choices that you make each day, each year, each lifetime. When you choose to Face Your Self, you do so with nonjudgmental awareness (that means to see what is and not what is not) and understand and accept the effect that your actions cause on your life. You know that you can change your actions and responses if they are not supporting your highest good. This chapter on body anarchy is not a chapter to get you to lose weight, though you might. This chapter is not about an exercise and health maintenance program, though you may desire to put one into effect. It is a chapter written to make you aware of what could be body anarchy situations in your life, and to give you some food for thought (no pun intended... – of course it was intended!) on how to undo the disorders of your body.

You have basically six systems of interior design of your Planet Earth physical body:

1. Blood and Plasma Channels - your heart pumps blood 24 hours a day, non-stop, your whole life.
2. Muscular Systems – move your bones and protect your nervous system.
3. Fat Supplies – create a natural cushion of food for your body.
4. Skeletal, Bone and Cartilage Framework – act as a supporting frame to allow your body to stand upright.
5. Nervous system – allows you to feel the touch of a loved one and the warmth of the sun.
6. Reproductive Channels – provide a channel through which new life is brought forth.

All of these systems work together, and if one is not functioning well, the others will be adversely affected. For example:

- Your nose is the opening to your lungs, which sends oxygen to your blood, which sends it to your bones, muscular and nervous systems.
- Your kidneys and your bladder clean out excess fat and toxins from your body.

- Your kidneys clean your blood, which affects your liver and your skin.
- Your heart revitalizes your blood and sends it throughout your body, nourishing your brain, nervous system, muscles, skin, digestive tract, reproductive system, and skeletal system.

Good health depends on:

- Cleansing and purifying the body
- Regular deep breathing habits
- Exercise
- Essential nutrients taken in foods
- Positive mental attitude
- Water for constant elimination

In order to create the life that you wish, you must look in your own Magic Mirror and clean up and change your unwanted grooved patterns of behavior and the disorders from your mind, body and home, since they all are interrelated. Once you have addressed your personal issues, you are better able to work in alignment with the universal principles of: **mentalism, correspondence, vibration, polarity, rhythm, causation, and gender**, to create the life of your dreams. (For advanced reading on these principles, see Appendix IX.)

TYPES OF BODY ANARCHY

The following list of body anarchy situations will open your mind to an awareness of different types of body disorders. They are in no particular order of importance. Read through this list with an open mind, and place a check mark in the margin if anything rings a bell for you. After each, you will find a Face Your Self affirmation and suggestions to bring your attention into focus. You may add other body anarchy situations to this list if you think of them.

1. Foods.
Not all food is anarchy. I bless everything I eat for it now is a part of me.

Additives. Do you know what you're putting into your body? You are what you eat. Read the ingredient label for additives. Check out what high fructose is and educate yourself about preservatives, colors and additives that are in processed foods. Question what the cumulative effects on your health may be.

Not Fresh Food. Does your food taste fresh? The more food is handled and the longer it is off the vine, the more opportunity there is for it to become less healthy with another person's energy, and food will be of a lower energy (prana). Purchase food grown locally whenever you can. You will be supporting a local farmer *and* your health when you purchase fresh, locally grown (organic) food.

2. Body Waste.
Body waste is normal. I am releasing all that I do not need. I live and let go.

Excess retention. Are you retaining more than you need? Do you feel bloated? Foggy headed? Muscle pain? If so, it may be excess body waste, which will begin to affect live tissues, thus causing degeneration. Drink more water (though not in excess) and consider fasting on pure fruit juice for a day. Consider getting routine professional massages.

3. Air Quality.
Air and oxygen are good. I revitalize and am born anew with each inhale.

Stale or poor quality air. Do your eyes feel dry or tired? Sometimes indoor air quality is worse than outdoor air quality due to use of cleaners, synthetic materials, building glues, etc. Breathe clean air – it makes a big difference to your head and lungs! Why would you choose to go to a hotel, office, hospital, or store where you cannot open the windows or where the air is not fully filtered from the germs of the guests and people before you? Choose to support hotels, restaurants, and stores where you can breathe fresh, clean air. Breathing should be easy.

4. Water Quality.
Water is a beautiful thing. Each sip I take brings me into balance. I bless the natural rains of nature, which cleanse my soul.

Impurities. Water is odorless and tasteless. Can you taste your water? Does it leave stains on your sink? Could there be a heavy metal band in your tap water? Heavy metals can be: copper, iron, zinc, lead, and magnesium. These metals can interact with free radicals and then attack the collagen fibers in your skin, causing your skin to age more quickly with lines and sags. (NY Times, 4 Feb. 2006) Have your tap water tested. Purchase a water filter for your kitchen and bath water and vegetable or herb garden.

5. Mind Chaos.
The mind is a beautiful thing when it is not cluttered with thoughtless thoughts. I have an open mind. I am open to the universal mind to guide me in everything I think, say and do.

Not being present. Do you feel scattered? Do you worry? Your mind affects body anarchy and vice versa. So be aware of what is on your mind. When you sit down to eat, be aware/present in the act of eating and concentrate on what you are tasting, seeing and smelling. When you eat, eat. Leave all the mind stuff for after the meal (newspapers, television...). If you stub your toe do you get angry at the dog or just accept that it hurts and you stubbed your toe?

6. Your Senses.
Your senses are important to know and understand your world. I listen, feel, smell, touch and see with understanding and awareness.

Hearing, not listening. Are you told that you are not hearing what others say? Suppose you hear someone tell you that they do not want you to do something, but do you listen? Are you as the child who may hear the call to come inside from play, but does not listen? Do you touch things but do not feel them? When you see do you really see what is, or what you think you see? Tune into your senses and be present – enjoy.

7. Insomnia.
Sleep is a needed commodity. When I lay my head down to sleep I release the day with thanks. I feel safe, whole and complete. All is in right order.

Sleep disruptions. Are you stirring most of the night? Do you get up in the middle of the night to go to the bathroom? Do you lie awake because you have something, which is very heavy on your mind and heart? Acknowledge your need, and then gently hug yourself and stroke your shoulder. It is natural to awake around 4:00 in the morning – use this time to allow your intuition to bring insights to your life.

8. Cosmetic Surgery.
Cosmetic Surgery is a good thing for reconstruction and uplifts of spirit when your motivation is to do it for yourself. I love me and I am loving to myself for I am mine to behold. I am beauty.

> Obsessing. Do you look at every little thing on your body and face and feel a need for surgery because you are unhappy? Or, do you feel that you need to keep yourself looking a special way because of other people's expectations? Ask a trusted friend or family member their thoughts. Remember to love yourself and to honor the wisdom of your body.

9. Recreational Drugs, Alcohol, Smoking.
Be aware. I am life and happiness.

> Self-destructive behavior. Do you find yourself popping a pill, a smoke or a drink whenever you are faced with: work, Mondays, your mother, pressure…? You may be missing the root mind disorder situation as to why you are abusing these substances in the first place. Talk to your friends, family or counselor about your situation. Be honest with yourself.

10. Pharmaceuticals/Prescription Drugs.
Prescription drugs can fix and maintain certain body/mind illness situations. I express self-knowledge and allow the truth to operate through me. I know my own body.

> Side effects. Are you taking several prescription drugs? If you get to a point where you feel that you do not have domain over your own body and mind and are taking pills to correct side effects caused by other medications, ask yourself: Are they worth it? Look into alternative methods to solve your illness and work closely with a medical doctor who will spend time with you to help you uncover what is happening with your body and support your body's innate ability to heal itself.

11. Toupees and Hairpieces.
It's a look – do you love it? Within me is the possibility of limitless experience.

Shame. Do you wear them for fun and looks or are you hiding something behind and under them? Do not deny the world the beauty of your perfect being.

12. Hair Colors.
It is fun to play. The hair on my head is a privilege I wish to enjoy.

Dyes. Do you dye your hair to hide grey or your natural color? Ammonia and unnatural dyes may become toxic to your body. Look to using hair colors without ammonia and with natural dyes.

13. Jewelry.
Jewelry can be a fun accent to any outfit. I wear the stones and trinkets on my body for protection - to enhance my health and well being.

Reason for wearing. Do you wear your jewelry to show off? If you find yourself wearing your jewelry as a method to show off the fact that you have diamonds, Rolexes and pearls, then jewelry may be a defense or armor you are hiding behind. Look at yourself and ask why you need jewelry to make you feel like you are important. Try going out for a day with no jewelry.
Some old pieces of jewelry hold the energy of the previous owner, which may not be healthy. If you are in love with the piece, try putting it out into the sun for 24 hours (which may mean a few days – bring it in at night) to allow the sun's energy to clear (burn) away any negative aspects.

14. Personal Hygiene.
It is good to take care of yourself. My body is the temple of my mind.

Poor Personal hygiene. Do you live like a good-for-nothing? Even if you live alone, dirty, unkempt fingernails, toenails, hair, teeth and breath are types of body clutter - clean up your act.

15. Allergens and Airborne Toxins.
Pollen and dust are naturally in the air. I breathe easily and freely.

Multiple chemical off-gassing. Do you find it hard to breathe inside malls, hotels, office buildings or even your own home? Many building products, cleaning products and interior design products such as paints, glues, pillow stuffing, window cleaners, furniture polish and soaps – to name a few, all have odors, which if you can smell it – it is off-gassing or emitting particles into the air. Meaning you are breathing in particles (fumes) of the product. When you put them together with other off-gassing products – what is the multiple effect? Multiple sensitivity? Purchase products that are environmental and biodegradable and have little impact on you and nature.

16. Body Movements.
When you move your body intentionally – that is good. I am always aware of my whole body. My fingers and legs do not have a mind of their own.

Nervous Twitches. Do people tell you your foot is moving? Twirling hair, biting nails, chewing on a pen, sighing, shaking or tapping your foot, leg, stuttering, blinking too much, are nervous results to your mind humbug. Integrate Face Your Self breathing exercises from the end of this chapter into your life.

17. Tattoos.
Tattoos are a work of art and you are the canvas. I highlight my body with honor.

I love Mary. Do you still love Mary? If you do not love Mary any longer – the tattoo is body disorder. Before you get a body tattoo, think about how you will feel about your tattoo when you are ninety-nine.

18. Chemicals Used in Commerce.
Modern life is filled with new wonders. I am safe and live my life in perfect harmony and freedom.

Nanotechnology. Chemicals that are being used to keep oils from seeping through the popcorn bag, stain-resistant clothing, food additives, fire retardants (even though they seem good – especially in children's clothing) … these are improvements? These particles can easily penetrate cells in your lungs, brain, and other vital organs. There are still major unknowns about how these chemicals will affect the human body 25 or 50 years down the line. Be aware of all packaging from which you drink and eat. Try to eat products, which come from local farms. Follow the concept that less is more, meaning less packaging and less added sprays and chemicals.

Toxic Cleaning Products. Are you scrubbing with scented, smelly products to get that "clean" feeling? What types of cleaning products do you use in your home? Try using environmentally friendly cleaners.

19. Deodorant.
Do you need to mask your smell if your diet is healthy? I smell sweet, natural and clean.

Aerosols and Ammonia. What chemicals are you spraying or rolling onto your body? When you wash yourself, do these chemicals run down onto and into the pores of your breast? Buy natural, pump sprays, which do not hurt the environment and which do not have ingredients that can potentially harm your body's balance. Try going without deodorant a few days of the week – less is more in terms of your health. If you eat a healthy diet, you will not smell offensive.

20. Past Lives.
In this lifetime, do you have many lives? I have no bondage or limitation. I am a free spirit.

Reincarnation. Do you feel that you have lived a life before this birth? We come into the world with issues to learn, and/or to teach. See things as they are in the present. What you do today will affect your future.

21. Pregnancy.
It is a most delightful thing to bring a new life into the world. On a golden strand from my ancestors to the children of the future, my life is a blessed continuation of love.

Unwanted Pregnancy. Do you practice safe sex? To be unwanted is a sad event – there are many people who would love to take care, raise your child and make them their own. Be wise when you have sex.

A THOUGHT TO REMEMBER:

Do not speak too much – use your energy to heal. Talking takes a lot of energy. My Aunt Rita had a stroke when she was around 103 years old. She was in the hospital and was not talking much – all the doctors were concerned – but I knew she was just trying to put her energy into healing herself and not be bothered with being social. She healed beautifully and went on talking for another two good years.

WORDS, ACTIONS AND PLACES TO LOOK OUT FOR

Warning signs that you should look out for: (Please feel free to add your own.)

1. You find yourself hiding food, drink, drugs or your lack of exercise (saying you worked out at the gym when in reality you took a nap).
2. You defend your unhealthy behavior. I like loud music in my ears where I can't hear myself think.
3. You find that you live in denial of your body disorders. What do you mean I am fat? I'm still walking.
4. You feel that you need to compete with your neighbors or friends to match their bodies.
5. You eat, drink and/or use drugs when you feel low or to socialize.
6. You eat or do harm to your body after talking with other people: Parents, children, spouse, neighbors, brothers, sisters, friends, business associates, others (remember, other people affect your vitality and energy).

A Few Situations and Places that Trigger Body Anarchy:

When you go food shopping be aware of what you buy. Do not go food shopping when you are hungry or in a rush, for you may find that you buy the quick and easy food fix, which in reality is not in the best interest for your health.

I recommend that you eat a nourishing meal before you go to parties. This way you will not be tempted to overeat. Be mindful that alcohol will make you hungry, as do many recreational drugs and you will tend to eat more than you would normally. When you are talking on the telephone with a perpetually needy family member or friend you may find yourself reaching for a drink or a bag of chips to fortify yourself – be aware.

When you are on vacation or holiday, keep a pouch of personal power bars with you. Try not to over indulge just because you are a vacationer.

Do you recognize any of these phrases?

I'll just have one more. (It's a holiday /my birthday/ it's so good.)
I'll start tomorrow…
Pass me the clicker…
Do you have a light?
I hate my hair.
Could you put three olives in my martini?
I like a drink with lunch.
I wish I was taller.
I eat chips because my body needs the salt.
Just relax, I only want a taste.
I hope I come back in my next life with prettier feet.
I don't remember; remind me again tomorrow.
My shoulders are too broad.
It's Christmas/ New Years/ My Birthday/ Your Birthday/ Someone's Birthday/Five O'clock somewhere
I'm bored, what is there to eat? Do?

MINI EXERCISE:

What anarchy is being held in your body? Answer the following questions right now.

- Do you feed yourself to nourish your body or are you feeding your body mindlessly with food to feed some mental longing?
- Do you display a twitch or a nervous action when you think about a certain subject?
- Do you grunt every time you stand up after sitting?
- Do you blow your nose and dab your eyes frequently?
- Do you feel tightness or heaviness in your stomach, chest, or back?
- Do you wake up happy and bounce out of bed ready to greet the new day?
- Do you sing and whistle for no specific reason?
- Do you love to cook fresh meals?
- Do you feel sharp, creative and focused?
- Do you work out, play tennis, walk or exercise weekly?

THE MIND BODY/CONNECTION

A THOUGHT TO REMEMBER:

The story of the tortoise that won the race over the fast running rabbit.

The slow tortoise just kept going – he kept his sights on his goal. He did not get distracted, nor did he worry about not completing the race. Sometimes when your body or life is cluttered either by weight, disease or desires, you need to put blinders on and focus on the task at hand – health and healing.

Illness or a body situation is your body telling you that something is not right. Illness can be a good thing when you take a look at your life and make changes that your body is calling for. The reality is that your physical body will die one day – it is that aspect of you that is connected to the Earth (your breath of spirit is not bound by the Earthen body). When you look at your body, try to box off the illness and approach it with a clear, unattached mind. This can be difficult because the illness and medicines you take can affect your mind as well. (Sometimes it is helpful to seek a practitioner who can see the holistic, overall picture of you). Sometimes an illness can be something we bring upon ourselves, like smoking, partying or drinking too much. Sometimes we inherit certain body tendencies with our genes or sometimes through our environment (air quality, too much sun, water, chemicals in cleaning and household products).

HOW PHYSICAL ILLNESS CONNECTS WITH YOUR MIND:

You have heard the phrase, "A sound body is a sound mind." Poor nutrition is associated with mental and emotional disturbances. But sometimes your mental state affects your physical health when your nutrition is fine. Sometimes, your home environment affects your health. Never think that when you are sick that you only have a sick body. Look at your situation and see if perhaps part of the dis-ease is caused by how you are thinking or how you are living. Often the cause of the dis-ease is not in your body alone, but in your mind and home environment as well.

Your body holds on to memories in your nervous system and in your muscles (massage is a good tool to release body tensions and blocked muscle movement). It is important to remain present. Once I experienced a very troubling time in my life. During this time, my life exploded on every front. There was nothing to hold on to. I lost my home, my marriage, my identity. I had no money to pay bills, and my life was being threatened. I was frightened and scared. Twenty-five years later, every so often, something will remind me of that time. If I am not aware, my nervous system and muscles are triggered - my breath becomes shallow and my palms moisten. This post-traumatic stress brings me right back to that period of intense fear as if it was yesterday. To use my own terminology, I become tight in my shoulders and back, and my breathing is quicker and short. I have to remind myself that the past is the past and today is filled with peace, joy, love and protection.

The following, is a short list of possibilities on how your mind can affect your body. The suggestions are food for your thought. Ponder the thoughts and see if you feel that there is a truth here for you:

Pain – Dwelling or focusing on pain will increase it. See your body as being perfect, whole and complete.

Headaches – These may be related to emotional confusion, worries or anxiety over some event. Headaches are like a mental traffic jam. It is helpful to think of something peaceful and relaxing. If you take on too much personal responsibility, develop time where you can let go and be peaceful.

Lung situations – With every inhale we breathe in health and wholeness and with every exhale we release and give our worries away. If you are holding on to your breath, perhaps you have an unexpressed emotion or desire, which you need to breathe into and work out.

Vision Problems – Your eyes are the vision of your soul. If you are experiencing eye situations, perhaps you can use your inner sight – that of your soul – to better understand why you are experiencing a vision situation. If you are fearful or depressed your eyes will appear with no luster or shine. When you are happy and light, filled with love, joy and good purpose -your eyes will shine.

Constipation – Are you having feelings that you are limited or burdened with something? Eat when you are relaxed. Change your thinking to create greater self-expression, which may mean breaking with old traditions.

Cancer/Tumors – Maybe you are not living or expressing your truth, or you may be believing that your private desires, personal ideas, or self-destructive emotions of depression, anger or frustration are physically a reality and they ultimately take hold of your body as growths expressing on the inside of you that which you have believed. Get a fresh new thought process - change your life style.

Skin – Your skin offers you protection and reflects your inner security. If you feel vulnerable, stop and do what you need to do to feel safe and strong. Perhaps you need to change your job or make a move.

Heart – Your heart is your center of love. Are you an overly controlled person who is afraid to let people see the real you? Must you keep up an image of who you think you are? Keep loving thoughts for yourself and others flowing.

Asthma – This is a your breath being constricted – could there be, perhaps an emotional connection? Keep your thoughts free from anxiety through daily meditation and walks in a natural setting.

Anxieties – Your nervous system is very responsive to your thoughts. Keep yourself free of tensions – tensions are not just of the moment, but of years of build-up. You must repeat to yourself until you believe it, that there is nothing from the past, which can hurt you today. You must heal yourself of worry. You want to work on keeping thoughts of peace, poise and power in your heart and mind – and be present.

Blood – This is a symbol of life. Blood is the reviving action of Spirit. Ask yourself if you have any hardened opinions. Are you bucking the system and experiencing frustration (high blood pressure), or are you feeling defeated and have no plan or purpose and no fight within you (low blood pressure)? Develop a sense of self-worth and harmony by finding a new hobby, or doing volunteer work. The Face Your Self exercises are designed to help you recognize your clutter blocking issues to reveal the flow of your divine worth.

Obesity – Being overweight is an expression of unexpressed longings. Food becomes a symbol for affection. Bless your food each time before you eat it. Do not eat under tension.

Colds - Ask yourself if you feel any confusion or chaos (by the change of season, lack of sunlight hours, different clothing requirements…). Look to create order and harmony in your life.

Stomach and Intestine Problems – Your digestive tract is related to retaining old ideas and not allowing or accepting new ideas in your life.

Sleeplessness – Non-sleep is fear of death or fear of what life is, and fear of being. Live your life to its fullest and give thanks for each day.

A THOUGHT TO REMEMBER:

All in nature changes – yet remains the same. Be fluid and ready to change and to adapt to new situations and ideas. Always see whatever changes come in your life as an opportunity and a prerequisite to your new growth and to health. Without change, you would stagnate. Actually, the "you" that you were at five and will be at ninety-five is the same core "you". All of life's experiences are like a picture show – they show you opportunities to know the "you" of yourself.

LET GO OF IT!
RELEASING THE ANARCHY OF YOUR BODY

The following are hints and suggestions for how to release your body anarchy. Remember that your mind, body and home are all interwoven – each affects and causes effects in the other - there is a correspondence. When you make a change in one, changes will take place in the others. These hints are meant to give you the nature of ideas you can implement in your life to be better in alignment with your health and body.

Be mindful of what you eat. I don't like the word diet, for it already seems to me to be a painful, unsatisfying way to eat and live.

Massage is a tool for health. Feel the toxins getting moved out of your body and mind. Past issues get stuck throughout your body. Think about that monkey on your back – get it massaged away. What images come up while you are being massaged?

Drink water and flush the disease away.

Breathe in fresh air and exhale old air and unwanted disease.

Feel the sun. In moderation the sun is healthy and life-giving. Hold your hands up to the sun and feel it come in through your palms and forehead – let it run through your body and out your feet – feel it cleanse you.

Yoga and Pilates. Keeping your body flexible is a key to youthfulness. My Aunt Rita always told me this and she lived to be 105.

Walk in a place of nature, in the country, or along the sea, or in a city park, or on a college campus and allow the wind or breeze to caress your body.

If you have an illness, surround yourself with healthy things and have nothing that is broken in your home. Fill your home with healthy plants and fresh flowers. Look at your artwork on the walls – is it healthy? I once had a client who was diagnosed with cancer of his groin, which was related to electromagnetics in his home. Right outside of his bedroom and office was a painting of a joker with a noose around his neck. It was very colorful and very expensive painting– yet it conveyed death to the fool. Who was the fool?

If you feel weak and need strength, bring in something strong into your home – a rock, a statue, or a bamboo plant.

Move – literally pick up your things and find a new home.

Vacation and relax.

Shower and wash the day away.

Share your life with someone.

De-clutter your home.

Buy new clothes – hang up a garment in your closet with the size you want to be.

Play sexy music and dance – feel your body move.

Play like a dog.

Get a lover.

Hug yourself. (see the Face Your Self Exercise #1 at the end of this chapter.)

Get a manicure/pedicure – give yourself a red toe chi lift.

Sing in the shower.

Yell into your pillow

Get a colonic for bowel cleansing.

Have a professional teeth cleaning, and smile.

Start loving your natural self as you are. Talk and refer to your body in a loving way.

Control your speech and tell no lies – it will make your nose grow if you lie.

Talk to your body in the places where it hurts – mentally massage it and play music for it.

Fast to cleanse and rebuild your body, and for spiritual growth of your soul.

A THOUGHT TO REMEMBER:

No matter where you live or what your physical conditions are, see everything as a gift from the divine source, which you – the being in your body – have been given to use as wisely and as constructively as you can. Whatever your situation, you can increase knowledge (by showing people how to deal with similar situations), wisdom, and use your situation to radiate love into your environment and into your heart.

WEIGHT, HEALTH, HAPPINESS: WHAT IS YOUR LIFE DIET?

Eating well is a way to unite with heaven and earth - you are the bridge.

Have you ever tasted an apple right off the tree?

Have you ever pulled a carrot out of the ground and taken a bite?

Have you ever eaten a freshly made berry pie, made with local berries?

Have you ever noticed how red and luscious an organic tomato on the vine looks?

If you had a choice, wouldn't you prefer to buy your food from local farms rather than foods shipped across the country in trucks and trains?

Wouldn't you rather know the people who touched and prepared the foods you eat?

I am an advocate for eating foods that are in season and eating products that come from local farms. The quality of our foods has changed in the past 50 years. With the use of refrigerated trucks and advances in food processing and large storage facilities, most of the foods offered today in major food store chains depend on preservatives and additives. Many of the foods in the major chain stores have traveled long distances and have been stored in storage facilities for weeks before you purchase them and take them home. There are many opportunities for contaminations to happen. With long distance food travel, there is a need for more packaging. There is a lot of waste – not to mention the added gasoline needed to run the trucks and trains.

You are an individual. Food is a blessing and becomes a part of you. You are the food that you eat. Right now, before you eat another thing, understand that ALL the foods that you eat become a part of your body and your consciousness. From this day forward, tune into the foods that you eat. In a sense, when you eat something, you are giving it life – your life.

Your body is made up of many elements: oxygen, carbon, hydrogen, nitrogen, calcium, phosphorus, potassium, sulphur, sodium, magnesium, iron, iodine, chlorine, silicon and manganese. In order to regain or maintain a proper balance of health, most of the food you eat should contain live vital organic elements, which are found in fresh, raw vegetables, nuts, fruits and seeds.

MINI EXERCISE:

Are you unhappy with your weight?

Are you eating because you are empty or unhappy with some aspect of your life?

Walk to your kitchen right now, open the refrigerator and your pantry closets. What foods do you see? Do you see food and nutrition for your body, or are you seeing foods that reflect and support your weight gain and foods that you escape to, to fill emptiness in your heart and mind?

Food not only feeds your body, it feeds your sanity. Do you turn to food for emotional reasons? When you were a child, did your parents give you food to stop you from crying? When you achieved something good, did your family celebrate with a big ice cream sundae or meal? With your own children, learn to give them hugs and empathetic conversation when things go wrong (like losing a game or not doing well on an exam or having a classmate make fun of them). Give them tools for self-awareness and support. Do not satisfy their hurts and upsets only with ice cream and cookies and make them believe that food will pacify them and make all their troubles go away. And do not always reward a child with ice cream and cookies and candy if they do something good like cleaning up their room or mowing the lawn or getting a good grade on an exam. Find other encouraging ways to reward your child.

It is important to check on your weight monthly. It is helpful for you to own a good scale and to have an upper weight limit and a lower weight limit in mind. If you see yourself getting close to either, alarm bells should start going off in your mind so you can make the needed adjustments to your eating and exercise program. I have spoken to many healthy, active people who live into their nineties and hundreds. When asked the secret to their long, healthy lives they all mention not overeating (portion control), eating a balanced meal (and that includes fats and protein in the diet) and keeping flexible (exercise).

The energy that you put into thinking and dealing with diet, weight and the clothes you will fit into could be put into more productive things. Keep a food notebook. Begin by jotting down everything you eat each day and at what time. Soon you will catch the places where you need to make your own personal diet adjustments. I have a friend who I play tennis with who always tells me she wants to play around 3 PM because that is the time, if she is home, that she starts to snack.

Other Tips While Dining:

Bless and acknowledge your food before you begin to eat. This food that you are about to eat is going to become a part of you – thank it.

When you eat, eat. Do not be distracted with driving, putting on make-up, talking on the telephone, working on your computer, watching television, or juggling a million other things.

While you are eating, do not talk about upsetting things, listen to awful news or read upsetting, scary books.

Do not dine with people who upset you.

It is very important to chew your food thoroughly.

When you let go of your excess weight you will feel liberated and experience a whole new sense of self. You will feel lighter and happier when you eat that which becomes you.

A THOUGHT TO REMEMBER:

It is easy to feel happy and healthy when you feel good. It is at your lowest and weakest moments that the most powerful affirmations need to be made. It is at your lowest and weakest moments that clearing out any destructive mind chaos and body anarchy are most effective.

HEALING AND REGENERATION

One way to change your health is to change your vibration. Use your will to intentionally and deliberately fix your attention upon a more desirable state of being. Making a short affirmation each morning will give you clarity and help you identify that which is real regarding your body. Your will directs your attention. Where you put your attention, you create a vibration around you (mental vibration of mood or mental state), which attracts (polarizes) the pool of creative mind stuff (PCMS) into motion. Your body has joined with your thinking to create your health.

By using the principle of **polarity** to destroy any unwanted mental (or physical) vibration, you must concentrate upon the opposite pole.

For example: Do not think or say: I need to lose weight.

Think and say: I am healthy and expressing my correct weight. Feel yourself as you wish to be. (The fact that you are walking around with ten to fifty extra pounds on your person does not matter - there is a slim, healthy person in there right at this moment.) Allow your extra weight to fall off of you. Walk it – talk it – polarize with it – imagine you are the weight you want to be.

You will learn in Chapter Six (Achieving Your Personal Best in the Game of Life.) that by applying the principle of **rhythm,** you can keep to the top of the swing of the pendulum and not get caught up in the natural swing of highs and lows. You can apply this concept to your food intake: drinking/not drinking, eating/not eating, exercising/not exercising. When you do this, you are not affected by the mental (desire) pendulum, which carries you from one extreme to the other, feeling depressed that you overate, to feeling high because you have not eaten at all.

By **polarizing** yourself on a higher goal, you raise your mental **vibration** and you put your self above the extreme **rhythmic** swing of the pendulum in your daily life experiences.

CAUSE AND EFFECT PLAYS A ROLE IN HEALING.

Every cause has its effect and every effect has its cause. No matter what the cause was that created your ill effect (of illness, mental stress), love is a major part of the cure. Love is the path toward healing and regeneration. Sending love toward yourself and toward others and toward the situations, which brought you to where you are today, is healing. Love may imply sacrifice - you may have to let go of old angers, beliefs and pains. When love is invoked in any situation, your acts and thoughts readjust and healing begins.

MINI EXERCISE:

You can try doing an experiment where you imagine yourself having the mind of one of your spiritual leaders (Jesus, Buddha, Mohammad, Moses). Look to imagine and realize what they would do in your place, faced with the same situation and problems that you have. Attempt to see the situation with their eyes – the eyes of selfless love – hear with their ears, the ears of compassion and use their hands – the hands of enlightened service. This is your higher self that you are calling upon.

A THOUGHT TO REMEMBER:

Age gives you more wisdom and depth of character. Be proud of your face no matter how old or young you may be. It is the beauty in your eyes that captures the eye of those who are beautiful.

HOW TO HEAL YOURSELF

The body knows how to heal itself if you help it find its own balance. Honor all your medical doctors for their wisdom, knowledge and training in helping to restore you back to health, but healing is up to you. The following are listed to offer you some suggestions to aid in your work of healing and regeneration.

- Learn to listen to your breath. Breathe in health, love, healing, goodness. Exhale all the bad things you want out of your system. Allow the sun's energy to burn them up.
- Sleep Therapy – Sleep gives your body time to rest and heal.
- Feel good about yourself - Put on special clothes, get a haircut, manicure/pedicure – go shopping for something new (as long as you are not shopping to fill an emotional need which, would be more mind humbug).
- Clear your house of all clutter.
- Reflexology and Massage - These can loosen and relax tense muscles and move old toxins out of the body.
- Laughter and Crying – Both release heavy tension energy.
- Play Music of Your Youth – Listen to music from the time when you were between 10 and 18 years old – it will charge you and you will feel younger with the stirred up youth energy.
- Cologne or Perfume - If you wore a cologne or perfume in your youth, get a bottle and put it on every once in a while, such as when you exercise or before you go to bed at night – your sense of smell will bring you back to that time of health and your body will remember.
- Allow grace to come into your world.
- Eat Foods Full of Life Force - The sooner you eat them from the vine – the more life force you are putting into your body.
- Healing With Herbs – Different natural herbs and over the counter teas provide a gentle yet powerful way to adjust your body chemistry.
- Aromatherapy and Flower Remedies – Use your sense of smell to heal, balance and feel good. I keep a small bottle of lemon grass in my purse and smell it when I feel that I need a lift.
- Gemstones - Enhance your energies by their molecular structure. By holding a stone, you can align with its properties. I wear a large tanzanite ring, which has a deep blue color. This ring, to me, has qualities of peace, poise, and communion.

- Crystals – These are used as a form of healing and communication with light. You can intentionally use crystals to break up old patterns of diseased or blocked energies in your body, thus raising your healing vibration.

MINI EXERCISE:

Hang a crystal, multi-faceted ball, in a sunny window. Allow the sunlight to pass through it, sending all the colors of the rainbow around your room. See this brilliance breaking up all your old, caked up clutter and purifying your mind, body and life.

- Colors - They heal. Surround yourself with a color that feels healthy. Color is food for your soul.
- Chakras - These are vortexes of energy systems in your body which can become blocked and unhealthy. Tuning your chakras into balance is like tuning a musical instrument into balance – when in balance, you have beautiful music.
- Music/ Chanting - Allow peaceful, clear sound vibrations to come into alignment with your being, and bring yourself into balance with the tones.
- Therapeutic Touch or Reiki - This is soothing and it opens your heart and allows you to relax and to release tensions that may be interfering with your health.
- Reflexology – Use your feet as your connection to the earth, allow the acupressure points on your feet to correlate to all aspects of your body's health.
- Visualization is used to see yourself separate from your disease, alive and well.
- Healing Rituals

Native Americans work in aligning you with nature and your natural self.

Chinese Medicine works with herbs to balance your system. It includes balancing your chi (your energy).

Ayurveda is an Indian tradition of balancing your body type and balancing your prana (your energy).

A THOUGHT TO REMEMBER:

The Life Force is ageless - whether you are 5 or 95 - it is the same.

WHEN YOU ARE FACED WITH A SERIOUS ILLNESS

There is a circle in life. You live your life within time, space and circumstance.

Disease is impersonal. Disease is an experience, an experience that is not you. You are a spiritual being, perfect, whole and complete. You always were and always will be. YOU are not your body. When you are diagnosed with an illness you may feel that your body has betrayed you and you may take it personally. Even though I have stated that so much of disease is subjective and mind related, you should not fault yourself or berate yourself. Much of disease is related to our cultural mindset and many diseases are environmentally related. For example, many of the baby boom generation are now experiencing skin cancers. We did not even think to put sunscreens and blocks on our bodies. What did we know about the hole in the ozone layer? We oiled our bodies and put aluminum foil on record albums!

A THOUGHT TO REMEMBER:

There is a circle in life – a rhythm in life: an inhale and an exhale. The tides flow in and then out, the sun rises and falls. We all have our season to live and to die. All is in right order. Death is in the natural order of things and it is good for it makes way for the new. Honor those who are going through illness and honor your self by living a good life of love and happiness.

CHAPTER FIVE:
FACE YOUR SELF EXERCISES

EXERCISE # 1:

LOVE PATS

This is a 3-part gentle exercise and meditation to align your body with your mind and spirit. The benefit of these exercises is in the process so make the process fun.

You can do one or all three, depending on your time. Or you can make an effort to do one in the morning, one during the day, and one in the evening before you go to sleep.

OBJECTIVE:

To bring your body into alignment and health, no matter what your physical condition.

WHAT YOU WILL NEED:

Your body and an open mind

EXERCISE:

Part 1
- Stretching:

    Stretching will keep your body flexible. Hug each part of your body that you can reach. Hug your shoulders, hug your head, your stomach, your legs, your arms. Hug your feet, and your hands. Hug your Knees. Hug your back. While hugging – feel the muscles you are using – Hug with feeling – put some music on and do a hug dance. Make it up. Move your body, feel it, love it, hug it. Do this for at least 5 minutes a day.

When finished: Pat yourself all over and feel good.

Part 2

- Walking:

  Brisk walking is one of the easiest and best methods of feeling your body as a whole. It keeps your body in shape, regulates blood sugar by reducing the amount of insulin, metabolism is increased, fat is burned and your weight is normalized. Walking builds up your heart muscles and keeps arteries clean and elastic, bringing more oxygen to the heart and circulatory system. My grandparents always took a walk after dinner around the neighborhood. Walking aids in digestion. When you walk, walk as briskly as you can and keep your head held high and mind humbug free. Take a power walk for at least 15 minutes each day.

  When finished: Pat yourself all over and feel good.

Part 3

- Deep Abdominal Breathing Exercises For a Positive Mental Attitude: Your breath is a major bridge between your mind and body. Breathe in. Breathe out. Watch your breath. Do you often hold your breath? Do you find yourself sighing over events in your life? Do you breathe heavily when doing routine activities, walking up a hill or when you think about certain issues?

  The principal muscle used in abdominal breathing is the diaphragm.

- Unlike shallow breathing, diaphragmatic breathing fills the lungs completely, providing the body with sufficient oxygen.
- Diaphragmatic breathing forces waste products (carbon dioxide) from the lungs. In shallow breathing some carbon dioxide may remain trapped in the lungs, causing fatigue and nervousness.
- The movement of the diaphragm up and down gently massages the abdominal organs, which increases circulation to the internal organs and aids in their functioning.

1. Lie on your back with your feet a comfortable distance apart.
2. Close your eyes and place your hands on your abdomen.
3. Inhale and exhale through your nostrils slowly, smoothly, deeply.
4. Consciously pull in your abdominal muscles while exhaling.

If you need to, you can use your hands to gently push your abdominal muscles in when you are exhaling. When you are inhaling, be aware of your abdomen pushing out. There should be little or no movement of your chest. Practice this every day for three to five minutes. Soon you will become aware of and understand the movement of your diaphragm and your abdominal muscles.

When finished: Pat yourself all over and feel good.

EXERCISE # 2:

LOOK IN THE MIRROR

The following are two powerful meditations, which will aid you in discovering and healing personal issues and forms of body anarchy. Through use and practice, your body language will shift (the way you hold and use your body). You will become stronger and more gentle. These meditations are offered as a sacred tool. Please give an offering of thanks before you begin. Feed the birds, call a friend in need, or say a prayer for world peace.

One:

This exercise requires you to have an open mind and not to become fearful at some of the things that you may see. With practice, you will be able to see past or future lives, experiences and events. By doing this exercise, you will become more aware. Your psychic and intuitive abilities will develop.

Do this exercise during the daylight hours.

OBJECTIVE:

➢ To be able to become fearless. This exercise will also develop your clairvoyance.

WHAT YOUR WILL NEED:

➢ Large mirror

➢ Your Magic Notebook

➢ A pen or pencil

EXERCISE:

- Close your door so you will have no distractions. Sit in a comfortable position in front of a mirror where you can see your whole face. Comb your hair off your face and take off your sunglasses and face make-up.
- You are to look at your face but keep your focus on your third eye (the area between your eyebrows and above the bridge of your nose).
- Squinting ever so slightly, so you are seeing/but not seeing fully with your eyes, keep looking into the mirror – at your face – into your eyes – into your third eye.
- Allow the images to come. At first you may see nothing – then you may begin to see animals or scary looking images – keep looking – do not become attached or fearful -remember to watch as you would a television screen. Do not blink too much. Just watch.
- Keep this up for about five minutes. Stop if you feel uncomfortable in any way.
- Note what your experiences were in your notebook.

Two:

OBJECTIVE:

You will be able to have private conversations with others who may have passed on or who are in other parts of the world. You do not need the other person present. This method of private conversation can aid in negotiation and it can aid in communication, understanding and support between two people who may be having differences or who may not have spoken in a long while.

WHAT YOU WILL NEED:

A Private Room

EXERCISE:

- This meditation is to be done with only love and compassion – if your intent is to manipulate another this meditation will not work to your liking.
- Relax your mind and body – take a walk in nature, say a prayer to open your heart or hum a happy tune.
- Keep your hands folded in your lap and allow your thumbs to twiddle toward you throughout this meditation.
- Sit quietly and visualize the person whom you want to speak with sitting in front of you.
- Allow your Chi – your essence – to leave your body through the top of your head and go to the other person through the top of their head and greet them.
- Ask them if they would come with you for a while to talk. If the answer is yes, (and only if you have permission – you will know) leave with them back to your own body through the top of your head, keeping the other person always connected with their life cord to their body.
- Move from the top of your head into your heart chamber. (Visualize your heart room in any comfortable way to promote conversation – you can design this room any way you want) Ask them to sit down in front of you. With only love, compassion and understanding, begin to tell them everything you want them to know - How you feel, what you think, how you hurt, etc. Take your time and always remember to treat your visitor with respect.
- When you have finished telling them all you need to say, bring them back to their body through the top of your head, into the top of their head and lead them to their heart space. Thank them for their willingness to listen and their attention.
- Leave back to your own heart space. Sit quietly for a few moments, allowing the experience to settle with you. Then slowly open your eyes. When you come back to your day, say a prayer, take a walk in some form of nature, drink some room temperature water, and go to sleep early. Try to avoid getting back into the fast paced world for a few hours, and give thanks. Know that the communication you had was complete on a psychic level - beyond space and time. And it is good.
- Recognize your own perfection. You are a Divine Being. Smile, for it is good. You do not have to prove anything to anybody. You are your real savior. No one can save you but yourself. Forgive yourself, love yourself.

CHAPTER SIX

ACHIEVING YOUR PERSONAL BEST IN THE GAME OF LIFE

The Main Event:

Did I ask to be in this game?
Well, here I am
Where all the players train.

Whatever challenge is given to me
Whatever fouls are called
I sit on the sideline and ponder it all.

When I make a point
I let the world turn
I don't get my ego out of joint.

What is the meaning of this game?
How do you know you have won?
Ah… that is the fun.

Fall down seven times

Stand up eight

Japanese Proverb

In the game of life, there is no race to the finish line. We each have our own paths, directions and speeds. We each have our own end. But we do all have the same basic goals; to live our lives in balance: healthy, happy, prosperous, creative and loving. Winning in this *game of life* is mindfully doing your personal best. Others may judge you but only you know in your heart the truth of whether or not your intentions were honest and true. And only you and you alone will have to face your self at the end of this game we call life to hear your score.

This chapter is reinforcement. From looking at your restless mind syndrome to looking at your body anarchy- it is all part of the game! In this chapter, you will be given techniques and ways to look at the game of life. Face Your Self is not a philosophy to joke with – it needs to be worked. Life keeps throwing things at you. Knowing that there is a mind/body connection, it follows that the art of living well is a mind/body pursuit. If you can clear your old, unwanted, programmed, grooved patterns of thinking and behaving, you can play your life game with ease even if you are not athletic. You are given certain cards to start with when you are born. You roll the dice (or have someone roll them for you if you are either very young, not aware or very ill) and move along the game board nicely when suddenly you land on a chute and slide backwards. You pick yourself up, re-train, regroup and continue to carry the ball – touchdown - you reach a goal! In life, there is no race to the finish line (I said that before but I believe it is important to say it again and again until you get it! This is it! Life is right here, right now.) You win when you know deep in your heart that you did well. And that, in the end, is good.

LIFE MADNESS

- Before you walk into a big meeting, a final exam, onto the beach, onto the fairway, the court, or the grocery store, do you have anxiety or nervous tension?
- Do you feel tight and hold your breath while you wait to hear the results of your investments, final term paper or a health exam?
- Do you experience more than the usual amount of injuries and illnesses in your life?
- Does opportunity fly by you, seeming to have a mind of its own?
- Are you a poor loser?
- Do you get all anxious when you know that you have to spend time with certain family members?
- Do you get upset if someone makes a suggestion to you?

If you answered yes to any of the above questions, you have experienced some life madness.

In today's world, sports have become a big business. Elite players have coaches, private trainers, wardrobe consultants and a public relations staff. They have accountants and agents. They have fans. Unless you are an elite sportsperson, chances are that your life game does not have such a team. That is where friends and family could come in, but be aware that sometimes other people have their own agenda. Life is like a game and you need to give yourself backing. The phrase, *for the sport of it*, means to have fun – not to take the game too seriously. But everyone likes to win. You want to win and triumph. You want to achieve your personal best. Right?

The following situations are forms of sports madness, a phrase I coined that suggests a certain lunacy or folly in playing your game of existence – whatever that game may be. Do you recognize any in yourself?

1. You are more interested in how you look - the clothing or outfit than the game and get upset if someone has a nicer outfit than you.
2. You are thinking about your hair, your next date, yesterday, tomorrow… everything but the present moment of life's game.
3. You have body fatigue from the night before from too much to drink, too much partying… too much.
4. You have mind fatigue from a personal disagreement or stress about something.
5. You are distracted, watching the cute umpire, the guy or the girl in the second row at the theatre, the birds flying by, the clouds…

6. You have guilt or fear of winning – not wanting to beat Dad or your loved one at their game, or always wanting to let the other person win.
7. You are afraid you might hurt yourself, fail, or be embarrassed if you push yourself out there too hard.
8. You think that you are so great that you do not need to do any training or planning ahead.
9. The Rambo-type life player psyches you out every time.
10. You get so down on yourself for flunking that exam or killing that plant, or not getting that call you wanted that you create an injury to stop or quit in the middle of the game.
11. You think too much… about your age, health, wanting to win or lack of training.

Part of playing any sport is focus, concentration and attention. In life, if you have a vision and clear understanding of the game you choose to play (your goals), you can match your intellectual skill with your heart and body's ability. When your body is in a healthy state you feel at your best – this feeling of balance affects your mind – when you feel good, you look good, and to say it simply, you think good.

LISTEN TO YOURSELF

When you are walking down the street with a friend or out to dinner with family, be aware of the words that come out of your mouth. These words, which are shouted out in frustration or muttered in jest, actually can tell you volumes about where your lifespan game garbage is located. Once you tune in and hear yourself and recognize your lip dis–service, you can then focus in on it and remove it by changing yourself (and your words) into the desired state of the professional life-sportsperson that you want to be.

Do you recognize any of these?

1. I don't care if I win
2. Why don't we get together for a little romance
3. I am: not up to par. old, aching, tired, bored, not good enough.
4. The wind is against me. (add: people, life, my friends, karma)
5. Oh my, what was I thinking? I don't want to play any more. I can't do it.

6. I give up.
7. My knee is hurting/ I can't go on/ I'm getting too old. - Excuses
8. I drank too much last night/I didn't eat breakfast – I'm too fat – body anarchy
9. It's not fair - the rules keep changing.

Listen to your voice. Listen to what you are saying inside your head.

MINI EXERCISE:

When you catch yourself and hear yourself uttering any sports madness: stop, exhale the thought with your breath (let it go), pause and remember your good. Then, inhale the intended positive attitude (words) you want. Continue on with the game. Do not dwell on the negative. Check the Face Your Self exercises at the end of this chapter for further suggestions on how to clear out the old mess that keeps you from your game.

EXCUSES

Are you afraid to succeed? Or are you afraid to fail or lose? Are you afraid of relearning or retraining your body and mind? Are you afraid of criticism, even if it's constructive? Are you afraid of solid, roll up your sleeves, work?

Usually, life-as-a-sport madness boils down to one or the other of the above fears. Winning or losing is not a bad (unhealthy) thing if you have done your personal best. Losing can teach and encourage you to improve your game. Winning all the time can make you feel too complacent where you can get into the trap of the ego. When you really give it your all and you know in your heart that you played the game honestly and to the best of your ability at the present moment; that is all you can do. When you miss the mark try again. You can practice and train (keep the Japanese proverb at the top of this chapter tucked in your mind to refresh yourself).

A THOUGHT TO REMEMBER:

There is no race to the finish line – that is the joy of life's game. It is a game that is ever present and now.

Relearning a new grip on a tennis racket or a new technique in the kitchen or a new job at the office may frustrate you in the short run but you will improve your game in the long run. Life is about creation and expression. As in life, if you are serious about achieving your personal best and being at the top of your game, you must be willing to break old habits and retrain your body and your mind in the suitable way. Face Your Self is a game you can play within the game of life. It may take weeks before your adjustment feels comfortable, and you may feel like a fool when you play, cook or go out with your friends – but your friends will be in awe of you when your life game improves (though this is not the goal of life – to awe your friends). Most important, you will respect yourself for taking the time to break an old habit. This respect you will feel will not be ego related – it will feel all empowering and satisfying – holistic in nature – a quiet joy. It may be helpful to remember the story of The Three Little Pigs and remind yourself that the work you put into your game today will pay off in your life tournaments tomorrow.

DO YOU LOSE GRACIOUSLY?

I once had a friend when I was around eight or nine years old, who really hated to lose, and on top of everything, he was a very bad loser when he did lose. One day we were playing Monopoly with our younger sisters. My friend was losing by quite a lot when all of a sudden he stood up and knocked the bridge table over - the money, hotels and houses went flying all over the room. He yelled proudly, "Sirvan, Sirvan, Sirvan." The game of course ended and no one won.

This was an early example for me of playing with a poor loser. Sirvan was a word my friend had made up – it meant nothing to me prior to that day but it made a great impression upon me. To this day, my sister and I will use that word with each other to express, in a fun way, when somebody thinks they won by destroying others' chances of winning. Actually they are the bigger loser because they have lied to themselves and hurt others.

LET GO OF THE MADNESS IN LIFE

Using your mind, body and home connection, the following tools will help you to let go of your sports madness.

If you feel uncertain:

Understand that if you feel uncertain, worried about your competition, or worried about what others will think about you, that this is really an issue with how you feel about yourself on several levels. Your competition, life and circumstances give you a backboard to play against. Thank them, for they all help you sharpen and become aware of your game.

- Wear empowering articles of clothing (red is a strong color), or a special ring (think of the Green Hornet or superheroes) to give you super powers. (Realize it is not the shirt or the ring, which give you the powers – they are only a reminder about the powers you already have within you to pull up when needed).
- Follow a specific ritual before competing, such as touching the tip of your hat, or looking to the sky for the sun's energy to fill you.
- Place an image of a person you respect and want to emulate in your private office space.

- When you work out, listen to empowering music, which has a beat to get you psyched up, and keep the tune in your head as you play.

If you are afraid to fail or lose:

Usually this form of grooved pattern has to do with a poor self-image and not loving yourself. Or that you give too much attention to what you think others may be saying about you. You are too hard on yourself or you have not cultivated a strong inner strength.

- Wear some comfort clothes, something that you feel nurtures you, makes you feel good and looks professional for the job.
- Create a space in your home which is just for you, and use that space to support you in developing a positive self-image – maybe the place where you do your Face Your Self exercises.
- Take lessons from a pro and implement their advice and guidance into your game (or listen to your mother!)
- In your mind know that there is no finish line – other than death (which is the beginning of a whole new game) – and play to always achieve your personal best. Repeat the proverb at the beginning of this chapter in your mind. (Note: Do not go to the other extreme where you begin to feel so cocky and attached to your ego that you fall over your own shoes.)
- Get your ego out of the way – if it is in the way – perhaps you are not sincere with yourself and your goals may have ulterior motives - look at your motivation.

If you are afraid of winning:

Do you ever feel that it is more polite to let the other person win or have old grooved patterns of thinking regarding gender issues (Mom or Dad should win)? Do you ever feel that you do not want to show up your opponent for you think that they would feel inadequate and sad? It is all right to win. It is good to succeed. That is what life is about – expressing your highest good, otherwise, why play the game? If you have been taught to be second fiddle in life Face Your Self: You are a winner. So look like a winner – act like a winner and reread this book again and again to unlearn old patterns of thinking and being. All that we do is for the highest good of all and that includes YOU.

- Check your posture – stand up tall.
- Get your hair cut and styled and let go of extra pounds.
- Clean your eyeglasses, and the windows in your home. Do this with the intention of no longer being in the shadows.
- Get rid of extra clutter in your life and home. Do all the Face Your Self exercises until you feel like a winner.
- Eat foods, which are winning foods – (in your mind, what do winners eat? Drink?)
- Empower and surround yourself with positive, honest and good friends who are in the game for the sport.

WHY YOU SHOULD PLEASE YOURSELF

In life (as in sports) it is important that you enjoy the game. We are all born with different bodies, opportunities and with different minds filled with different thoughts from our personal life experiences. Yet, in more ways than one, we are all the same. You know from earlier chapters that the energy of your thoughts creates a magnetism. This law of **attraction** is a major principle in creating the life that you want to achieve. The game of life is not over at your last breath. Your essence lives on in those you love, in those who you have touched in this lifetime. How you think, feel and act carries on energetically with your spirit too. Your breath, so to speak, should always be an honorable, happy breath. Part of Face Your Self is the knowingness that if you are not doing well then neither am I. We are all one and if one of us is not happy that will ultimately affect us all.

The way I understand quantum physics is this: Imagine that a pool of invisible creative mind substance surrounds you. This substance has no intelligence on its own. Your mind's thinking (your thought) electrifies and sparks this substance, which then swirls around and surrounds you with your mind's creation (which is magnetic and grows into a reality) – it is a circle which only your thinking and feeling – (which are mind connected) can change. If you think you can't – the pool of creative mind substance (PCMS) will create that for you – and you can't!

MINI EXERCISE:

When you focus on an outcome, what is your focus?

Are you worried about missing the point/the goal?

Or are you focusing on getting to that the point/goal?

The difference between the above two questions is very subtle. Can you see how the first question will undermine your success?

You do not wish your competition ill – you wish always for the highest good of all – even if you win, your competition (so to speak) wins too for they will learn to improve their life game. We are all winners.

What kind of player do you think you are? It is so.

Take time out for introspection to Face Your Self. Ask yourself questions and reflect on your life, your visions and your current life situation. Then take time (even if it is only ten minutes a day) to sit quietly and allow your mind to relax. Meditate with it. It takes work – work it. Do not be afraid to face discomfort – be truthful to yourself and face your unpleasant truths. When you intentionally tune into the Pool of Creative Mind Substance (PCMS) you will have a clear channel to achieve and receive your dreams in quantum leaps and bounds and create the life of your dreams.

My aunt Rita was, and still is a wonderful influence in my life. She did yoga and dance every day until she was 103 years old. One day, when she was about 101, I brought my new husband, Barry, to her home to meet her for the first time. In the course of conversation Barry remarked to Rita how wonderful she looked.

Rita looked at Barry and said, "Do you think you will live to be 100?"

Barry shifted in his chair and said, "Well Rita, I don't know…"

Rita immediately shot back at him, "Then you won't!"

After that day, whenever Barry is asked if he will live to be 100, his answer is, "Absolutely!"

Rita passed on at age 105.

> *The key to youthfulness is a flexible spine.*
> *Rita Dombroff*
> *(Rita practiced hatha yoga and dance until she was 102.*
> *She lived to a healthy 105)*

BREAKING BAD HABITS

What have you "thrown" yourself into with your mind, body and soul to truly achieve your personal best? This is a very powerful question. There is a mind-heart connection to everything that you do. If your heart is not really in the game you have chosen, can you ever really win? Listen to your heart. What does it say to you about this game you are in? Life – you've got to love it!

What is your game? Is it fooling yourself into believing that you are in the right game at the wrong time or place or is it being honest with yourself and having the courage to change that which is not of your heart?

You create your own self-obstructions. If you are not happy with your life, hobby, or achievement, you must have an open investigation as to why, and Face Your Self to discover what clutter and unwanted grooved patterns of thinking and believing are hindering your game (your life).

You know that your physical health affects your mental health and vice versa (As within, so without – the principle of **correspondence**). There is no division of mind/body – they are in reality one vibration – dancing together - in the polarity and rhythm of life that surrounds you – your essence – your true self.

MINI EXERCISE:

What do you want to achieve? Take some time right now to think about that.

To change your game, or your life, you need to change your vibration. How do you do this? You focus your intention (always for the highest good of all) on your goal and continue to practice despite your upsets. With quiet time in meditation, and knowing your true motivations, in time, you will see remarkable change. Use your <u>will</u> to intentionally and deliberately <u>fix your attention upon</u> a more desirable state.

A THOUGHT TO REMEMBER:

You are working in conjunction with the Pool of Creative Mind Substance.

For example: Let's say that you feel that you cannot hit a particular stroke in tennis. And you say repeatedly that you can't do it. With that kind of thinking and believing, your body and actions will follow and most likely your result will be that you will never hit that particular stroke well.

But, if you summon your will (imagine your will as a special force of courage and wisdom within you) and focus your attention on the proper way to do the stroke – seeing yourself achieving the mastery of it, while you practice...,eventually you will achieve success. Your body will know how to do it. You will feel it. You will be it. This is different from creative visualization, for here you are actively summoning your will and including your body to learn new muscle patterns of behavior.

Your will is like a laser beam. Use it as an instrument. Do not attach yourself to your will in the sense that it is you or who you are. This is very sophisticated awareness – and with this awareness comes a great responsibility: you realize that you always work for the highest good of all. Your will directs and controls your attention and your intention. Where you place your attention creates your mental vibration (your mental state), which affects your emotions and bodily reactions (your breathing and oxygen intake, your muscle tensions, your heart rate and rhythm). This focus of your will polarizes the invisible pool of creative mind stuff (PCMS) into motion. By using your new vibration, you create (attract) your <u>game</u> (your life, or, ____, fill in the blank). (This will be further and more fully explained in Appendix Part IX.)

You can use the principle of polarity to destroy an unwanted mental vibration when you concentrate upon the opposite pole.

Do not think: I need to improve my game.

Think: I am healthy and a sportsperson who is playing at the top of my game – my personal best. Place yourself at the positive end of the polarity. Feel yourself in there with a winning vibration.

Do not think: I need to lose weight to become more athletic.

Think: I am athletic. Through my athleticism, my body is projecting its perfect weight.

VISION, PRESSURE AND FOCUS

The principle of rhythm will help you to keep focused on your game of life (your goal) even under pressure. This section may seem esoteric so please read this section through. Then read it again and play with it - work it.

So many people get caught up and blinded by the swing of the pendulum – the highs and lows of life. They get caught up, tangled, and attached to the mini successes or loses they experience along the way and lose focus on their goal or vision of what is really important in life – love and joy in the present moment (love of self, love of life). Some people get dejected, yell at themselves, lose faith and give up when faced with thinking that they are losing. Some people get too relaxed, boastful and sure of themselves when they think they are winning (and then they lose). There is a **rhythm** to everything – a high and a low – a breath in, a breath out – a sunrise, a sunset... the constant remains the same – the dream does not change – it is from that apex point - that dream - that the metaphoric pendulum swings.

There is always a measured reaction to a measured circumstance (an equal and opposite reaction), meaning that the pendulum swing to the right is the same distance as the swing to the left. For every action there is an opposite and equal reaction. Translated into your game of life: if you get bummed out by missing the ball one moment you will get equally ecstatic if you hit the ball the next moment – you and your emotions are being swung by the pendulum and are under the influence of this principle of **rhythm**. But, by being aware of how this principle operates, you can work with this principle by keeping your attention and focus to the top of your game. When you do this, you will not swing as much back and forth like a pendulum, cursing yourself out or degrading your self one moment and jumping for joy the next. If you are not affected by the mental (desire) pendulum swings, which affect so many people with their highs and lows carrying them from one extreme to another, you will be able to rise above pressure and focus more clearly.

Of course, you will need to attend to each pressure and make adjustments and evaluations. And, of course you merit the right to enjoy each success. The point, again, is to not attach mentally, emotionally, and bodily to losses and successes – see the pendulum swings of your event (life experience) and rise above them. See them for what they are – you are not them - by keeping your attention focused on the apex – your game - your life's goals. You are perfect, whole and complete – doing your personal best.

MINI EXERCISE:

Draw an equilateral triangle in your notebook. Write your vision or a long-term goal at the apex of the triangle. Write all your pressures or obstacles to this goal (Lows) at the bottom left and any of your successes toward this goal on the bottom right (Highs). Notice that the obstacles and the successes are just natural swings of your goals pendulum. They are nothing more than that. This is the **rhythm** of your particular goal. Use this drawing as a tool to aid you in not getting attached to the daily ups and downs or highs and lows on your path in life.

DEVELOP YOUR GAME

You are aware of the principle of **cause and effect** and know on some level, that whatever you sow, so shall you reap. But how many times have you reaped not what you wanted?

Look at your life right now. Can you trace your present circumstances to past decisions and actions that may or may not have been wise for you and brought you here to your present moment?

If you are older than ten years of age, you can understand cause and effect. It is now time for you to become the sower, (the creator of your life), to affect and effect your life's game in a positive way so that you reap and harvest what you intentionally, with wisdom and awareness, planted in your garden of life.

MINI EXERCISE:

Playing this game, ask yourself:

Are you on the defensive or the offensive?"

Do you have a game plan?

Are you willing to take responsibility for your actions?

We are all affected by time, space and circumstance. Yet, ultimately we are the masters of our game of life. We create our world. This is important: nothing ever happens in your game that can be higher than its own source and that means, you (or us as a people). The first question to ask yourself is: If something happens in your game of life, is it an effect from some cause within you?

Your game can never improve with just blind energy or force. You can't win if you run around like your hair is on fire or you sit back and think; but never take action. You must have a clear uncluttered vision and plan of what your goal is. One primary goal is to clean up the chaos of your mind and body and to work with the universal principles clearly and honestly to achieve success in your game and your life.

When you are up against a wall:

imagine roses.

CHAPTER SIX
FACE YOUR SELF EXERCISES

EXERCISE # 1:

UP AGAINST A WALL

This exercise will have you intentionally place or imagine yourself in pressure situations where you can practice changing your mental vibration.

OBJECTIVE:

You will be able to shift your mental vibration any time you are under pressure to a positive, winning vibration.

WHAT YOU WILL NEED:

To pay attention when you are working out, cooking, practicing flute, dining with friends, or playing your game of choice.

EXERCISE:

Look for the non-winning Face Your Self mind set in the following paragraph.

Imagine placing yourself in a pressure situation in your sport or in life or business. One where you have to anticipate, concentrate and judge what is going to happen in your game:

You have to dig down and exude confidence. People are watching. A trophy and big money are on the line. You need to keep a positive attitude and play aggressively. Who will crack first when you are in this dogfight? You can't make a mistake. It is a sudden death situation – you are up – it is your shot – your play – you go for it...

In the situation above:

First, if you feel that you have to dig down and exude confidence you have lost the game already. You should not care if people are watching – your confidence is not based upon their thoughts, or is it?

Second, if you start sweating to keep a positive attitude and aggressively try to force a win, you have lost the game. You can't force anything.

Third, if you are thinking about who will crack first you probably are beginning to be thinking about how you will screw up. Just play your game.

Fourth, if you are thinking you can't make a mistake, you probably are getting tense and tight and soon will make a mistake.

In the toughest times of any game (and life) – you must create momentum – you must stay loose and not see a dead end. Tension will only tighten your muscles and freeze your brain. If you think, I can't make a mistake, you slow your vibration down and create a frozen moment in your body and your game will follow. These examples are to make you aware of the subtle things we do to ourselves with our thinking – of course we are all human – do not get down on yourself while you practice – make a game out of the game – remember, we are all in the same game.

Create your own kinesiology (the scientific study of human movement) experiment. Think different thoughts and notice how different thoughts affect your body (while you are working out), which will affect your performance in the game and life. Follow this basic workout plan – you can apply this metaphorically to anything you do:

1. Warm up
2. Stretch
3. Aerobic or strength training
4. Cool Down
5. Stretch

A THOUGHT TO REMEMBER:

Everything is in motion – everything vibrates. If your mental vibration slows down or freezes to a slow frozen movement– so will your ability.

Keep a reminder handy: carry a bell or a pendulum in your pocket or sports bag (pocketbook) to remind you not to get caught up on the little things and to keep to your game. Or keep a happy scent in your bag. Dab it on your wrists or neck to break up any tension of your mind or body. Use it to keep your thoughts and muscles strong. Sometimes I even put a note on my dashboard, computer, or bedside lamp to remind me.

EXERCISE # 2:

PRACTICE, PRACTICE, PRACTICE

How do you get to Carnegie Hall? – Practice, practice, practice. You must practice your sport (your life). Working with the principle of cause and effect, you want to be the causer of the effects of your game (and your life). Do these exercises below. You can practice them before you go off to sleep at night.

OBJECTIVE:

➢ To understand how you affect your game.

WHAT YOU WILL NEED:

➢ Game time

➢ Personal Meditation/Visualization time

➢ Your Magic Notebook

➢ Pen/Pencil

EXERCISE:

A. Yoga strategy:
Close your eyes and visualize yourself playing your game (whatever that may be).

1. Watch yourself; how you handle the competition, how you handle stress and pressure, how you handle winning a point, how you handle losing a point. While playing your game, put yourself alternately on the offensive and the defensive. Does your thinking change? How does your mindset change?

- Observe what feelings come up.
- Observe what thoughts come up.
- Write down what you learned about yourself.

2. A Little Breathing Room: Give yourself time to just play free form -without any rules, goals or pressures. Watch your body and mind. Do they free up? Observe your self. Bring that relaxed freedom to your game.

B. Before you go off to sleep, spend a little time playing your game in your mind. Practice your shots/swings/hits. See yourself a winner each time.

Sweet dreams.

CHAPTER SEVEN

YOUR HOME IS A MIRROR IMAGE OF YOUR SPIRIT

I trip, I fall, I stall.

Here I sit in the midst of my stuff,

It is an interesting circumstance which I pence.

Why am I so dense?

"You acquire stuff, and then you have to maintain and store your stuff and insure your stuff and make arrangements for what will happen to your stuff after you die."
George Carlin

YOU ARE THE DESIGNER OF YOUR OWN LIFE

Do you constantly say, I have to get organized?

You now should have an awareness of your mind chaos and body anarchy. After that, looking at your home space becomes easy. Your home reflects your spirit.

A THOUGHT TO REMEMBER:

As within, so without. Your property, your home, and its contents can support you and your life, or undermine your well-being.

Sloppiness and disorganization is not a natural way of life. Being organic and natural does not mean being dirty or slovenly. When I see a disorganized, dirty, untidy, sloppy home, I see people who are either depressed or selfish. I do not see people living in harmony with nature nor in a spiritual manner. It does not matter if your excuse is that you have final exams, your children are little, or that you have no time or more important things to do than to keep your home in order and clean. Spirit = clarity, which translates into cleanliness, order, and light (and I am not talking about white glove clean). To leave your trash on the floor or on the couch, wet towels on the furniture, gum on the floor and toothpaste on the sink and walls of your home or at others' homes – including hotel rooms – expecting the maid to clean it up – is just plain selfish. It is not necessary to be obsessive about your cleaning and clutter; it is important to be mindful of how you live in your home.

Let go of all those things that you do not love and/or things that do not function any longer. We are living during a time when over consumption has become the norm. People actually overbuy and hoard extras of everything from shoes to paper towels. Never before have people had the time or money to purchase items that they really do not need. There are people diagnosed with compulsive shopping disorders. Our grandparents would never think of hiring a professional organizer – for major clutter situations did not exist during their time. Stores have been created to *Hold Everything*. It is becoming a specialized science to learn how to deal with your stuff. There are closet planners and garage organizers.

You want to create your surroundings as well as your life! In de-cluttering and simplifying, you actually create a more prosperous life. The more you have, the less free you are, to paraphrase the George Carlin quote. When you let go of extra possessions - your inner self will feel free and unencumbered too. I once heard an interview with a young girl who was preparing to become a nun. When asked how she felt about giving up computers and cellphones, she said, I feel so free!

Your home is a reflection of the inner you. If there are clogged areas of your home, you can be sure that there are related clogged areas in your mind, body and life. Feng shui is an ancient art and it is also a science. It is a tool – a very strong tool, when done correctly – to allow you to create a home that mirrors for you the life that you want to experience and live. Your home can be used, when you are aware of it, to support you on your path in life. You cannot feng shui your home and then sit back and eat potato chips on your couch and expect the world to come to your door; you still have to work your life. Feng shui is an integral tool to use with the rest of your mindful life. You will still want to eat healthy. You will still need to make telephone calls and go to meetings for your business. And you will still need to exercise and live a holistic lifestyle to keep your body and mind refreshed. Your mind, body and home are all inter-related and *vibrationally* connected to each other.

One of the basic principles of feng shui, and this book, is that by intentionally designing your home – you are intentionally making adjustments and changes to your life. As within, so without – as without, so within, this universal principle of **correspondence** is a basic essence of feng shui. Your home is a reflection of you. Your home is a reflection of your spirit. By first removing your clutter from your home, you allow more magic to happen. In a sense, you begin to unclog *the garden hose of your life-force,* so the waters of your life will flow more freely and naturally. When this happens, then you can make the positive adjustments needed and the water will flow where and at the speed you want it to go.

When you hire an interior designer, a good designer will want to sit down with you and understand your lifestyle, your likes and dislikes and how you imagine your home to look. It is important that you do take a purposeful role in designing your home to create your own personal space, which reflects to you a vision of your happiness, prosperity, success, health, peace and love.

Would you want to live in a space that reflects discord, misery, sadness, poverty and lack? Of course not, yet so many people do live in such spaces and it does not matter if they are rich or poor (so that cannot be an excuse). Feng shui is about change and living in harmony with nature - living in harmony with your nature - living a natural life yourself by being a natural being who is always changing and growing. When you live naturally with the laws of nature, you find that life is no longer a struggle. You accept the winter times of your life as well as the summer. Each of us may be different in our nature and each of us experiences life differently at different times – yet we are all one and the same - we are all natural beings.

When you hold your wishes next to your heart and reflect them in your home design, your wishes will have better opportunity to manifest because you are living with a reflection of your wishes all around you.

HOW TO IDENTIFY HOME CLUTTER

Is it Clutter? Or is it healthy? How do you know? Ask yourself two questions about any item in your home: Do you love it? Does it have a function? If you do not love it or it does not have a function – ask yourself why it is in your life?

Can you get into your closets and medicine cabinets? Have you moved from a big house to a small house or a smaller space? This happens a lot with college students, retired people or to people going through a divorce and moving into a smaller place

Sometimes you inherit things either through death or divorce or from generous relatives or friends. There may be items that you do not like but feel guilty about letting go. Old birthday, holiday, anniversary cards that are boxed, old photographs, letters, old bills of sale and tax returns all fall into this category.

A THOUGHT TO REMEMBER:

Be aware – there are many types of clutter that may be affecting your life. The clutter may be in your mind, body or home.

Make a note on the side of the following pages or in your Magic Notebook as to which forms of clutter you relate to. Then follow the suggestions for eliminating or donating.

- Dirt and dust. Dust is comprised primarily of old skin cells, pet dander, or pollen from plants:

    Vacuum, dust and give yourself fresh sheets on your bed and you will feel much better.

- Things that you do not love. Such as an ugly gift you received:

    If you do not love it let it go.

- Things that do not function or are broken. Non-working appliances, light fixtures, switches, broken window glass, an old necklace, or that old lawn mower you have been meaning to fix:

    If you really need it, fix it. Or get rid of it and get something that functions. Broken things in your home may make you feel less whole.

- Things that don't belong where they are. Fishing poles in the foyer of your home. Skates in your bedroom on the floor. Stacks of mail from weeks and weeks on your kitchen counter, shoes under your bed:

Clear your pathways for fresh energy to flow in your life.

- Having too many things in too small a space. Shoes, lipsticks, or cloths that are crammed into a closet or drawer:

    Keep what feels good, but do not clutter yourself up where nothing new can come into your life.

- Things that you think may become of use one day. A big box of ribbons bought at a garage sale, or old textbooks:

    Be aware: this thinking might be a poverty mentality and may be actually affecting your prosperity and wealth. If you haven't used or enjoyed something for at least two years, let it go.

- Previously owned objects and things that you were given or you inherited. Antiques, that old jacket from your dad or the couch that your mother-in-law gave you:

    Inanimate objects have their own energy and emotional attachments. If something doesn't feel right – let it go.
    Give away what you do not like or want.

- Collections. Elephants, dolls, cars, photos, shoes:

    Offer them to a good friend who admired them or have a sale – Don't let your collection own you! Put your photos into boxes, files, frames or albums.

- Expensive items that you bought, later realized it was a mistake, but you keep because it was expensive. Art work, too heavy drapes for your living room, wrong color carpet, a shirt or skirt:

    Cut your losses and let it go.

- Being constantly on call. Telephone, fax, beeper or e-mail and Tweet messages that you need to return:

    Have at least one room in your home where there is a no phone zone- no television – no fax or computer.

- Old Stuff. Towels, shoes, dishes, clothes, projects

  Shoes and old pillows hold a lot of energy of past experiences. Get a new pillow at least once a year to refresh your dreams. Let go of old, worn out shoes. Definitely do not keep your shoes in view while you sleep. Shoes hold so much of your old energy. Close your closet and do not keep them under your bed.

  Old magazines or newspapers that you think you will read one day or old textbooks and books that are outdated, including phonebooks. Old legal papers or tax forms. Just the weight alone can be overwhelming. Information can become clutter. Know that if you need to find out a certain piece of information there are libraries and Web sites that can help you out quite nicely. Make a file with clippings of articles if you need them for your work.

- Things that marketers or society tells you should have. Certain cars, watches, clothes, sneakers, computer gadgets:

  Do you really need three watches or 20 pairs of summer shoes, or a car bigger than your house? It is clutter if you are buying these things only because someone or an advertising campaign made you believe that you needed to buy it - feeding your ego. What is your real reason and need in purchasing the item?

- Other people's clutter. Clutter from your children, family or friends:

  Offering to store stuff for others is a very nice gesture, and fine if there is an agreed time limit. However, it can get to a point of you having your own clutter and others clutter as well.

PLACES WHERE HOME CLUTTER CAN COLLECT AND HIDE

Keep an eye out for these areas – they are notorious places where it is easy for Clutter to collect.

<u>Refrigerator Door or bulletin boards</u>
I recommend that you clean off the refrigerator door and bulletin board of all things each season, and than intentionally place back only what you want – leaving room for new things.

Desktops
Keep your desk as clear and clean as possible. Keep all projects, folders, and lists of ideas off your desktop. With fewer distractions in your view, you will better be able to focus on the project at hand.

Any flat surface – dining tables, pianos, beds, floors, kitchen counters... Beware of all flat surfaces. It is so easy to drop the mail, keys, library books, magazines, sweaters, etc., on a flat surface. Unless you are working on a special project that requires a large flat surface, get in the habit of putting things where they belong. I realize the convenience of dropping your purse or the mail down on the counter – what I am really talking about is where days, weeks or years go by and the pile is still there.

Under Beds
Keep the area under your bed clear of all things. Having old tax papers, photos, old books, clothes or shoes under your bed creates a subconscious heaviness that is not conducive to a restful sleep.

Junk Drawer
Everyone needs one. We have to have someplace to put the little giggly, niggley things such as old keys, glue, paper clips, screwdrivers, menus, tape, chopsticks, string, matches, pens and pencils. Clean out your junk drawer seasonally - at least make it so that you can open and close the drawer without too much difficulty!

Basements
Basements can be a metaphoric space of your subconscious. Issues from the past and issues not dealt with can cause depression and make your feel burdened. As a rule, keep your basement empty other than your heating and water equipment and perhaps your washer and dryer.

Attics
Attics can be a metaphoric space of your future. Your clutter can block your vision and limit your high aspirations. You may worry more about the future if your attic is cluttered. Go up there and clear out your clutter.

Spare Bedrooms
Do your spare bedrooms offer you a place to store extra clutter? Clean them out.

Personal Bedroom

Do you hide stuff in your bedroom when people come over? Get organized. By keeping your personal bedroom a catchall, you show disrespect toward yourself.

Front Door

Do you pile things by your front door, main entrance or vestibule, meaning to take them out of the house, but they sit there for days, months or maybe years? Do not block your health. The front door to your home mirrors your mouth - how energy comes into you for life through your home.

Behind Doors

Do you load up things behind your doors where you cannot swing the door back fully? Allow your door to swing freely – your joints will move better too.

Kitchen

The kitchen is the heart of your house – even if you do not use it. It represents nourishment – it reflects how you are fed and how you feed others. Are things in your refrigerator or cupboards there for too long? Clean your cabinets out at least once a year and give your can goods away and buy fresh produce and ingredients whenever possible.

Living Room

Are you living in your living room or are you using it as a storage room for furniture you do not use but only look at? Live in your living room.

Dining Room

Formal dining rooms often become stagnant and/or a place to put old newspapers or projects that you will get to one of these days. Clean up your act and dine in your dining room at least once a week. By eating in your dining room you balance your digestive system and create a family center.

Hallways

Hallways are pathways of your home. Open up your pathways – clean up your hall clutter.

<u>Bath - Medicine cabinets, cosmetic drawers or vanity tops</u>
Do you have many bottles of half-used shampoo? Do you have towels that are never used or are so ratty that your neighbor might think them a rag? Renew yourself with an uncluttered bath and fresh towels.

<u>Closets</u>
Hidden and unknown aspects of your life lie in the deep recesses of your closets. Open up your closet doors and come out of the closet. Be free to move and be yourself, with nothing to hide.

<u>Garage</u>
If you can't drive your car freely into or out of your garage you may develop burdens and not feel fully independent and mobile in your life.

<u>Storage Sheds</u>
Whether it's on your property or a storage unit that you pay for, clean them out. The extra stuff that you really do not need adds extra weight on you and your heart.

<u>Trunk or Backseat of Your Car</u>
Clean up your old lunch wrappers and last year's old tissue box. You will move more freely and open up the passages for more to enter your life if your car, your mode of transportation, is clean. You'll get better gas mileage if you don't use your trunk to store dog-food, books, or clothes.

<u>Pocketbooks, briefcases and pockets</u>
Empty them out and regroup on a daily or weekly basis.

EXCUSES AS TO WHY YOU KEEP CLUTTER

Why do you collect clutter? You are human, that's why. There are many reasons for why you may find yourself keeping clutter. You may be defensive or need justification about something in your life (I am a good mother – look at all the photos/drawings/memorabilia I have of my children). You may be gripping on to a situation or an object from the past. You may think that you might use it sometime in the future.

A THOUGHT TO REMEMBER:

Your clutter is not clutter if you love it or it functions for you.

MINI EXERCISE:

What are your excuses? Jot down right now a few notes in your Magic Notebook about why you are keeping something, which you know you really should and would like to let go of.

Do you find yourself saying any of these things?

It is still as good as new.

I've had it a long time.

They don't make it like this anymore.

It just needs fixing.

It is too good to use.

It has always been in the family.

It was here when we moved in.

I might need it someday.

It reminds me of someplace I have been.

I'll decide later what to do with it.

HOW TO LET GO OF HOME CLUTTER

Before you purchase anything new, ask yourself if you truly need it. If the answer is yes, buy it. If no is your answer, ask yourself if you really want it. Ask yourself why and be honest with yourself (this will also help you with recognizing your possible mind and body clutter). If you do decide to buy something new, before you bring it home think about where you will put it or how you will use it. I recommend throwing out, letting go and giving away something in exchange every time you bring in something new to your home. Your new item will replace an old item. For example, if you really need a new pair of shoes, throw out an old pair.

Depending on how much clutter you have and the nature (papers, clothes, old furniture) of your clutter, it is always good to start with a plan. If you feel overwhelmed, start small. Small projects breed success - just work on one drawer or one closet at a time. Make a clutter plan; mark on your calendar what you wish to accomplish each day. Keep three boxes or large bags handy. Label one, Junk (trash), label one, Transit (to move to another space), and label one, Out (to give away). As you go through your space, sort your stuff into one of these three boxes. Before you know it, step by step, your home will be clutter free.

WHEN TO THINK ABOUT DE-CLUTTERING:

Each season or at least once a year (Spring Cleaning).
Before a holiday.
When you get a new job or begin a new relationship.
After an illness.
Each morning or evening.

The following are suggestions to help you in de-cluttering your home:

Make it fun: have a friend over, share wine, put music on.

Start by cleaning your house. Dust, vacuum, change the sheets, do the dishes. Give away chipped dishes, worn out sheets and towels in the process. (If you can't do it yourself, hire someone to jump-start the process)

Keep a note pad nearby to list the new things you want to bring into your home.

When you buy something new, let go of something.

Take a few days or week's vacation and do it. Create your own clutter - free spa!

When you are ready, you are ready. I lived one whole year in my grandmother's home after she passed away before I moved one of her things. I felt safe and nurtured during that year - I needed that.

Pay your bills on time – feel happy to pay them and release them. Mounting bills add clutter to your heart and mind – not to mention your accounting.

Make it a family project, respecting that everyone has different opinions about what constitutes clutter. It is not your right to throw out or give away something that belongs to another person, even if you feel it to be so ugly, or that your spouse would not miss it.

Keep the faith – the universe does not like a void - it is an abundant universe. More of what you are getting rid of will come if you need it in the future – keep an attitude of prosperity and wealth. Know that you will be able to buy whatever you need or you will receive it again if you need to.

Bring in flowers and natural scents to your home, to inspire you to create a natural, healthy, uncluttered, beautiful home.

Take time in the morning to sit quietly to just be. Imagine all of your baggage (the clutter of your mind, body and home) sitting by a riverside, safe and ready for you when you need to go pick it up. Now visualize that you step into a little rowboat and cross over the river. When you are on the other side, step out and even let the boat go (it will come back to you if you call for it) – but feel and imagine the freedom of being you alone on this new side of the river without your clutter – the you that was you when you were five and who will be you when you are ninety-five. Rest in the uncluttered joy of that state.

Take time in the evening to let go of the day. There is nothing else you can do, so lie your head on a fresh pillow and rest, knowing that you are safe, protected, and your life is abundant with all good things. Count your blessings.

If you are lucky to be a past president of a country, you can create a library for all your correspondence and stuff. You can let other people keep your clutter while you get on with your life. This way you can go and visit it from time to time and feel accomplished. If you are not a former president, keep the history of your life to a few photo albums, journals and framed diplomas. If you live only in the past, you have no present and no future, for the past is always in your face. And think about what your children will have to pour through when you knock on heaven's door - have mercy!

Create a de-clutter schedule and write it down on a calendar, i.e. Monday, clean out top dresser drawer. Tuesday, clean out medicine cabinet. Wednesday, the pantry. Thursday, relax. Friday, clean out the cabinet with the glasses. Saturday, the garage ...

Have a garage sale and let other people buy your stuff – or better yet, just give it away. You will have fun and make a lot of people happy.

Space clear your home (see Face Your Self exercise at the end of this chapter.)

HOW YOUR HOME MIRRORS YOUR SPIRIT
KITCHENS:

What bounty fills my kitchen.
Smells and tastes of wonder.
Such is life given
To love, work and play.
The kitchen of my home supports my existence.

When you sit at your kitchen table, what do you see? How do you feel? What do you think? What do you eat? How do you eat?

Food supplies you with your life force energy. If you eat well, you will have the energy to work well, and have good relationships. The kitchen is one room in your home that has a powerful impact on your health, vitality and your wealth. It is important to keep your kitchen clean, in order and well organized. By doing so, you will metaphorically reflect health and prosperity. Just imagine a dirty, disorganized kitchen or even imagine a kitchen that is not often used. Now visualize the family or person who owns it. Chances are they will look and act in unhealthy ways.

In feng shui, it is advised that kitchens should not be the first room you see when you enter the home. When you see the kitchen first, day after day, year after year this may enhance eating disorders of overeating, eating unhealthy foods or bulimia type behavior. This is because food is always subconsciously on the mind. It is important too, if you can, to situate your kitchen so that it does not back up on a bathroom wall or view a bathroom. Having a bathroom in view or having a bathroom sharing a wall with the kitchen can metaphorically and subconsciously deplete the life-giving forces of cooking and eating your meal by draining your energies with the downward drains of the bathroom experience. If you do experience this, try placing a screen or curtain in your view or intentionally place some fresh flowers in your kitchen or bath to break-up and shift the draining bathroom experience.

If your kitchen has the space for a dining table, it is suggested to choose a round or oval table, which symbolizes good blessings and fairness. Have an even number of chairs, for even numbers are more balanced, and avoid having just one chair even if you live alone, for this could symbolize loneliness. The table should be out of direct line of any entranceway into the kitchen for this provides a more stable-eating environment. The table should remain uncluttered, with only flowers or a bowl of fruit or vegetables in its center to represent abundance and health – which actually can mirror or reflect the center of your being.

When cooking, be mindful to use all of the burners on your stove, for in feng shui, the stove is related to your good fortune and wealth. If your food is prepared well and happily, you will assimilate that food into your bodily systems where it will nourish you and make you strong and therefore able to work well and be prosperous. Ideally you want to design stove placement so that it is not cramped or stuck into a corner, does not have a back door opening into it, is not next to the sink or refrigerator and is well lit and ventilated. It is also advisable to not have oppressive overhanging pots, shelves or microwave ovens over the stove. Basically, you want your stove to be unencumbered and ready to service you to cook any meal without annoyances.

Remember that humans shape their environment but the environment also shapes the person, so be aware of what shapes, textures, colors and artwork you surround yourself with. Artwork in the kitchen should reflect bounty, peace, love and joy. Remember that you want to surround yourself with images and accessories which will nourish you and ease your digestion, not make you nauseous and ill feeling. I often suggest whites or greens for the color of kitchens. White is a color of purity and cleanliness in our country and it allows the beautiful color of the foods to shine. Green is a color that reflects new growth, the garden, family values and abundance. But color is subjective; just be mindful of the color you choose and how it aids in your cooking and eating experience. For example, if your kitchen has bright red cabinets and orange walls – do you find yourself being anxious and arguing often in the kitchen? Think about changing the colors.

You are fed and nourished not only by the food you eat but also by all of your senses. Avoid televisions and newspapers while you eat. Be thankful and playful in your kitchen design and know that you really are what you eat.

May the foods that you prepare in your kitchen, support your life force and make you abundant with health, wealth, and happiness.

DINING ROOMS:

Candles lit,
Flowers in the vase.
Fine china and silverware.
My lips touch the crystal glass of wine.
Thank you life.
This is how we dine.

I am amazed at how many people do not dine in their dining room. They eat in bed or on the couch in front of the television. Or they eat in the car or have something while putting on make-up, or shaving in the bathroom. Office eating at one's desk has become an art as people eat while on the telephone or typing on their laptop. Eating has become very fast. People don't really chew their food. It seems to be shoveled into mouths at a fast pace and swallowed whole – almost as if there were a prize for finishing in the quickest amount of time.

Dine with room - a mindfulness of the importance and pleasure of eating, giving yourself space, ease and time while you dine.

What is eating or dining all about? First and foremost it is about nourishment. The foods that we eat are for our survival – to nourish our minds and our bodies. This is important to remember, though it seems very obvious. The food that you eat becomes you – and you take on the energy and nature of the food that you eat. Food can absorb the energy of the cook and those people who handle the food in the (sometimes long) process of getting to your table. That is why your grandmother's cooking probably tasted so good when it was made with total love and fresh, wholesome ingredients. Before you eat, stop and give a quiet thanks (for your abundance) and make an energetic connection between you and the food before you. This can be done so subtly that no one need know you are doing it, but it will make a difference toward your digestion, and bring a quiet, thankful happiness to you. Eventually you will find that you become far more particular of the foods that you eat and the places you go to dine.

Some people eat to nourish their emotions. Dining or eating also takes on a social aspect. Be mindful of how and why you are eating. You are the boss over what and when food goes into your mouth. To dine together is to share a certain intimacy. Think about it, you open your mouth and put a fork or spoon filled with food into your mouth. The tongue is involved in the tasting process as well as all the olfactory senses of smell. Then you chew your food and swallow it into your body. You take this food with full faith that it is clean and of no disease and eat it without any protection. The food becomes you as you assimilate it into your system. You are sharing a meal – a meal that will become assimilated into the bodies and minds of all present. I can think of no more intimate thing other than sharing sex with someone, where you merge on such a high level that you do become one for those moments of splendor – the same is the dining experience.

Sometimes dining rooms are used as offices or where the kids do their homework. Arts and crafts projects may take over the dining table and stay there for weeks. This is fine from time to time just become aware that the space does not become a clutter center of old bills, papers and magazines – not to mention larger items that need to be put away but are confidently placed on the table until such time comes when you can take it no more, or guests arrive. Even though your dining area or room may take on other functions, I encourage you to set aside a weekly time for the pleasure of dining in your dining room.

I think it a shame that many people are missing the joy of dining because they have gotten so caught up in a fast-paced world. Yet the sun rises and sets as it has for centuries. Bring a mindfulness to your meals that food is a wonderful gift. That dining is an art. There is grace in dining. The use of a particular serving spoon can become ritualistic. The conversation can be inviting, entertaining and cultured. The preparation can be a delight of making offerings to your friends and family. The eating can bring a fullness that is of joy and abundance, not bloated where you need to take some sort of antacid because you stuffed yourself and feel sick. Food and dining – the art - is to nourish and feel good!

I invite you to consider how you dine, with whom you dine and on what you dine. You may want to dine in a special room for your dinners or Sunday meals, or you will want to have all your meals in a sacred space called the dining room. You may want to take time out to stop rushing, and pause over a salad or lovely little dessert and give thanks. Or, you may want to buy wonderful dishes that will enhance your mealtime experience. Perhaps you will want to invite friends or family more often to your home and invite them into your Dining Room where the smells, tastes, textures and visual experience will delight all, while the sounds of laughter and conversation fill the room.

May all your meals bring you life, happiness and abundance.

BEDROOM:

I snuggle with you in my dreams.
I fly above the world.
Safe and warm,
The room I bed my head is
Peaceful and serene.

A bedroom is a room that you go to at the end of the day to be intimate, relax, retreat, and sleep. I do suggest that you not bring any work-related business into the room. The nature of the activities that take place in the bedroom including loving your partner, makes the bedroom the most intimate space than any other room in your home and that is important. Therefore, I do not recommend using or placing exercise equipment in the bedroom. When I do have a client with exercise equipment in the bedroom, most of the time it is draped with clothing and directly in view of the bed. This creates guilt on a subconscious level, where the client is always thinking when they climb into bed that they should be losing weight and exercising. This does not lead to a restful sleep or a sensual, intimate relationship! Things become mechanical and rushed.

The bedroom is a space that most people do not invite many people into. It is your personal space. Therefore, I go so far as to suggest that you do not have photos of children, family or friends in your bedroom - especially married couples, if their relationship is suffering. Too often I find that couples begin to lose their intimacy once children are born. So often I go into a client's bedroom and there are many photos of the children, even children's drawings and art projects hung around the room. On a subtle level - because these photos are in your face, your energy can be focused toward them instead of toward your partner. I suggest you place photos of you as a couple where you each are relaxed and in love – such as a marriage photo or one from a relaxing vacation. The family photos work well in hallways, kitchens or dens. Artwork that is placed in the bedroom should be of peaceful scenes from nature or images that feel sensual and safe. For example, I would not recommend a painting of a ship in a storm, no matter how well done and expensive it may be, for the bedroom.

Because of the nature of the bedroom, it is advisable to work with soothing colors that are not too intense or bright. You want to create a space that feels peaceful, sensual, and protective. You might try a stronger color behind your bed such as a deep brick red or a darker shade of a color that you love. This darker color behind your bed suggests a protective mountain behind you – giving you more power and strength. It is similar to having a headboard, which is also recommended.

Because of closets, windows, heating and air conditioning units and vents, there is sometimes only one place to put the bed. Place your bed in a way that if there is a bathroom off of the bedroom, either you or your partner do not see it while lying in bed. It is advised that you also do not place your bed in direct line with the entrance of the room because it can make you feel more vulnerable. Ideally you would want to be able to see the door from your bed, but not be in line with the door.

I like to choose fabrics for the bedroom that feel rich, soft and sensual, meaning that they move. Think in terms of silks, velvets, chenille, and high thread count cottons. Again, remember, as within, so without. Having fabrics that feel good, warm and cozy on the outside will make you feel that way on your inside.

People always ask me about mirrors in the bedroom because they have read in many feng shui books that they are bad. I do not recommend hanging a mirror over your bed because if it fell it would hurt (so it's not good to sleep under a heavy mirror). Otherwise, I see no problem in having a mirror in your bedroom as long as it is not reflecting the dirty laundry or the toilet in your face. If you have a mirror in your room and you are not sleeping, you may want to try covering it with a sheet for a few nights to see if your sleep gets any better. If you do, remove the mirror. Sometimes in our sleep state the mirror may affect our astral body and sleep can become restless. Restlessness may also be from the thoughts we take to bed with us. You might try taking the television out of your bedroom too.

I invite you to walk over the threshold of your bedroom and leave the world behind - enter your own little retreat. Fill it with fresh flowers, scented candles and fresh air. Surround yourself with furnishings and images that you personally love. If you sleep well you will be good for the next day's adventures, good for your family and friends and good for yourself.

May you sleep in peace. Sweet dreams.

BATHROOM:

The journey of the day was long and my body needed to bathe. I dreamt of a private, special place where I could squat and eliminate the unnecessary elements from my being, offering them back to the earth for replenishment in the cycle of life. I longed for a space with a warm, secret pool and waterfall to bathe my tired body. A place with a stone shelf nearby holding the natural flowers, roots and oils I would use to cleanse my body, hair and soul. Then, I imagined the music of happy birds being carried by the light wind to my ears as I gazed into large reflection ponds, seeing my new face lit by the light of the golden sun and God's grace. As I stepped from the pool, I felt the warm soft, natural, absorbent cloth that was hanging from a nearby tree being wrapped around my body ... my feet felt secure and grounded on the earthen clay. In balance and refreshed, I moved the branches aside ready to face the world again!

If I had my choice I would put toilets and bidets in separate rooms off the *bath room*, for I see two completely separate functions here. Elimination is a normal, healthy body function where we relieve and purify ourselves. Yet why do we have to have it in our face while we bathe? The toilet is quite a downward energy drain, that when seen from tubs or the hallways of our home can, on a subtle level, pull us down energetically. I advise you to put a small screen in front of the toilet if there is space to screen it off from view. At least keep your door to the bathroom closed, especially if you sleep in a room with the bathroom in view from your bed. A fun solution to the downward energy pull of the toilet is to place an object on the toilet tank that represents explosive energy such as a jar of unpopped popcorn or an unopened bottle of champagne.

I see showers, bathtubs and hot tubs as places for meditation, nurturing and wonderful sensuality - as well as cleansing. It is nice to sit in the tub and feel the water cascading down upon you from the shower-head. Also, there is nothing better than being bathed and lovingly sponged by a loved one - either a mother bathing a child or lovers bathing each other. There are so many wonderful tubs and shower stalls to choose from. Pick colors that reflect a soothing scene for you and sizes that fit your body (bodies) and budget. If you are feeling angry or fiery, take a shower or bath, for water puts out fire, and bathing will calm you down. An affordable real luxury is to have a hot tub outside in your garden where you can relax and watch the movie of the sky in all seasons, either alone or with friends.

Mirrors can be your reflection ponds, where you see your self. However, be mindful of what else the mirror is reflecting - is it the toilet? the dirty laundry? the moldy wallpaper?

Ventilation is important in a bathroom. The best choice would be an old fashioned window that can be opened to let in the fresh air. Many ventilation fans are so assaulting to the senses making such a racket that you could never relax feeling that perhaps you, too, will be sucked up into the vast unknown of the venting system.

Sinks are sweet areas where we can smile as we brush our teeth, wash our hands and shave. Free-standing sinks are very pretty yet don't allow space around them for the tools of the trade, i.e. toothbrush, cups, shaving stuff, soap, washcloth and make-up. Beauty is important, but function is even more important from a design perspective. Combining beauty and function is the quest. (Although the Shakers may not agree with me.)

Bathrooms can become your private getaway and nourishing spa. They are rooms to bathe and refresh your soul. Allow the flow of the water's cleansing properties to wash over you. Elimination purifies. Surround yourself with natural sponges, candles, scented oils, sea salts and special goblets for wine or pure water. I invite you to create sensual bathrooms and enjoy the art of bathing for your self and your loved ones.

May your body revitalize and stay forever young in the magic mirror in your bathroom.

LIVING ROOM:

Once a man came to visit
And was invited into the living room.
He was not allowed to sit down.
He was not allowed to sneeze or blink.
Forget about a drink.
He left and never returned.

What is a living room but a room for living? This makes perfect sense according to its name, yet I find myself in a person's home where the living room is anything but a room for living. In early frontier times the living room was the room where people had their fireplace, cooked, ate, sewed, gathered and even in some places, slept – truly living in the space. Somewhere along the way of home design living rooms became places that were cordoned off like museum rooms. Places where one had to sit up straight and hold one's cup of tea with the pinkie extended out. Children were not allowed to enter unless chaperoned. In extreme cases, plastic slipcovers were even placed on the furniture to protect the fabric for a lifetime and beyond!

Today in many homes people have family rooms where most of the daily activity occurs. Many of these rooms are connected to the kitchen area and are truly today's living room. Yet, the living room is still designed into archetypal home plans. What do we make of these rooms? Again, it may not be a room used every day, but it can express or reflect the design preference of the family. Are you a formal or informal family? Do you like contemporary and trendy things, or do you like a more conservative and traditional design? Create your living room accordingly.

For example, I currently live an informal life – having moved to Northern Vermont. I created one large room that has my couch, dining area and kitchen all in one. With the lighting and large windows, most activity takes place there. I then chose another room to become the library/media room. Its walls and ceiling are painted a brick red and the windows are draped to create a room that is more cozy. A relaxed feeling exists there -yet the furniture is more formal than in the larger living space. In my mind this room can become a quiet space where the family can go to read, reflect, and write.

Designing your living room can be fun and full of self-expression. I have clients who place large artwork and expansive couches and funky lighting to create a room that is designed for large parties. Other clients like to see the beautiful space that they created in the heart of their home and just enjoy it as they walk by. If, from your living room and hall passageways you see other rooms, remember to choose a color and a pattern for the walls and drapes to compliment these other rooms.

If your living room truly is a room that you rarely use, you might want to consider placing a large plant or tree in it to bring a little life into the room. It is not a good idea to let any part of your home lie dormant for too long. Metaphorically, this is like ignoring a part of your life. By needing to go into the room to water a plant, you keep that aspect of your home alive. If you find that you do not use the living room much at all, keep in mind that you can make the living room anything you want. I have one client who is a confirmed bachelor after a divorce. He loves electronic things and has his living room stocked with all his gadgets, televisions, and stereo equipment. This is his room and he loves it. Another client is an artist and has transposed her family's living room into her studio space. I invite you to take a walk around your home and see where you and your family are doing the most living. Declare that to be your living room!

May your living room reflect the living space within your heart.

GARDENS AND PROPERTY:

Picture yourself walking down a garden path; its gentle curves lead you on a journey of delightful sights, smells, tastes and sounds.
You pass luscious fruits and bountiful vegetables. There are beautifully colored flowers of all shapes and sizes that look as if they are about to speak to you as they caress your fingertips. The trees along the path offer you shade, with their umbrella of leaves, from the afternoon sun.
Pause to breath in the beauty of life.
There are several large, prominent rocks and boulders in this garden, which you touch. You feel grounded to the earth and know your strength.
You slow down and sit upon an inviting stone next to a waterfall. A butterfly flies by as if to say hello. Feeling the earth between your toes, you gaze into the sky and watch a bird's flight of freedom.
A gentle breeze sends perfumed scents to your nose as you listen to the harmonious sounds of the water falling into the pond upon the lily pads with the croaking frogs. With your hand, you touch the cool water and notice your reflection in the currents you make which radiate out across the water.
You are at peace.
There are no fast moving computers, TV satellite world news, telephones, cars, appointments, must do's and must have's.
Here, you are alone with the natural world. You are part of this natural world - nature - man connecting Earth and Sky.
The peace you see reflected in the garden reflects the peace you feel in your being.
Life is good.
Breathe in and inhale this precious moment in time. The Breath of Nature, the flow of the Cosmic Breath, your Breath is in alignment – you are breathing with the flow of Life and it is good.
Exhale this goodness into the world.

In real estate the saying goes, Location, Location, Location. The great thing is that when you design your landscaping, you can create worlds within worlds on your property with places to sit and reflect and places to walk uninterrupted. You can create magical, protective, prosperous spaces on your properties, decks, balconies and terraces, which will allow the external world of nature to nourish the internal world of yourself.

Your property is the place you set your home upon, to live your life, raise your family, and play. Property reflects the families or people who live in the home. What does your entrance look like? Is it well lit and without clutter, dead or unhealthy trees and shrubs? Are the pavement or stones on the path in good repair? Is the path to your front door welcoming? The main door of your property, even if you don't use it, is still considered the entranceway of your home. It is important that overgrown trees do not block it. Trees are wonderful and can give you lots of energy, but if you have a large tree right in the line of your front door you may feel blocked and that your life is not going anywhere. Think about working with stone or slate walks that have a gentle curve in them rather than straight lines or 90-degree turns, which can feel sharp and cutting. If you already have a straight path, you can soften it up with ivy or floral plantings in season, which flow over the angles.

If you are having problems with being heard and noticed in life, make sure your house number is clearly marked– this allows people to find you. If you live on a busy road and you feel like opportunities are just passing you by, place big rocks or boulders on each side of the entranceway of your driveway, which will anchor your life and property down metaphorically. Opportunity will not pass you by.

My first suggestion with your grounds is to take a walk around and clean up! Get rid of the clutter: old dead trees and branches (which have no life force) will drain your energy, I have a client who has grown children in their teens, yet still keeps a broken old slide and swing-set on the property. This is an indication of the family not growing forward and not allowing new things into their lives. Your storage sheds can be clutter centers that have stuff in them that you haven't used for years and block new things from coming into your life. Spring-cleaning makes a lot of sense. Rake the leaves, throw out broken flowerpots and clean out the clutter of the property.

You create your environment and your environment creates you. Where do you want your eye to go? Where do you want most of the focus of your life to go? Think in terms of activating these areas on your property. You can work with water, plantings, wind chimes, garden furniture and sculpture. Begin by looking out at your property from each window of your home and use these areas to begin to create beautiful gardens. Eventually, you can connect all of these gardens with walkways and waterfalls and ponds. Whatever you choose, no matter how large or small your exterior space may be, create a space where you can feel at peace and at one with nature. You are influenced by where you live – ever so slightly every day, which adds up over the years to create who you are.

May you dance with the nature spirits of the flowers and feel their love.

COLOR:

I inhale.
In the darkness all is contracted and absorbed within.
I see nothing. No one can see me.
All is black. I am nothing. I am everything.
I exhale.
In the light a dance begins.
As the rainbow scarves the Earthen body,
I pull the ribbons of color to create a Maypole of woven de-light.
Red reflects the fire of my springtime passions, the earthen clay,
the sunset of the day.
I dance with Orange, juggling organic fruits from the Earth's womb.
Twirling still, Yellow fills my head with sunshine and daffodils, - yellow
birds and lots of frills!
The Greens of the summer grass send me on dance to treetops full of robin's nests,
which send my heart in flight
To the Blues of the sky where my voice sings out loud the love
I feel for life and living.
Indigo - I dance on toe – and know the wisdom of my play.
Violet is the prance that keeps me in the dance - weaving the colors of my life this
glorious day.

What colors do you have in your home? What colors do you love? What colors do you avoid? There are many books and studies that have been done on color. What is color? Color is energy. Very simply, you need light and an eye to see color. White is the reflection of all colors of the rainbow off a surface. Black is the absorption of all colors. All colors are the reflection of a color dancing from the surface of an object with the absorption of the other rainbow colors into that object. Color is a major tool used by interior designers in creating a mood, style and visual direction. Color can also be used to heal and balance you. In a sense, color can be a type of food for you that, when used intentionally will nourish you.

Color can bring up certain images and feelings from your past experiences. Therefore it is important to remember that color is subjective. For example, even though blues are considered a soothing and calming color, if you had an unfortunate experience of violence with someone wearing a blue sweater, blue may not be the color of choice to use as a means to soothe you. I invite you to play with and explore all colors. Get a set of finger paints or water colors and explore the colors. Ask yourself what images each color brings up for you. We can see, feel, smell, taste and hear color. The smell of a fresh cut lawn brings up images of a rich, healthy green color. The taste of grandma's Italian tomato sauce - a deep red color. Feel the sand and the earth; try to imagine them another color. Does it work? How does it make you feel?

All color has three dimensions, so it is, in a sense, very sculptural. You have the basic colors you learned in kindergarten, which you can lighten or darken by adding white or black (or light, which is like white). You can also change the intensity of a color by adding grey. So there are literally thousands of colors. Just look in your local paint store at all the choices.

By intentionally working with color placement in your home, you can enhance energies and aspects of yourself. Green is a color for new beginnings, growth, and abundance. Think about springtime, how the green fills in the land from light green to deep dark green. If you would like to enhance an area of your life, such as your career, you may want to choose some greens for your walls to mirror the growth of a new career. Red is a fiery color. It can bring a jump-start to an area. If you need to jump-start a relationship that has been a little sleepy, try some red! (Although bright red on your walls may cause arguments, for it is too hot). Yellows and gold are earth colors. They can give you a feeling of being grounded. Yellow is also good for communication. Think of purple and how royalty use it. Does it give you a feeling of wealth? Try it.

We will change the way we dress when we get into different moods. Sometimes we may be playful, other times more serious. Sometimes we feel the need to be quiet and comfortable in the way we dress and sometimes we feel like being out there partying. Often we will buy an item of clothing because of its color. I invite you to take a look at the way your home is dressed to fit your mood and personal expression. We can't change our home designs as often as our clothes; however, we can change a color of a wall, ceiling or floor simply with a can of paint or a decorative accessory such as a pillow. So if you are one who always played it safe with white or egg-shell walls and you want to keep your life from becoming stagnant, I invite you to be a little playful and try some color. Have fun!

May your life be filled with rainbows of light.

CHAPTER SEVEN
FACE YOUR SELF EXERCISES

EXERCISE # 1:

CREATING A SACRED SPACE (SECRET ALTERS)

All space is sacred for all is a golden thread woven into the whole.

The rituals and activities that you do in any space are sacred when you do them with awareness, intention, compassion, thankfulness and joy. In this exercise you will create your own intimate, private space, which you can later share with your family or friends (or not).

When you move unhealthy energies and vibrations, it is important to have a healthy base which holds the intention of your space clearing (next exercise). An altar can be used as a source of personal protection, awareness and strength. There is no need of any religion or dogma when you want to declare something special for you - something that has a special meaning for you and you alone.

First, let me tell you a little story:

There once was a man who was sitting barefoot under a tree relaxing in the afternoon sun. In India it is very disrespectful to point your feet toward an alter. It just so happened that a princely man came riding by on his horse and said to the man in a shocked tone, "How dare you sit there with your feet pointing to that temple door where God is at the alter!!" The man sitting under the tree looked up at the man on the horse and said to him, "If you can tell me where God is not, I will gladly put my feet there."

OBJECTIVE:

You will be able to set up private; sacred alters in your home that will support you in your poise, happiness, hopes and dreams. They will be reflections to you. You will receive all the blessings of heaven and earth in any space that you hold dear and near to your heart.

WHAT YOU WILL NEED:

The following items are suggestions of the types of things you may choose to include in your altar (use your imagination and your own items and images that resonate with you):

Gemstones, rocks, shells, minerals, fresh leaves, salt
Statues, photographs, paintings
Signs and symbols on cards or drawn by you or a loved one
Cloth and fabric designs
Fire, candles, lamps, light, incense
Colors (intentionally use the color of an object)
Flowers, oils, scent
Poetry, letters, e-mail
Vase or crystal drinking glasses
Special Objects that are dear to your heart, pictures
Bells
Earth, wood, stones
Holy water, lavender water
Anything that you give meaning to and that is meaningful to you

EXERCISE:

1. Choose an area that you see from your bed, your favorite chair, or a place in the hallway that you pass often. It can be on a dresser or on a table with a lamp and other decorative objects.
2. Place and arrange your sacred object or objects on the table, nightstand, countertop or surface of your choice.
3. State what your intention is that you want the objects to hold for you (love, abundance, health) and then infuse the object (s) with that intention by saying a prayer in your own words over the object. (For example, "This stone will represent for me a grounding influence. When I see this stone, I will feel perfect, whole and complete. I am grounded.")
4. Display your altar where it can be easily seen. Do not tell other people your intention with the altar. To their minds, it will look like

a decorative accessory (in the example above: it will look simply like a lovely rock sitting on your table.)

5. Whether you use your altar as a reminder of your spirit or as a place for your meditation and prayer, every time you pass your secret altar, you can smile to yourself and give thanks and do a little dance of joy, and live your intention.

EXERCISE # 2:

SPACE CLEARING:

Energy can get stagnant in a space because of illness, negative emotions, clutter, etc.

Perhaps you recognize times when you walked into a room where someone has been ill and notice how even the air in the room feels sick and sticky. Your inclination may be to immediately open the windows to let some fresh air inside. Have you ever walked into a room right after someone has had an argument? You can feel the tension in the space - the negative energy permeates the walls and floors. Have you ever experienced a rude guest in your home who left their toxic thoughts and manners behind? You may have felt like removing all the things that they touched.

Space clearing is a method to move negative, unhealthy energy and vibrations out of your home. You will want to break up the stagnant energy and move it out of the room and out of your home space through the door or windows. As you continue to work the stagnant energy, it will break up, lighten up, and disappear. Claim your healthy space back with space clearing.

Reasons to Space Clear:

- If you feel stagnant, stuck in your life or bored.
- To clear out predecessor energy from your home, office, hotel room, etc.
- To enhance your feng shui cures.
- To cleanse and rebalance your home after someone was sick or died.
- To cleanse your home while someone is sick.

- To assist you in gaining more clarity and wisdom and peacefulness.
- To help you feel connected to the space.
- To increase your health and vitality.
- To make you feel more sensual and present.
- To help set the stage for creating a sacred space.
- To sell or move from a space.
- To help you get in motion to remove clutter.
- To help move spirit energy.
- To open you up to joy and luck.

Do space clearing when:

- You have cleaned out your clutter.
- Springtime.
- In daylight hours.
- You feel healthy - physically, mentally, and emotionally.
- You will not be disturbed (i.e. by phone calls, pets, children, company, etc.).
- It is near a full moon (prefer waxing).

Do not space clear when:

- You feel any fear or apprehension.
- You are sick – physically, mentally or emotionally.
- You are pregnant, have your period, are sexually depleted or have an open wound.
- During the nighttime.
- The space may be empty for several days afterward.

Create an altar in your home before you space clear.

- While you are setting up your altar, think about your intention for the space clearing.

OBJECTIVE:

To be able to clear out any negative, draining or unhealthy energy from your home, and to keep your own energy healthy and strong.

WHAT YOU WILL NEED:

Depending on what energy you intend to clear and which approach you take to clearing your space, (see Techniques for Purification, below) you will need to choose one item, from the list below:

Air: incense, orange mist
Sound: bells, drum, clapping hands, sticks
Water: a mister, bowl of water
Fire: candles
Earth: salt

STEPS TO BASIC SPACE CLEARING PREPARATION:

- Prepare yourself with a bath/shower, meditation, and a good night's sleep the night before. After your morning meditation, eat a healthy breakfast, do a little stretching or yoga and connect yourself with a natural setting (take a walk in the woods, park, or along a waterway).
- Put all open foods and drinks away in the refrigerator and cupboards.
- Turn off music, fans, etc.
- Open the windows or doors if it is possible and keep them open during the cleansing.
- Know what your intention for space clearing is. (Each space clearing you do may have a different intention. See Reasons to Space Clear, above). Your intention sets up an energy field. The stronger you resonate and sense (feel) your intention, the stronger your work will be in the clearing. Set up your altar space in the center of the space to be cleared or in a nearby room. Bless your altar with your intention by simply stating your intention over the altar or by writing your intention on paper and placing that paper upon your altar.
- Have your hands clean. Roll up the sleeves on your shirt.
- Drink a large glass of purified water.
- Hold your hands about six inches apart and imagine a golden ball radiating back and forth between them. Allow this ball to purify and sensitize your hands.

TECHNIQUES FOR PURIFICATION:

Using one of the following techniques to break up and remove stagnant and unhealthy energy, walk around your space, starting at the eastern corner of the room or at the main entrance and work in a clockwise manner moving and removing the energy toxins that you feel.

Go around your space - along the walls and into corners, behind doors, and around bulky furniture, allowing the purification to penetrate (wash away, burn up or dissolve) the intended reason for space clearing.

There are 5 techniques that you can use to remove toxic energies in your space. Review the Reasons to Space Clear, (at the beginning of this section) to get clarity as to your intention for the clearing, then choose from these 5 ways.

Air: Penetrates and dissolves unwanted energy

Example: If you had an unwanted guest or after a party in your home to bring your residence back to itself, you would use air to clear your home.

Light sage or incense to penetrate and dissolve unwanted feelings. Sprinkle lavender or orange peels mixed with water around your room, imagine that the scent is replacing all illness and filling the room with: calm, happy, healthy energy.

Sound: Breaks up old energies and changes the vibrations of energy

Example: If there was a violent argument in a room, you would want to work with sound to break up the hard, violent energy and replace it with softer, happier tones.
Ring bells, singing bowls, gongs, tuning forks, cymbals, chimes, drums, rattles, clapping, toning, chanting, singing, musical instruments, imagining that you are breaking up and changing the energy in your room.

Water: Washes away negative energy

Example: If there was a long illness in your room, you would want to wash away the residual energy of the illness to bring the room back to health.

Place misters, holy water, fountains, aquariums, water systems throughout the house, imagining that you are washing away all of the unwanted energy.

Fire: Burns up unwanted energy

Example: If you felt a danger in a room, you would want to burn up that energy to bring the room back into balance. If you wanted to get beyond your past, you would use fire "to burn up" old Cluttered thinking patterns.
Light candles, oil lamps, or your fireplace, imagine that you are burning up all unwanted negative energy.

Earth: Absorbs unwanted energy

Example: If you wanted to balance your new home, you would want to absorb any old energy from the predecessors with earth.
Place salt, crystals, linghams, stones, earth, copper, in your room, imagining that you are absorbing all old energies and they are going back to the earth. You may want to leave the salt in the room for nine hours or for a few days, and then you can vacuum or sweep it all up.

TO CLOSE YOUR SPACE CLEARING EXERCISE:

Invocation:
Call a healthy, radiant light energy to fill into your space.

Preservation:
To keep your space clearing intention in the room, reaffirm your intention and place it in the space you have cleared. You can do this by writing a note on a piece of paper and then burying it in a plant that is in the room or by placing a crystal or stone from your alter on top of a dresser or table in the room.

When you have worked your way around the room, tie off each room by making the infinity sign in the air with your arm, which has strong power long after it is used.

No gust of wind or un-welcomed visitor

Can take your home from you, for you take your home

with you wherever you go.

CHAPTER EIGHT

YOU HAVE TO POLISH YOUR MIRROR: YOU HAVE TO WORK IT

The Jungle

I rode into the jungle
My backpack on my back,
Let me tell you about it,
All the troubles that I've seen.
The tigers were hungry
They ate my meal.
Let me tell you about it,
All the troubles that I've seen.
Hot, tired and hungry
I fought with all my might.
Let me tell you about it,
All the troubles that I've seen.
I screamed and shouted
To be heard over the lions' roar
Let me tell you about it,
All the troubles that I've seen.
Left alone,
Torn to shreds on the side of the road
Let me tell you about it,
All the troubles that I've seen.

I rolled over and picked up a stone
And uncovered a gold mine.
Let me tell you about it,
Amazing grace.

Give service with a light heart and all your days become enchanting.

WORKSPACE HAPPINESS

This chapter is about working it. Your personal work (what you may do to earn a living is one type of work) - the work you do, which addresses your personal purpose in life, your path in life, your journey; is another type of work – and is the work we are talking about in this book. In reality, all work connects to your inner work. This chapter is about your place in the workplace and your work in the world. In truth, the whole world is your workspace.

I once knew this man who was an artist and a teacher. He struggled to make ends meet financially– but he was working his life. One day his father died and left him quite a bit of money. This artist let go of some of his old friends, bought fancy cars and went out with many women. He spent much of his money on cocaine and alcohol. He partied. His life spiraled downhill to a point where he became very sick and died at an age of 43 years old. He had nothing more to live for – he had no goals – he had lost his purpose- he misplaced his own self.

There is an old Chinese proverb that says, House done, man dies. What does this mean to you? Think about it. If you have nothing left to live for – you die. Having a goal and work to do is a good thing.

This chapter is about your inner work and your outer work, and how the two reflect each other. Clutter, personal issues, disorders, difficult situations come at you every day. It can be exhausting and debilitating to the point that you just want to give up. Please don't. Your true work in this lifetime is to know yourself and how this self of yours fits in (connects) naturally to the whole world around you. We all are trying to make sense of existence.

MINI EXERCISE:

How do you feel about: work, labor, employment, a job, a vocation, and an occupation? Write down your reactions and thoughts or emotions to each work word above.

Do you feel control, drudgery, exertion, effort and toil? Or, do you feel success, part of something good, healthy and happy?

If you keep doing what you have always done before, you will keep getting what you have always gotten. If you keep your old patterns of doing - they will hold you back and you will forever not only be where you are today but also in the same place in your future.

You are the authority of your life. From today forward, set an intention; make great choices. You may feel that you made good choices in the past, or had bad luck in the past, either way, if you are not happy today in your work (life), you must ask yourself why not? Whether you work for yourself or another, whether you are an entrepreneur, capitalist, industrialist or a sitter under a tree-er, it is not good enough to just read about and have book wisdom about <u>the work</u>. In working your life and your dreams – you have to experience it – use it - work it, and have living **proof** of it through *your own wisdom*. You must make a commitment to yourself to actually work the exercises and live your life from a Face Your Self perspective of heart. Knowledge becomes wisdom by your personal experience; through your wisdom you gain significant knowledge.

MINI EXERCISE:

How do you define your business or your work? What is your business about? What is your mission in life? Do you have a purpose for your work? Is it just to make money? What is your reason for being on this planet? What is your calling in this lifetime? Part of this chapter on work is, once again, for you to un-clutter your life so you can see yourself clearly and know what it is that will make you joyous and what you can offer the world - no matter what that work might be. You are worthwhile. You are a love. You are important. Let the world turn and hug yourself whenever you feel exhausted.

A THOUGHT TO REMEMBER:

We each have something uniquely ours to offer. It is ok to change your mind.

BUSINESS

Each business has its own life force. Each business is, in a sense, alive, and is a reflection of the owner, CEO, president, manager and the people working for the company. When it is your business or your work – you must align yourself, or adjust your chi (energy), to make your energy fit with your work. If this is impossible, you will experience the predictable, ultimate situation of attempting to fit a square peg into a round hole – you just will not fit and you and your work will suffer for it. This is perhaps the biggest, most toxic form of work disharmony that you can experience – for when you do not align with the mission, purpose or life force of your work, you and the work suffer.

Are you following in what your parents want you to do? I once had a client whose parents insisted that she work in the family business as the bookkeeper. They felt it would be a good experience for her. This client was not in love with numbers – she loved music. After several years of unhappiness in her work, she finally left the family business and started to teach music to children where she blossomed and felt much joy and happiness in her life.

If you find that you cannot adjust your chi (your energy) for the period of time that you are at your workplace and align with your business at hand – you must ask yourself honestly if perhaps you are in the wrong place? How many times have you gone to a local restaurant or a checkout counter and have gotten miserable service because the person working was actually miserable themselves?

If you experience this most basic form of work disharmony, not aligning with the work you do, you will find that you will sooner or later:

Clash with other workers and clients
Not do the work well
Harm your vital, alive, positive life force
Become more and more mentally and bodily ill
Ultimately, damage not only the business but also yourself

ARE YOU ON YOUR CAREER PATH?

Your path in life is not necessarily the work that you are doing to earn a living. Many people confuse their career path with the work that they do. You may be working as a car mechanic by day and play the saxophone by night. Your day job provides you with the money to live and your night work is your passion. Face Your Self and know that you are always on your path in life when you do all your work (including your laundry) with awareness of who you are. All work is important in the great scheme of things, just as each little piece of a clock is needed to make it tell precise time.

MINI EXERCISE:

Answer the following questions right now in your notebook: (Make three columns) What does your work, your business; do for you physically, spiritually and emotionally? How does your work, your business, help others physically, spiritually and emotionally?

If your work is not supportive of you and others, then ask yourself why you are staying with your current job. Remember not to judge your answers - be honest with yourself. Is it for the money alone (that is fine, for we all need money to pay our rent and buy food (since most of us do not grow our own))? The benefits? Is it because your parents thought you should become a…. (you fill in the blank)? There is no right answer – just be honest to yourself right now. First you need to know yourself and not lie to yourself any longer. When you are in right alignment with yourself, you can't help but be successful. What is success to you?

A THOUGHT TO REMEMBER:

Wealth comes in many ways – not just in money.

MINI EXERCISE:

You Have to Work It! Make your work like a fairy tale. Make your life a story. Pretend the big bad wolf and the obstacles you must overcome all translate into a story – your story. You've got to believe… believe in yourself. What is the story about your true work? Write your story out now in your magic notebook. Have fun.

A THOUGHT TO REMEMBER:

The world is abundant. Look to nature. Just one watermelon has many seeds to make well over one hundred new watermelons.

HOW DO YOU GET RID OF CLUTTER IN THE WORKSPACE?

Workspace disorganization can be very subtle but it can mirror problem situations in your business (your life). Do you find yourself either holding on to old business projects- standing on past glories, or do you tend to focus on a failure or defeat in a business transaction, to a point that either way you will not and cannot go forward? Refreshing your office space by removing the clutter will help you to regain fresh clarity of your goals. Once you have removed your office/work clutter, your business will feel refreshed and you will notice newfound positive energy flowing into your life and work.

Whether you are an owner/executive or a worker bee, look at the space where you conduct your business/career and answer the following questions:

- Does your space reflect your business in a professional manner? (Even if you work at home in your basement or garage.)
- Are your signs clear, and reflect your business?
- Is your office space clean and in order?
- Are your files in order?
- Is your library outdated?
- Is your office furniture worn or broken?
- Is your staff productive and happy?
- Are your air vents clean?
- Are there buzzers that can be replaced with a more soothing sound?
- Is your desk clear so you can work on one project at a time?

MINI EXERCISE:

Imagine your business already operating successfully (or your career advancing) and answer the following (you can write your answers in your Magic Notebook):

- What are your business opportunities to increase/succeed and grow?
- What is your greatest challenge?
- How do you distinguish your business/career from others in the same field?

BE AWARE: BEWARE OF PLACES WHERE PHYSICAL CLUTTER HIDES

- The Conference Table

     Do you use your conference table for storage? Flat spaces are ideal places for clutter to pile up. Even if you use your conference table for other tasks or projects – be mindful that clutter does not start moving in, piling up and taking over your business. It is important to keep a clean pallet (in this case your conference table) for new and fresh ideas to spring forth to create and grow new business.

- The lobby

    Are there old projects hanging on the walls and sitting on the shelves? When I see this in an office space – I wonder, what has this company done lately. It is good to display past accounts and projects – showing a history of the company – but do not rest on past laurels. Keep it fresh and up-to-date.

    Are the magazines and office brochures outdated? I find this the highest reflection of a company that does not seem to care about its clients or even, itself. I suggest that you sit in your lobby and become a client for that moment – see what they see. How is what you see reflecting on you and your company?

    Is there dust and grime on the walls and floors? There is no excuse for dusty air ducts or grimy doors. Once again, if this is how the company feels about themselves, how would they care about taking care of a client?

- Behind doors

    Do you keep and store things behind doors in your office? Metaphorically, things behind doors do not allow freedom of movement – Is your company stuck and not getting accounts? Perhaps it is that clutter you have stuffed behind the doors that is mirroring that stuck experience for you.

- Cabinets

    Is your desk and are your cabinets full of old files and/or do you keep outdated inventory on the shelves? Look at what is at your fingertips? Are there current files and telephone numbers and projects at your reach? Or, do you have to fight every time you need to find something? Again, this shows someone who is not organized and ready to do the current work at hand. Why are you doing this to yourself?

- How you represent yourself:

    Is your logo clear and are your business cards and stationary updated and professional? Your logo, business cards and stationary are an image of your company? What do they say about you? What do you want them to say about you? What about your website? Does it match your logo and other materials your company sends out?

Do you dress appropriately for your position? You would not want to see your pilot or doctor dressed in cut off shorts and an old tee shirt if they were going to fly your plane or perform surgery on you. You would want them to project some kind of professionalism in their dress, which gives you added confidence of their skills. The same goes for any business – dress the part.

- The personal home of the president, CEO, or office manager and your home.

If the head of the company's home is cluttered (energetically in discord) he or she will bring that energy to the office or workspace. It is important for a healthy business to know that its people are healthy and have a clear perspective on life and the business.

EXCUSES: WHY YOU KEEP OBSTACLES IN THE WAY OF YOUR WORK

You may find that you really want to succeed in your business (your life); however, you keep missing the boat. Ask yourself what mental obstacles you are living with. (You may want to reread Chapter 4, or look at your notes).

A THOUGHT TO REMEMBER:

Face Your Self: You can only be what you think you can be. That sounds like a great bumper sticker or tee shirt.

You can only experience that which you have the mental ability to personify. For example, if you want to be successful, but your underlying reason (your thinking and feeling) is to prove to others (and yourself) that you are (or are not) a failure, either way, the failure energy surrounds you. Your Pool of Creative Mind Substance and you will eventually fail. If you feel that you need a job to make money (because you feel that you are poor), then you have surrounded yourself with poverty thinking and will always experience a feeling of poverty. And remember, it is good to have a job where you earn money – respect it as such. Continue to pursue your passion and be who you know you are – bring your creativity to what ever you do – even if that has no monetary income – it feeds your heart and gives you wealth in your mind and body and soul (which is worth more than gold or platinum).

See if you relate to any of the following:

- I need this job to pay my bills. This is fine if, while you think this, you realize that you are not poor but abundant with all types of wealth. The universe is abundant – it is your thinking that stops you from receiving your greatest good. If you have a poverty mentality you will always feel poor. Instead of saying, "I am poor.", it is better to say, "I am broke right now." or, "I do not have the money right now – but, I am divinely supplied and I am prosperous."
- I need this job; my good comes to me from this job. NO! Your good comes to you because of who you are – it comes to you from the One Source. Do not look at any one job or person as your source of good – they are what the Source uses to deliver your good.
- That's what everybody does:

  Comes in late.
  Wears sloppy clothes to the office.
  Doesn't return telephone calls.
  Doesn't smile.
  Makes their own private telephone calls at the office.
  Takes long coffee breaks.
  This is a lazy, non-creative, selfish, giving-away-your-power and thinking approach. You should always perform your best. What you give you receive back ten times over.

- I need clients to keep this business going. Do you care and support your clients as you would yourself? Do you make fun of your clients and treat them behind the scenes as if they were jerks?

  You are a magnet. The laws of attraction bring to you what you really deep down in the middle of your soul and heart believes. If you think it is, it is. It is as simple as that. Realize that you draw to you all that you experience, with a power, which is within yourself.

Even if you may be experiencing lack or frustration, that may be the Universe in some way testing you to see how real you are in wanting your dream. Know that the truth is that you are success when you are on your path in life.

A THOUGHT TO REMEMBER:

You must continue on a daily basis to Face Your Self. If you feel unsuccessful you must get to the root reason for your feelings, motivations and face them – once you honestly do, then you can turn everything around and say, "I am a success just waiting to happen."

How does your workspace support you? How do you experience your office or work environment? Does it feel like your space? Does it reflect the belief you have about yourself? Does it remind you that you are an abundant, vital being?

Everything has energy. Round tables, for example, can reflect work of the heart and fairness. Too big a desk may make people feel that they can't come to you. Glass desks can seem weak or unstable, (you may want to put a blotter on the desk so the energy of the work does not fall through to the floor).

Be mindful of what you look upon as you sit in your work-space. Hopefully, you are not feeling cramped into a corner and looking at a bare wall. Place something from nature in your office such as a plant, water fountain, painting of a beautiful landscape or some interesting stones or sculptures to support your spirit. Intentionally allow these natural items to give you a sense of global connection to your clients, other offices, to yourself and to the earth.

The following suggestions will make your work-space more supportive of you and your work. These are meant as suggestions – you decide if they feel good to you:

Foyer and entranceways:
- Should be visible and easy to find from the main entrance or elevator of the building/floor. You do not want to hide – put your face out there.

- Your business' main door should be in proportion to your overall space.
- Clients should clearly see the receptionist, who should be seated in a comfortable, supportive chair upon first entering your space. How many times have you entered an office space and wondered where everybody was and where to go.
- Use colors from your company logo in your color scheme. Keep consistent the look of your stationary, office walls, business cards, and advertising.
- Have an inviting seating area for guests where they can see the front door and also see into the company's interior space. Make your clients feel comfortable and welcome.

The office of the President/CEO:
- Locate the chief executive offices as far as possible from the main entrance, in the rear corner office.
- Angle the desk to provide a wide viewing angle to the door – but avoid direct alignment with the door for that may seem too unfriendly.
- Have a picture of the company logo/name behind the seat of the president on the wall – this will show that the company is behind him. You can do this even if you are not president – you will be looked on as a team player.
- Personal pictures should face the executive (you). Avoid having others see your personal pictures. This is a place of work – it is nice to reflect upon your loved ones from time to time but others need not see them.
- Make sure that there is space behind your chair so you do not feel cramped.

Office layout, desk placements, design:
- Expansive views are great for creativity. Open the curtains when you need to do creative thinking. If your conference room has expansive views, and you have business to work upon, you may find that people's energy and their thoughts are going out the window. Close the drapes or blinds to get down to business.
- Keep your sales and marketing offices close to the front doors. Their job is to get out into the world and sell. You can keep the creative design team farther into your office space.
- Use your company logo and colors to create a unity in all of the offices. Use that color on a wall in all the offices.

- When clients or employees are seated with their backs to the door, they tend to become less communicative. Give everyone a view of the door – if not possible, you may be able to use a mirror hung on the opposite wall so they can see the door.
- Give everyone in the office the same chair, to create unity.

CREATING A HEALTHY WORK ENVIRONMENT IS IMPORTANT TO CREATING A HEALTHY BUSINESS.

Some workspace clutter you may clearly not see, like the level of fresh air, natural light and environmental toxins. But your productivity and health of body and mind are affected by environmental factors of the workspace.

- When cleaning, use only natural products to clean the office space. Toxins cause illness and dull thinking.
- Color and light affect your mind, health and business. Use natural light when you can. Or use full spectrum lighting, which feels like sunlight. Use colors that are strong, yet peaceful on the walls and floors (blues, golden colors, greens, or earth tones).
- Design your office with products, which show you care not only about your staff, but the global environment as well.
- Filter your office air system.
- Bring in pleasant sounding ambient noise, such as a waterfall, or music – especially if your office hears traffic or other unpleasant sounds.

WORK/PLAY

I play as I work and work as I play
Either way same one day.
One me in the middle,
I am what I am
Whether I work or play
Tis I.

To divide your life into two aspects of work time and playtime is a normal perception to have, given that so much of our taught perspective divides time as such and stresses the thank God it's Friday mentality. But, we miss. There is another way to look at work and play: look at them as opposite sides of the same one thing - YOU. When you get caught up into believing that these two activities are separate, you miss the present joy of being you - a centered, poised and joyous individual. Everything has its duality, that is true, but do not forget that there is one mind behind that duality. Everything has its yin side and its yang side and every side has its lesser and greater – its good times and bad times (so to speak). But, in reality it is all of One – there can be no other.

One mind – when you are not living from the back of your brain with old notions and thoughts – lost as a zombie in your mind field, you may notice that your mind has a unique ability to be a transmitter and a receiver. Your mind is the transmitter – concentration and focus to get a job done – transmit your creation. It is the receiver – open and clear (without preconceived notions) to receive new thought. Whether at work or at play, if we do anything under duress and pressure, we will not feel any satisfaction and certainly not be present. If we only work to get money or play with an intention of an ulterior motive, we do not get any gratification and we lie, hurt and deceive only our self. Work, play, devotion, entertainment, relaxation, mopping the floor and study: all when done with attention and without any ulterior motives or distraction of preprogrammed thought (such as, I hate to study.) allows you to experience your life as joy. You always will be you whether you are at work or play – so why not be the best you can be?

How can you set up your work and home space to support you in this goal of enjoying the moment regardless of whether you are at work or play or doing something that you love or not especially enjoy? Choose a reminder. This reminder can be as simple as a piece of jewelry such as a ring that when you look at it, it "reminds" you to be your joyous, present you. Reminders placed in your home or office can be a photo of a scene of beauty or one of a person who means much to you. It can be a happy plant or a special rock or even a statue of a bunny rabbit. Infuse this reminder with your intention to be present with no pulls of attention and allow it to remind you to appreciate the moment and task at hand. Do your work as an offering and your play as a thankfulness.

There is an expression that says, When you eat, eat. This means to not let your mind wander – not to read or watch TV or think of other tasks that may need to be done. Just eat – enjoy your food - appreciate the tastes, colors, textures of your food. Allow your food to nourish you, otherwise you will miss the experience of eating and on a major level – not get nourished properly. This is the same with your work or your play – do not wish to be somewhere else while working or feel guilty that you should be doing something else while you are playing and relaxing.

Life is here and now – right now – This is it! No matter what you are doing if you are not in the present, you miss life. Design your home to support you in all the things you need to do and take joy in the mundane and allow simple everyday moments to become special.

A Prayer for Survival

When I respect nature.
I respect life.
It is in the daily gestures that I can make a
difference.
Today, when I inhale the morning air, may my face
reflect thankfulness, beauty, wisdom and prosperity
to all.
May my spoken words, that I exhale, be pure.
And, may the moon's silver light be a mirror to the
universal principles that govern us all.
All is in right order.

CHAPTER EIGHT
FACE YOUR SELF EXERCISES

EXERCISE # 1

DAY OFF – WHO IS THE BOSS OF YOUR LIFE?

Have you been giving the power and the vision of your life over to someone else? Do you procrastinate, saying to yourself that you will get ambitious and do it tomorrow? Who is driving your car? What are you doing? Have you been sitting in the backseat of your life, allowing someone else to drive your car and take responsibility for your life? Do you believe that you can succeed?

OBJECTIVE:

This exercise will force you to expand your mental ability to embody the success that you imagine. Know right now and accept that the choice is yours: to either give your power away or to keep your own strength and use it for the highest good of all. You can choose to either believe in yourself or to give in to your doubts.

WHAT YOU WILL NEED:

➤ Your Magic Notebook

➤ Paper and Pencil

➤ Full Body Mirror

➤ Privacy

EXERCISE:

- Open your windows and breathe in fresh air.
- Psych yourself up with 10 jumping jacks or running in place for five minutes.
- Jog in front of your mirror and while jogging in place, in front of your mirror, shout out your pain, anger and frustration to the person in the mirror. Tell that person what you hate about them.
- (Just let it out – you may be surprised what you hear but keep shouting until you have no more to shout.)
- Bend from your waist, putting your hands on your knees and blow out nine breaths in a row without inhaling – visualize blowing out all your mental gunk.
- Inhale a big, fresh, new breath. Give your self the biggest hug. (If you find that you are crying, that is ok, it may be that you have broken down some walls that you created (illusions you had to hold onto for some reason). Take some time to sit and be with this release.
- Next, imagine in a light-hearted, positive way, all the possible things that you would want to happen in your future (without all the walls - be real – from this moment on). Tell them to the mirror person. Be outrageous and let your imagination soar- anything you can think that is good. Acknowledge to yourself what changes you may need to make. See yourself full of inspiration and inner strength. Use your imagination to see that you are the hero of your own life.
- Sit down on the floor in front of the mirror with your pad and pencil and write out your goals for 10 years, 8 years, 6 years, 3 years, 2 years, 1 year, 6 months, 3 months, one month, 2 weeks, 1 week, tomorrow, and the rest of today.
- Keep your goals nearby (perhaps in the top right drawer of your desk or next to your bed). Reread your goals every month and make adjustments as needed.
- Refresh your magnetic energy of what you intend to attract by repeating this exercise as needed.

You are a magnet, attracting to you and your business all that you need to succeed. Now Work It!

CREATING A HEALTHY WORK ENVIRONMENT MAKE ALL THINGS NEW

If you want success, you must have a healthy work environment, which starts with having a healthy mind and body.

OBJECTIVE:

- You will be able to Face Your Self in any work situation, then apply and use that awareness to continue to go on with your work (your life) in a joyful, detached (as an observer), loving, compassionate way.
- You will be able to enjoy your work.
- You will be able to recognize the relationship between your business and your spirit.

WHAT YOU WILL NEED:

➢ Your Magic Notebook

➢ Paper and Pencil

EXERCISE:

Yesterday is over and done with. All you have is today. Right now, where you are, you can magnetize yourself to focus and attract that which you want.

Explore your world with a fresh face:

- Greet people that you know as if you are meeting them for the first time, and avoid people who are angry or distrustful in nature – it is not worth it in the long run.
- Eat your meals with a fresh new awareness. Intentionally taste each sensation of sweetness, salt, sour and savory as if they are all new to you.
- When you say you should do something, ask yourself why and how you got that opinion. If you still think that you should, – do it.
- You must Face Your Self every day – de-cluttering, regrouping, and realigning your self with that which you visualize and imagine. Think of your work to be like sailing a ship. If you do not keep on course the waters and winds will take your boat somewhere you most likely, do not want to go.
- Think with a positive perspective. See problems, as situations.
- Use caution before you take any new action. If you are about to embark on a new business, consider all of the disadvantages as well as advantages first.
- Do not send yourself in too many directions, which will dissipate your energies.
- Always try to help yourself before you ask for help, but ask for help if you really need help, explaining clearly your plan of action.

Review all of your notes and written work from all previous exercises.

A THOUGHT TO REMEMBER:

Blessings come in many ways. Wealth and happiness come in many ways. You are blessed, wealthy and a reflection of joy right here, right now. Respect yourself.

Life: cause and effect, mentalism, vibration, polarity,
correspondence, rhythm and gender.
Life is a multi-dimensional, continual spiraling process
Spiraling forward for the highest good of all.

THE LOOKING GLASS: MAGIC IS IN THE EYE OF THE BEHOLDER

Dear Progenies

There is one Life.
This life is flowing in and through you.
The Earth and all of its wisdom is speaking to you.
Allow it to show you the way.

There is one Life.
This life is flowing in and through you.
You are part of an ocean of existence,
That has no beginning and has no end.

Two circles that are joined as one.
There are no walls of separation.
No community that lives in isolation.
No life ever dies or fails.

Around the world
There is one breath.
You are me
Om Shanthi.
Our song – our dance – our scent
Ever-flowing - ever-spiraling
Like smoke circles from a pipe of Father Time.

Where You Go From Here

There is one life that flows in and through everything and everyone. This life force is all knowing, creative, healthy and prosperous. You are Nature and move by natural laws. By clearing the chaos from your mind, the anarchy from your body and the clutter from your home, you open up pathways for this force to flow freely in and through your life. You'll feel its natural ebbs and flow. You will see clearly through any problem and situation, knowing the right course of action. You'll feel more creative. You will look more vibrant. Your eyes will shine more clearly. You will have an inner joy – an inner peace.

To look to the future you must release, yet honor your past. Use your past as a foundation upon which you can spring forth for your present life. Do not dwell on your past, otherwise you will always bring the past into your present, which will naturally bring it into your future.

A THOUGHT TO REMEMBER:

Grounding yourself is important, but like anything it has its opposite polarity where too much grounding creates a weight where you cannot move freely – and the weights we are talking about are those of your body, mind, heart (emotions) and soul.

Everything between birth and death is a gift – your family, your friends, your troubles (to learn from), your homes, your jewelry, your cars, your pets, your plants and your toys. Keep your inner life simple – you come into

245

this world with nothing but your personal vibrational force field and you leave your earthen body with nothing but your personal vibrational force field - created by how you choose to live your current lifetime. Choose to live a life with unconditional love toward yourself and others - you will live a life richer than a king.

MINI EXERCISE:

There are three frogs on a log – one of them thought about jumping off.

How many frogs were left on the log?

Answer: Three

Thinking about it is not jumping into the pond.

You need to work it.

HOW TO MAGICALLY TRANSFORM YOUR LIFE

You are the magician. You can make real magic when you understand the laws of nature. You can change your life to a life of prosperity, love and beauty right now. Yes, there may be obstacles - the world is multidimensional; not only do we have to live with our own choices – we live in a world with many people with many different motivations. The Universe is in right order. If you believe that you are not entitled, or that others are better and more deserving than you or that you want others to suffer by your gain - you skew the field of vibration to create what appears as chaos – which is only the natural ripple effect of your cause. Chaos is actually order when you recognize the laws of Nature operating.

By doing the exercises in this book and Facing Your Self – your true, unlimited, self – you now know that you are powerful, brilliant in your own unique way, and strong with inner strength (and that does not mean you are ever the bully). You must work it otherwise, all the inspiration and motivational tapes, books and people you meet will never open that *magic* door for you. It is all right to be powerful and successful – in fact, it is your birthright. It is all right to be soft and yielding - in fact, if you are not, you will break. You are worthy. Your words are important when spoken with this mindfulness. Within this book are the tools that enable you to take back your own life and break up and destroy your harmful habits and self-abusive ways of thinking, eating, acting, and being. Own your own stuff, love yourself, get strong and get on with your life in a refreshing, positive way. Each moment, everyone starts anew with each breath - so can you. Fix your past mistakes. You are not better than anyone, nor are you lesser than anyone. You are who you are. You can see (when you remove your personal Humbug) that you are complete, whole and divine. You are YOU right here and right now – no one has control over you except YOU (except maybe the tax department! – Remember: you need to make jokes and laugh).

This final chapter is your beginning. It is filled with reminders: secrets you have discovered, and practical actions you can incorporate into your life. I know that life is difficult at times. I know that we suffer not only for ourselves, but also for others. The lines of communication must be kept open. Sometimes you may want to run and hide and not Face Your Self or your situation, even face others. That is understandable and that is all right. Give yourself a hug and carry on. You can only be true to yourself.

When you are true to yourself and face and admit your own faults, fears and delusions - a magical wave of relief comes over you. You stand naked to yourself. A weight is lifted from your shoulders and back. You stand in a beautiful space with no pain in your stomach. Everyone who is anyone has been in a funky space in his or her life. It truly is by the grace of God (whatever you may feel that God to be) that we all are loved, protected and guided.

You want to manifest a dream –a new business, health, relationships. Do you clearly understand your motivations and intentions? At what point as you go along do you say, "Enough, this is just not going to work out?" They say that when you are in a hole, the first thing to do is stop digging. Question: Is it a hole when you believe in what you want to manifest? How do you balance the thought to stop and cut your losses with the thought of, never, never give up? I'll tell you how: If you find yourself getting sick or if you find that your money flow has stopped, regroup and look at your priorities and intentions once again. Sometimes obstacles in your way are ways the Universe has to get you on your right path - either to see if you are really serious or to give you clues that you are not on your right path. You decide - Face Your Self. Let the world turn for a few months or even a year.

THE CYCLES OF NATURE

Keep life simple. Nature is your best teacher, since you are a natural being, learn from the Source. Sometimes you may forget about that reality because much of your time is spent in artificial places such as malls, schools, office buildings, homes and cars. Do days go by where you do not go outside? You can have bright lights in the middle of the night and darkness during the day. You can escape the winter season by flying off to warmer climates or putting the heat up in your house. You buy your food in a food store where you expect to find all the produce, meats, fruits and grains any time, any day, any month any time of year. You do not think about the weather, other than how it might affect your plans for the weekend, a date, or if you may need to take your umbrella or snow boots before you go out. In our culture/society the seasons are related to by their holiday appeal, not their effects on your Being or of the growing season. When you correspond yourself to nature you notice that you are a natural being and experience within yourself high energy and low energy times – winter cocooning times and summer exuberance - times to plant a new idea - times to harvest what you planted.

Everything reflects the cycles of nature, even a telephone call. Think about it: You think about calling someone (this is like late winter when you have cultivated in your mind what you want to plant in the coming Spring. You make the call (the very early spring when you plant the seed). The telephone is answered and your conversation Springs into action – "Hi – How have you been – what is new…" (this is like the early budding time of a plant, when it is popping its head out of the soil. Your conversation develops and you get into deeper topics – the "high heat" or Summer of the conversation. Slowly – your conversation begins to wane – "It has been good talking with you, you sound so well." This is like the Autumn or harvest time of your conversation – you feel good and reap the joy of having made the contact. You say goodbye and hang up. This is the Winter of the conversation. You know the other person is out there but your conversation is on hold until you decide to Spring forth again.

This cycle is true for all things: businesses and relationships. For example – you want to meet someone – your eyes meet and your relationship develops as you get to know each other (Spring). Soon you find yourself in the heat of love and passion (Summer). You then become comfortable with each other and have a wonderful harvest of good relations (Fall). You may find that your relationship is not so heated, and you regroup (Winter) until you cultivate a new beginning with your partner and the spark reignites. The cycle spirals forever forward through the seasons.

There may be times when you are experiencing a *dark of night* - what seems like depression – winter, cocooning feeling. This is not a bad thing. You need time to go within and cultivate, reflect and gain wisdom as to what you want to plant in your life for the next cycle. This wintertime feeling may come to you in the actual middle of summertime. That is all right. We all have our own cycles of life. Take time to enjoy the process – remember, your friends may be on a different cycle than you – it is all right if you need a day or two to stay home and curl up with a book or retreat. With your wisdom of the law of cause and effect, be aware of what you choose for your next step. Then plant the seed. Water it and allow it to spring forth. With good nurturing and care it will blossom and bear healthy fruit for you to harvest. Then of course you will start the process again – building on your successful past cycles.

LIGHT THOUGHTS FOR LIVING A HAPPY LIFE RIGHT NOW - WHERE YOU SIT

Laugh at your toes.
Smile toward the sun with your eyes closed.
Smell the air around a flower.
Inhale and say – "Here I am, and this is good."
Exhale and say goodbye to all that you do not need.
Listen to uplifting music.
Take a nap with sweet scents upon your pillow.
Drink a toast to life – your life.
Help someone in need.
Call a friend or loving family member.
Take a walk in a natural setting.
Pet your dog.
Sing out loud.
Count your blessings.
Close your eyes and listen to your heart.
Look for rainbows on your walls or create them with a crystal hanging in a sunny window.
Get up and dance around the room.
Clean your home.
Make plans to do something you really want to do.
Make plans to move where you really want to live.
Write and journal - including only positive things.
Express yourself by painting or writing a poem or song.

THE SECRET OF A HAPPY LIFE IS A HAPPY HOME

When you do activities with awareness and with clarity - not gripping on
to any outcome or situation - you allow your joy to come through.
Your real nature is happiness.

Wherever you go, whatever you do, whatever happens to you, you are
always home in your true home - the center of your self. The following are
seven things you can do to have a happy home.

Let go of Clutter. You feel better when you lose weight in any form. This
will clear your pathways for clearer thinking.

Bring healthy, natural things into your home. You feel better when you
eat healthy foods and wear natural, comfortable clothes. As within, so
without.

Balance the yin / yang of your home and life. Everything has its other side,
but you do not want to always live in an extreme mode. It is fun to go
out partying all night – but a steady diet of *late nighters* will take its toll
on you. Balance - it feels good to stand on both feet. What is in the
center of your home? Where and when do you feel off balance?

Understand, accept and live with your cycles of life. Dawn moves into day -
to noon - to eve - to night. There is a time to play and a time to ponder
and a time to rest.

Move things around, with the seasons, change patterns of movement and
flow and try on different hats.

Bring in something new and let go of something. Non-attachment and
giving.

Invite friends and family to dinner or drinks at your home. Speak of your
goals and how you plan to make them happen.

To change your thinking about something,
Correspond to that mental vibration to which
you desire.

This will change your mental polarity, which
changes the cause which changes the effect
which sets up a new vibration, which creates
a rhythm, which - with your will creates a
movement of mindstuff,
that manifests as creation.

CHAPTER NINE
FACE YOUR SELF EXERCISES

You are the magician. Real magic is a truthful, open-faced, unique (self) encounter with nature. Serious magical practice accelerates your karma. Your mind, body and soul are to be trained simultaneously, that is, your mental, physical and astral bodies.

EXERCISE # 1
CREATING YOUR LIFE CHART

Ask yourself these questions:
If you could take a quantum leap and change your life right now...

- Where would you be living?
- How would you be living?
- What would you be doing?
- What would you be wearing?
- What would be in the forefront of your mind?
- Who would you be having dinner with?
- What would be your plans for tomorrow?
- What do you want to harvest?
- What is your joy? What makes you happy?
- Are you living the life you want? Why or why not?
- What thoughts/fears/doubts keep coming through your mind?
- What is your general mood? Emotion?
- What values do you have? What is important to you?

OBJECTIVE:

➢ You will be able to write out and set both short-term goals and long-term goals that will aid in breaking any lasting Humbug holding patterns, which keep you from achieving your goals.

WHAT YOU WILL NEED:

➢ Your Magic Notebook

➢ A pen.

➢ A fresh new calendar

➢ Your list of goals created in, Day Off: Who is the Boss of Your Life Exercise #1 in Chapter 8 (you can update and refresh it if needed)

EXERCISE:

Divide your page in half and list the following headings, filling in under each title.

<u>Current</u>
List all of the things, which you currently do.
    1.
    2.
    3.

<u>Future</u>
List all of the things, which you want to do.
    1.
    2.
    3.

Use the following headlines as a guide:
Fun:
Exercise:
Health:
Friends:

Family:
People you can depend upon:
Work for income:
Work for love:
Study:
Finances:
Mind Concerns/ What is on my mind:
Travel:
Volunteer/Donations:

Hang this chart up in a private place where only you will see it (in your closet, bathroom, or private space).

Use your new calendar to list your goals on a daily, weekly, monthly and yearly basis. Find a time each week, (make it the same day and time – a time that you can personally look forward to) where you can sit down and list your goals for the week and write them down.

Activate your personal Creative Mind Stuff by reviewing your past week's goals and check your yearly goals and adjust them as needed. Make it a game and go with the flow. Remember, your goals are always for the highest good of all – and that includes you. Each time you reach a goal, note your feelings in your magic notebook. Do a dance of joy and add a newer goal. Onward and upward.

Uproot your character flaws

Be a natural tree of life.

You are divine.

You are the Artist.

You are the creator.

You are the light; the instrument

That rings a bell of harmonic tones.

Return to That.

Travel back in time and sustain the World.

Whether it be Man or the World

It is all part of One.

The Beginning is the end, the end is the

beginning.

MANIFESTATION AND CREATION

There are several parts to this exercise.

Manifestation is the act of showing or displaying. You give expression to your manifestation by gestures, facial aspects and body posture. You cannot manifest without the beginning point of a thought.

OBJECTIVE:

You will develop mental training and personal thought control. You will be able to be in touch with the entire Universe and human race when you create and manifest. (You will be upgrading your intuition and perception.). You will become an explorer who crosses the familiar boundaries of your old home and enters the unknown. You will recognize that your anger, tension, weight gain, general ill health, and frustration have been indicators that you have been resisting your own good. Step by step you will stop resisting your good, and notice increasing relief in your life experience.

WHAT YOU WILL NEED:

➢ A Magic Notebook

➢ Your Life Chart (that you created in Exercise # 1 of this chapter)

EXERCISE A:

1. List all the unproductive, non-focused thoughts that run through your head again and again (as opposed to conscious creative thoughts).
2. Go back and write down all the emotions you feel with each of the above thoughts. There may be more than one emotion attached to each above thought.
3. Look back and see if you can remember the times of day when your mind is attracted to thinking about these things, and why? What provokes the thought?
4. Develop an emotion check. Sometimes you carry old emotions, which affect how you think and act. Look at how you are feeling while driving, on the telephone, out with friends, at mealtimes, during sex, and shopping. Are you feeling, angry, sad, hurt, lost? Are you thinking about something other than what you are doing?

EXERCISE B:

1. List all your hopes, dreams, and wishes. Be very specific about what you ask for. If you created your Life Chart in Exercise #1, review and revise it (if necessary).
2. Now go back and list all the emotions you would feel with each situation becoming a reality.
3. Next, look at the time of day that your mind thinks upon these wishes and dreams. What triggers the thought to come? Do you feel it in your solar plexus, and around your shoulders? Do you see it clearly? Do you feel it in your chest?
4. Develop a mind check. Practice stopping all your activity for a moment to catch what you are thinking about. Try this while holding your tea or coffee cup, eating or speaking on the telephone.

EXERCISE C:

Every day, expand the time that you can hold a single thought of your hopes or dreams, suppressing any other thoughts. This is very advanced so do not get discouraged – it is fun to try. Practice keeping your mind filled with only one thought. Using a flame on a candle at eye level – stare at the flame and let your restless mind settle on your chosen thought. Or just watch the flame. Practice this for one to three minutes each day for three months.

The survival of any of us is through devotion and love. Do not try to do too much or too little – find a balance and never give up – even when you want to just stop because others do not understand you and treat you unkind - let the world turn a day or two. Consider this time as a great adventure – looking for joy and light when it may seem so completely dark.

Now is a time of faithfulness – think/meditate upon your inner flame – the inner strength that is within you, and do not forget your playful inner child. Play.

Everything that happens has a reason, though it may seem disastrous at the moment – it may lead you to a better place – do not attach to anything.

Hug to your heart reflective moments and allow your mind to be cleansed by the beauty of what was, is and what will be. Be receptive to all the good that comes to you. You have so much to be thankful for and so much to offer - do not turn your back on that!

Life is about evolution and there comes a time in everyone's life where they have to face something that is not easy. (For some of us it is at a very young age).

Know that you can only accomplish real growth and salvation through your own self by your own work. Though you may have other people and sources for support – they can only lead you so far to a place – they cannot walk you through it, nor can they cross the river for you. This is what takes real work and is the challenge of life – but, once you gain that wisdom, inner strength and inner peace no one at any time can take that from you - ever. Life will go on - the sun will rise – the seasons will change and love will always remain – it is a law of nature.

Your seeds are sown – be patient - wait – visualize and, act as if it has already happened. There is no timing other than the natural unfolding of things, which is all in right order. Think positive thoughts. Sow positive ideas. Implement positive actions.

Leave no negative wake on your journey while rowing your boat. (Row, row, row your boat gently down the stream. Merrily, merrily, merrily life is but a dream.)

There is no difference between you and any other person. That is why you cannot hurt another without hurting yourself or help another without helping yourself. My Grandma always said, "Do unto others as you would have others do unto you." Not because you expect to gain something, but because it is your natural joy.

The End is another beginning.

Good Work!!

Big Hugs!

APPENDIX PART I

ABOUT THE AUTHOR

In case you want to read more about my journey read on:
Personal Pam - Either I have a very active imagination or if Pam were
a tree...

THE ROOT OF PAM:

In the many years of my life, since I was a little child, I remember
questioning why? Most children do this. They ask, why is the sky blue? Why
is the world round? But I questioned why I got born into the family I did.
I questioned who I was? Where did I come from? What is the meaning of
time? I really wanted to know the answers to these questions. I remember
clearly, staring out of my bedroom window many a night looking up to the
stars and feeling a strong connection to the star belt of Orion. Thinking
that I somehow came from there and that I was still connected to it by an
invisible thread, I would often squint my eyes and see a light channel that
connected me to the star and feel somehow I could instantly time travel
there. Since I was five years old – I remember feeling that my parents were
not really my parents – though of course they were my earth parents – I felt
my real parents lived up in the sky on the belt of Orion.

Late at night, I would hear my parents voices talking to my grandmother
down the hall in the kitchen and think – here I am, five years old – going
to kindergarten and grandma is in her fifties – but one day in a blink of
an eye I will be the grandma in my fifties – (and now I am a grandma in
my fifties) another type of time warp or travel. How does it work? Where
does time and all of our experiences go? I am here now but in a day, a
year or a century when I am there it will feel like a moment. I realized very
early on that all we have is the present moment – wherever or whatever
that moment may be – it is eternal. We may come and go but the present
moment always is. In a breath, like the wind blowing out a flame we seem
gone.

Time does fly (and so do people I believe, but I haven't figured it out
yet except in my dreams). I realize that life is ageless; it is only our bodies

that change with the passing of years and that those changes can affect our happiness and joy when we identify ourselves with those changes.

Childhood was magical when I played in the woods. I spoke with little people who were up in the trees that I would climb - fairies and earthen gnomes I later learned. They would teach me joy and understanding – a way of living, dancing and breathing together without harm or fear. They were very gentle and beautiful beings. Under the rocks that I would hold in my little hand I would find other earth beings that would rather not have been disturbed, but the rocks told me stories of long ago. I could see proud and strong people who lived on the land I was standing upon. As I held the rocks they became warmer in my hand. They taught me a quiet strength and poise that I carry with me today. Mind you, this teaching wasn't spoken like we speak to each other. It was just sort of an unspoken communication - something I felt and knew through other channels or ways. I saw little flashing, dancing lights around flowers and trees. The wind and breeze seemed to bring me messages from faraway places. Often I found myself imagining that I was breathing the same air as someone in another country. I would speak my wishes into the wind and imagine them being carried off to the *wish god* who listened to the wind. I would also send a message to other lands knowing someone would receive it in some manner or other. I felt that I could fly and fly I did in the magical woods around my home. (To this day I have many flying dreams.)

I felt a strong connection to nature's gifts and found myself one day not understanding why many of the trees were being plowed over and the earth torn up as new housing was being developed. My parents said it was progress. I cried – for a part of me was devoted to those sacred places in nature. A part of <u>me</u> was being plowed over. It was a time of life when I could wander by myself or with friends deep into the woods without fear of molestation, kidnapping or murder. These thoughts never even entered my mind.

I was brought up with the Catholic religion. I was locked into a belief system that did not allow independent thinking. I remember one day in an after school class which was preparing me for my Holy Communion I asked the question, " How do you know that Jesus was the Son of God? " I got into trouble just for the asking and never got an answer. When I was seven, I had long hair down to the bottom of my back, where in the wintertime I wore a white rabbit's fur headband. One day in this class of holy learning for my Communion the Sister Nun had to leave the room for one reason or another. I was a very shy and a quiet girl, but given the opportunity I liked to make people laugh. My headband fell down upon my face and under my chin. It was maybe two weeks to Christmas so I started saying, "Ho, ho, ho," pretending that I was Santa Clause. The kids thought it was funny and laughed and I was happy until the Sister Nun came back into the room. She took one look at me and put the most terrifying face and pose onto her body armor. She took the ruler and smacked it hard down on my desk and told me how dare I do such a thing. Didn't I know that Christmas was about the birth of Jesus? I was taking the Lords name in vain or something. She told me to get up and wait in the hall as she went to fetch Father Kane to tell him of the horrendous crime that I committed and that she wasn't sure that I would be able to receive my Holy Communion in June with my class. Well, here I am a seven year old *shy, do gooder, always wanting to please* little girl having my first out of body experience that I was aware of where I saw myself getting up and walking into the hall – shivering and worried to death that my parents would metaphorically kill me. Yet in my out of body mind I was hearing – "Pam you are seven, you didn't do anything wrong." Father Kane came down the hall and talked to me. He was very kind and understanding and told me not do it again and I could continue to study for my Communion. I did, but from then on, organized religion all seemed a charade to me - all at the young age of seven.

THE BRANCHES OF PAM:

This work of facing your self is easy when you are sitting on the top of a beautiful mountain on a beautiful day – but in the muck and trenches of it all - this is when the pay off comes. Life affects us all and I went through trial and tribulations in my life that were beyond my own possible imagination. But there I was in the middle of a major real life soap opera. My life exploded on all fronts back in 1986 (which is another story). One night around 1:00 AM, I was sitting in my bedroom exhausted from all the mental anguish I had been going through and I became actually mindless for once in a long time. All of a sudden, I can't explain it any other way, a large light filled the room (actually it was in my head but I was blinded by it) and I heard a voice (though it was not a voice as you hear it spoken from another person) say very clearly, "FACE YOUR SELF." It felt loving and caring and all knowing and I was not the least bit afraid. To make a long story short, it is from that point onward that Face Your Self has been with me.

I went back to nature. My survival was taking five-mile walks, three days a week at Caumsett State Park on Long Island, New York. There I found myself nurtured and counseled by nature. The Spirit energies of the trees, earth, wind, and water fueled my soul as the fire of the sun's rays burned away old beliefs and warmed my heart. I practiced flying and time travel walking quickly to a large tree down a long path – soon the sensation was that the tree was coming to me and I was standing still. I made friends with *Mr. Angry* who was in a tree that had a very gnarled and angry face on its side. I knew that the turtle image on the base of the tree carried wisdom with it and that *Mr. Angry* was really a very wise old elf. Every time I passed him I would say hello and bring him a kiss. I know he is with me even today. I passed a tree with a large owl figure grown into its side. One day a large owl appeared – spread his wings and then flew right over my head. Often if you look carefully the trees and stones will shape shift to teach you things and they become what is around them. You shape shift too. You become what and whom you surround yourself with. You become what you speak about. You become what you eat. You become what you think.

There was one private place off the path, up a little hill where I would go to just sit. I would sit there literally for hours not moving – just listening, watching and smelling the air. It is there that the winds often spoke to me. Up on a hill in a wide-open meadow I would go to salute the sun and give thanks – then I would run down the hill and feel so free. At the water's edge were many wonderful rocks being caressed by the water. Pieces of time and earth melded together and shaped by the currents of the water and air – very much like we are. It was a beautiful place – one I will always keep dear in my heart. It was there that I became nourished and began weaving my new life into a beautiful basket.

Actually, I was on the beach weaving grasses and shells into a basket when someone came by and thought I should sell my work. It had never occurred to me – but galleries and stores and many commissions later, I was a working artist. I have created my art always with a spiritual intention: my Sculptural Baskets, based on the energies of life, the Chaos Vessels, based upon the chaos principal, the Artifacts, based upon West African Art of the Dogon. My sculptures were made with natural materials and often depicted nature spirits and dimensions of time and space.

In October 2001 I moved to Northern Vermont from Tribeca, Manhattan. I have been painting in oils, planting and tending to gardens, building rock sculptures on my wooded paths near the lake, creating a labyrinth, sacred circle and making offerings to the nature spirits.

PRACTICAL PAM:

My experience includes a BS and MS degree in Education and Instructional Technology. My work spans over 35 years as a holistic/lifestyle educator in the arts, yogas and feng shui. I have been a freelance writer for many newspapers and magazines including the *New York Post* and *House Magazine,* where my column, *Go With the Flow* has been published bi-monthly since 1997. I began the formal practice of yoga in 1971 way before yoga was popular – there was no hot or cold yoga – no fast or slow yoga – it was based upon a spiritual oneness – the hot and cold and fast and slow came naturally as one did the work. I began teaching yoga and meditation in 1986. I began to teach spiritual oneness through art and self-expression at Ananda Ashram in Monroe, New York and at The American Craft Museum and other art centers. I traveled to Mali on a grant and scholarship to work with Dogon and other African artists and came home to teach what I learned. My art is in many collections including the Clinton White House. I began teaching feng shui in 1996, again way before it was popular in America to students across the country from a little interior design school in Plainview, New York. It had 5 students when I began as its Executive Director and over 550 students for the year when I left. I founded the Mountain Institute of Tribeca where I taught feng shui and invited previous students to become teachers to give them an opportunity to manifest their dreams of becoming a teacher. I sold the school to a student and colleague when I married and moved to Malletts Bay in northern Vermont where I currently live seven months of the year. The other months I travel to Oro Valley, Arizona with my husband. I enjoy painting, playing tennis and good friends and family.

For 25 years I have been working with the message: Face Your Self. Though many friends and family thought I was strange and that facing one's self was the last thing anyone ever wanted to do, I carried on so much so that I created a company to teach through. I have never felt the need to bring this work to the great masses for it has always been a very private and personal work, my own life's journey to understand. I studied with knowing teachers and spent long periods observing Nature. But as life continued, I began getting the message to bring Face Your Self forth. Through the years I have developed **Face Your Self** ® with many different hats but always remained constant to its essence – *to be a better human one has to know themself and then they can live an honest and natural life for the highest good of all and manifest their good.* The real calling is to bring mankind back to mindfulness - to overseeing this world and each other with love, honor, harmony and peace.

My life is good. I feel rich – my Dad would say, "Pam, be happy with what you have because someone always has a bigger boat." Every day I give thanks for what I have. I know how close the disaster gods can be and I know that all is a gift – including the opportunity to write this little book. "Thank you, thank you, thank YOU."

APPENDIX PART II

BREATHING EXERCISES

DEEP BREATHING

Sit in a posture where your spine is erect and your hands are resting upon your knees.

Exhale slowly. Then inhale slowly. As you do, expand your stomach and then your chest. This allows the maximum amount of air into the lungs. (The abdominal muscles will contract, as your chest becomes full.) It is ok to allow your collarbone to rise as you inhale. Without holding your breath – exhale slowly.

With inhalation and exhalation – the breath should be one continuous flow. Every inhalation should begin from the stomach and every exhalation should start from the top of the lungs. Imagine filling and emptying a glass of water.

SINUS AND HEAD CLEANING (SKULL SHINING)

Attention is entirely focused on maintaining rhythmic diaphragmatic action – the speed of the exercise is of secondary consideration. Equal force is given to both exhalation and inhalation. There is no retention. * If you become dizzy – STOP!

Sit in a comfortable posture.
Exhale and then take in a deep breath through your nose

Immediately after completing this inhalation, expel the air through your nose by an inward jerk of your abdomen.

Involuntarily you will inhale again.

Repeat the jerking expulsion by your abdomen.

The expulsions are sudden and strong.

At first, aim at one expulsion per second for five or six times without a pause.

Then rest and repeat the process for up to three or four minutes.

After much practice, increase speed up to two expulsions per second and for a period of ten minutes.

BELLOWS

Do rapid inhalation and exhalation as many times as you can comfortably do, giving force to the exhalation.

Then, upon your next exhalation; inhale slowly filling your lungs. Hold your breath and while your breath is being held, bend your neck forward bringing your chin as close to your chest as possible. Retain your breath as long as you can do comfortably. Then raise your head up slowly and exhale the breath evenly through the nose. This is one round.

Aim to complete three rounds.

Benefits: Brings heat to the body when it is cold. Improves digestion, helps cure asthma. Exhilarates the blood circulation and stimulates the entire body quickly.

NERVE PURIFICATION

Here the breath current moves in and out with an audible sound.

Inhalation and exhalation are through one nostril at a time only. To begin, press the thumb on the right side of the nose and the two extended fingers on the left side. Release your two fingers and exhale through your left nostril (keep your right closed)

Then inhale suddenly and quickly through the same nostril (left).

Close with the two fingers and allow the air to move out forcibly through the right nostril.

Inhale again through the right nostril, keeping the left nostril closed.

Exhale through the left and then inhale again through your left while your right is closed off.

Exhalation is always followed by inhalation through the same nostril. Respiration is at first short and sudden with a vigorous impulse from the abdominal muscles in expelling your breath. Breathing gradually becomes deeper until a full and deep breath may be drawn in evenly.

Benefits: increases the breath span to capacity and purifies the entire respiratory system. It is an excellent method of arousing the internal vigor of the body. Also, enhances alertness of mind, good appetite, proper digestion and sound sleep.

WHEEZING BREATH

The breath is drawn in through clenched teeth (hissing sound) with your lips slightly open and the tip of your tongue in contact with your teeth. Your lips are closed for exhalation, which is made through your nostrils.

COOLING BREATH

Your tongue is extended well forward beyond your lips and the two edges are rolled upward to form an aperture (like a tube) through which your breath is sucked in. Your mouth is then closed keeping your tongue against your teeth and exhalation is done through your nostrils.

Benefits: Cooling off your body and helps remove heat, thirst, hunger. You also will sleep better.

With daily practice of the breathing exercises, you will find that you will develop better lung capacity and wisdom.

APPENDIX PART III

ADDITIONAL WAYS TO LET GO OF MIND CHAOS

Cultivate friendships

Do a project (paint).

Start or write in a journal.

Spend a day of silence – no television or radio – have a quiet day and self-cultivate.

Make lists for the future.

Walk in the woods or by the sea. Find a place of natural beauty.

Exercise.

Cry – Crying is good when it is used as a release of pain and sadness – allow the tears to wash the pain. (You do not want to avoid the pain – you want to go through the pain out the other end)

Go to school.

Feed the birds.

Listen to music.

Volunteer your time.

Get a haircut and go for a manicure and pedicure.

Buy some flowers or plants for your home.

Work in the garden and get your hands dirty.

Change how you look at a situation – is the glass half empty, or half full

See a therapist or a psychologist.

Do a dance of joy every day and be thankful.

Check the clutter in your home – broken things, where things came from, memories, photos. Shower each evening before you go to bed and wash the day away.

Change your name.

Watch your speech. What do you speak about? This can tell you where you are cluttered.

Speak your mind if you do have something that is on your mind and speak it clearly.

Too much talk – sometimes it is good to just keep quiet.

Pay your bills on time and be thankful.

Return calls in a timely manner.

APPENDIX PART IV

I wrote this one night in 1994 and dedicated it to my children
(though they were too young to read it then):

Live with Peace and Rest in Peace
A simple little book to live in peace and harmony – simply and quietly
in our world as it is today.

1. Develop a daily routine of yoga, breathing mindfully, and meditation.
2. Eat to nourish your body and mind.
3. Connect to the Earth – spend time with nature and natural things.
4. Thoughts:

You are a spiritual being living in the human existence.

> You came into this life with nothing but your soul and you will leave
> this life with nothing but your soul. Therefore, everything in life
> is a gift to enjoy – from the sweet smell of flowers, the people in
> our families and those we meet, to the things we choose to buy and
> where we choose to live. Enjoy without attachment.
> Move with freedom and ease.
> All lives are connected – interwoven - share.

You are in control of your body and mind.
> Not the other way around.
> Breath controls the mind –take a deep breath when you are upset,
> you will quiet down some.

The only constant is change.
> Go with the flow
> Bend with the breeze
> Many of life's lessons
> Are learned from rivers and trees.

Give us this day our daily bread.
> Let go of the fear of not having enough. Our needs are always met.
> Live in the present – most people are locked into the past or the
> future. Sense the present. The past is gone so learn from it and let it

go. What you do today will create your future – plan – do – then let go of the future, it will unfold naturally from your today.

As a flower blooms, so shall you.
> A seed needs time to germinate, strengthen, bud, flower, and bloom. So do you – so do your goals.
> When things don't seem to be going right – let them go – sometimes you just have to allow the world to turn for a day or two. Do something else – clean a closet – take a walk.
> You can't force something to happen – you must allow it to happen. Release.

Detach.
> Sometimes it is good to hibernate for a while. Sleep, eat well, think of nothing in particular, just hang out and talk to no one. Enjoy and be with yourself.
> Sometimes it is good to do your work with blinders on – not seeing or comparing your self or work to others – just stay your course.

Ask yourself what you want.
> List the good things in your life. Count your blessings – no matter how small – do this often.

Don't judge yourself or others.
> Detach yourself and see it for what it is – be honest – than changes can be made.

Read about other lives.
> Know reality vs. make believe life.
> Develop a sense of your community as if there were no mass communication networks – see it and feel it. Be a part of it.

When dissatisfied or unhappy – be happy!
> This is God's way of pushing you forward to better things.
> Don't take things too seriously – laugh.

Be Aware.
> Listen and see messages – amazing grace – for your good.
> Don't forget the story about the truck, boat, helicopter that was sent to save that man.
> Remember that I always love you.
> Mom (Most Optimistic Map (Pam spelled backward))

APPENDIX PART V

Amazing Grace

Words: John Newton, 1779

Amazing grace! How sweet the sound
That saved a wretch like me!
I once was lost, but now am found;
Was blind, but now I see.
'Twas grace that taught my heart to fear,
And grace my fears relieved;
How precious did that grace appear
The hour I first believed!
Through many dangers, toils and snares,
I have already come;
'Tis grace hath brought me safe thus far,
And grace will lead me home.
The Lord has promised good to me,
His Word my hope secures;
He will my Shield and Portion be,
As long as life endures.
Yea, when this flesh and heart shall fail,
And mortal life shall cease,
I shall possess, within the veil,
A life of joy and peace.
The earth shall soon dissolve like snow,
The sun forbear to shine;
But God, Who called me here below,
Will be forever mine.
When we've been there ten thousand years,
Bright shining as the sun,

We've no less days to sing God's praise
Than when we'd first begun.

APPENDIX PART VI
Imagine

By John Lennon
Imagine there's no heaven it's easy if you try
No hell below us
Above us only sky
Imagine all the people
Living for today...

Imagine there's no countries
It isn't hard to do
Nothing to kill or die for
And no religion too
Imagine all the people
Living life in peace...

You may say I'm a dreamer
But I'm not the only one
I hope someday you'll join us
And the world will be as one

Imagine no possessions
I wonder if you can
No need for greed or hunger
A brotherhood of man
Imagine all the people
Sharing all the world...

You may say I'm a dreamer
But I'm not the only one
I hope someday you'll join us
And the world will live as one

APPENDIX PART VII

Living in a world of hell
Surrounded by hellish people,
Breathe love and feel the winds of grace on your face.
Heaven is here – you are here.
Magnetic attractions pull heavenly people toward you.
The hellish people all look at you – jealous.
They try to break you.
They try to steal from you.
They try to kill you.
They don't seem to get it – they can't seem to get it:
Heaven, peace and happiness.
There is a box, which no one can get out of except the heavenly people.
The hellish people kick and scream. They curse and rage.
The only way out is
To let go and love

APPENDIX PART VIII

ON MEDITATION

A majority of the people of the world would like to meditate but fear that they do not know how to do it or are fearful of losing control of their mind. I remember when many laughed at and feared yoga practices and now yoga is a mainstream tool used to balance body vigor. Many laugh at and question feng shui but it too is a major tool for healing and balancing one's life. Meditation is a tool for healing and balancing your life, letting go of your mind clutter so you do not live in a dream.

Some just do not have the patience or want to find the time to even concentrate for three minutes on anything. It is funny to hear some say that they do not have the time, when they spend hours watching television or going to the movies to pass the time and twitter the day away with texts and talk about the same things over and over – just to kill time.

There are many paths and many ways to meditate. Basically all require putting your mind's ego aside so that you can just be. The Face Your Self book is one long meditation and will aid you in this process.

WHAT IS MEDITATION AND WHY IS IT SO WONDERFUL TO MEDITATE?

The behavioral objective: To be aware and present, experiencing a joyous life.

The importance of meditation is that it can be used as holistic medicine – it is like love, you lose yourself in it. It can be used by anybody at any time in life – in sickness and in health, during prosperity or poverty, young or old, day or night. Meditation is not religious – it is not attached to any religion. Meditation is a tool to quiet the mind, unlike prayer, which one speaks from their perspective of heart and mind. Meditation is a discipline, which will transform you. It is a freedom from all outside limitations and freedom from the tangle of your mind chaos. Approach mediation like a science. At first you may feel a separation or strangeness for you will begin to see your life experiences from a fresh perspective and this may make you go through an awkward stage. You will see yourself as you really are – no lies – no illusions. You may even see that you are not real. Through

283

practice and exploration as a scientist, you will sooner or later feel a silence within - a silence that will blossom and be with you always no matter what is going on in the world around you. You will know your center. You will not attach to that ego part of you. In fact you will laugh at that part of you. In this silence…you will be more aware and present than you ever have been in your life.

Meditation is a means you use to better know who you are – to see with clarity what is real and what is made-up illusion. Meditation is a way to connect with your heart and listen from a place of just knowing.

Meditation helps quiet and clears the mind of its mental clutter. Meditation is great to reduce stress, gain clarity and increase concentration – all of which allow you to achieve your true potential with greater ease and increased benefit all around. Meditation will help heal both your mind and body.

WHAT AM I SUPPOSED TO DO OR THINK WHILE I AM MEDITATING?

You may ask, "Am I supposed to NOT think at all? Should I push all thoughts that pop into my head away? Do I have to close my eyes? Can I just lay flat on the floor?"

Technique:

When you choose to meditate, it is good to sit in a comfortable position – either on a sturdy chair with a good back or on the ground with a mat (or towel) that you choose to use only for this purpose. Why? If you lie down you may find yourself falling off to sleep. Honoring your meditation work is good – respect yourself and your sacred work, which is why I would suggest that you do not choose just any towel or mat from your closet that you may use for other things. You can meditate any time of the day – but most people find that they like to practice meditation in the early morning before the day's activities begin or at the end of the day after one has washed the day away. Find a place where you will not be disturbed by a telephone, a pet, or another person. Turn off all electronics and the world around you. When you feel safe and secure, you are ready to begin the meditation practice. It is suggested to close your eyes during meditation so that other things in your room do not distract you and keep you attached in the self-made world you created around you. But you can leave your eyes open – see how it works for you. You might want to focus on the tip of your nose or keep your concentration on a candle flame (which is good practice to develop your concentration just be careful not to fall asleep with the candle burning).

OBSERVE YOUR THOUGHTS MEDITATION

One type of meditation, which is good to begin with is to simply (ah, there is the challenge) observe your own thoughts. Sit quietly and watch your thoughts until your mind gets quiet. Your breath will settle down too for thoughts need breath. When thoughts come into your head see them as you would a movie – a movie that you do not get emotionally attached to. Just watch your mind's doings - it can be fascinating when you are the watcher. Be neutral – no judgments If you find yourself following a thought down the garden path to other thoughts, just mentally let it go and bring yourself back to your meditation practice of observing and being the witness. It takes practice like anything else you want to learn – the more you practice – the better you will be at meditating until one day your whole life will be a meditation.

Take baby steps if you want – there is no race to the finish line – as a matter of fact – you are already there – you may not just know it yet. Truth is always present - you do not need to seek it. Accept it. Just give yourself a hug right here, right now.

YOUNG TO OLD AGE MEDITATION:

The process of life – the old are wise so they say – why? Because life is a meditation whether you know it or not. As you live your life you are practicing a form of meditation. As you go through life you see and observe, you try on different hats, you travel far and wide, you jabber and talk, you do different activities, you hurt and cry, you laugh and sing. As you begin to reach your 50's (if you live so long) you may even find that you resist, fear, feel anxious and do not like what you see. You may try to go back to attach to and to recreate feelings and body shapes you long for from your youth. But eventually, if you are fortunate, you can only resist so long, you begin to let go and come to a place of joy, peace and serenity (and I am not talking about the graveyard which my Dad would always call the quiet place). You surrender. You see what is real and what is an illusion. You begin to see what people create as frustrations to complicate their lives and what is the natural reality of life. In this letting go and simply being – the practice of life's meditation is complete. You have succeeded and can live the rest of your life in a silent meditation of your heart – even when you laugh and dance – eat, sing and make love. You smile to yourself, a knowing smile and you give yourself a hug. You realize that you are nothing but everything and you are complete just as you are. And you are happy – you say that you have no problems and you ask, Is everything good? to your loved ones.

ADVANCED READING ANCIENT WISDOM: ATTRACTION IS IN THE MAGIC MIRROR

The water flows,
Its sound refreshes.

The flower blooms
Its beauty purifies.

The night sky illumes,
Its mastery mystifies.

There is a joyful creative intelligence
In the world within and without.

There are no miracles, only unknown laws.
St. Augustine

YOU ARE THAT YOU ARE

You have completed – and applied - the work of the past nine chapters. With practice (I do advise that you reread the book again a year later for you will find that you will see things you missed the first time you read it through), you will begin to see quantum changes in your life.

A THOUGHT TO REMEMBER:

Life is multidimensional. Life is like a flowering plant that unfolds in time in all directions with its roots firmly planted in the earth – the scent being offered to the heavens.

There are seven principles and laws that are operating in all of your life situations - in and through all life situations. These laws or principles work on you whether you are cluttered or not. You can see their actions better when you are clear and presently aware and you can live your life in alignment with them. I have highlighted these principles in bold and italic print in the past nine chapters to subtly plant the seed of their importance. I have worked consciously with these principles since 1972 when my Aunt Rita gave me a 1930, copyrighted edition of The Kybalion – Hermetic Philosophy. The Kybalion, is a book based on the teachings of Hermes Trismegistus, a contemporary of Abraham who lived in old Egypt. These laws are not dogmatic or religious in nature. Note, as with all things, these laws may look like they can be manipulated for evil or selfish intent but that is only to the person who is stupid and unaware, for they boomerang back to those who do so with a force that is most unpleasant.

A THOUGHT TO REMEMBER:

Your thinking is a circular creative force, which mirrors back to you that, which you think. (For a refresher, reread Chapter One: The Magic Mirror: The Secret to a Happy Life.)

Are you ready and willing to receive this powerful information? Work with these principles, apply them, and understand how they apply to you and your life always for the highest good of all. Otherwise, they are just words – words that will confuse you if you do not apply them with an open heart. It is also important that you do not let this work become crystallized into a religion or a creed. You are the explorer of your life. You are encouraged not to believe anything unless you can convince yourself of its soundness, validity and make it real for you. Make yourself the researcher. Most importantly, I ask you to play with this knowledge and stay light. Pretend that you are a spiritual scientist as you continue to Face Your Self and Know Thy Self (a Hermetic axiom).

The following seven principles or laws operate in and through you and your life at all times, just like the laws of gravity on this planet. These are multidimensional ways that you and your life circumstances move and dance. It is your job to see the possibilities: How your mental chemistry and alchemy can change and transform the mental states, bodily forms and conditions in your life - all for the highest good of all.

Each principle is directly quoted from The Kybalion, Hermetic Philosophy in bold type, followed by an explanation of how it works in your life, and how, with your awareness you can live in the sea of life with ease. The Kybalion is in the public domain. If you would like to read more, it can be found online by simply Googling: Kybalion.

PRINCIPLE # 1: MENTALISM: ALL IS MENTAL

THE ALL IS MIND; THE UNIVERSE IS MENTAL. -The Kybalion.

This is a foundation of Face Your Self, to understand the power of your thinking and how the collective thinking of a group or nation can affect your world.

You can call the All a deity – many do: God, Allah, Moses, Jesus, Buddha. To me this All is the Fundamental Truth with no dogma attached. You live in the All and the All flows in and through you. You are part of the Ocean of the All – not separate from it. The All is infinite living mind (life and mind not as we know it as limited or finite). This principle is a major key in knowing yourself.

The art of alchemy deals with the mastery of mental forces, not that of material elements such as turning lead into gold. The gold is living a life of joy, peace and happiness in a world, which is filled with pain and unpleasantness. If the universe is a mental energy (vibration), this applies to your well-being, as well. Do not use your mind's thinking in a haphazard way. For example, when you want something, think as if the prayer is such – that it is already answered and in place (no need to plead). Any mental thought otherwise will shift the degree of your mental prayer ever so slightly (and we all know that if a line is not straight, it will be way off course the farther it goes from the point of origin). You must believe and know in your heart - know the existence or presence of something even if it is not yet seen. The potential of the seed in the soil is the power of this mindset: plant the thought and manifestation of your thoughts happens.

Be aware of your body actions: your gestures, facial aspects and body posture - actions of your body and your breathing show and display your thinking not only to others but to the universe, by giving expression to your thoughts. Not only are these gestures clues to your real thinking, these actions also compound and lock your thinking further into the reality of your existence.

Creation is the beginning point. The point where your thought ignites a spark with the One Mind (All), which then vibrates with the mental universe in accordance to your thought. The foundation of this creation is your words and your actions. In the beginning was the word and the word was good.

Your Mind creates. Put power (will) behind the energy of a thought and you can create matter or circumstance – in an instant – even though you may not see the manifestation on the material plan for years to come. In the Christian religion the symbol of the cross represents the sacrifice

Christ paid for showing people a way to God. Perhaps another meaning of the cross symbol is to teach us to focus at one point (the 90 degree intersection of two lines) to achieve creation. Note that this intersection is also located in the heart. This focus would require you to sacrifice other thoughts to achieve your creation. When you focus with your will and put your power of intention behind your focus, you must sacrifice other things in your life. For example, you may want to become a dancer. You must work out and stretch every day. You must be mindful of your diet. You must practice while your friends are playing. If you start to focus on eating chips and doughnuts and watching television all day and mildly thinking of being a dancer – your creation will not manifest for you, for you did not focus and sacrifice – you just had a thought here and there - now and again, of how nice it would be to be a dancer.

Energy, power and matter are all secondary to the mastery of Mind – your right thinking. Henry Ford said, If you think you can, you can. If you think you can't, you can't. Once you have said your thought out loud it is crystallized – it is manifested to the degree and power that you speak it. (See Face Your Self Exercise #1 – The Power of Your Word, at the end of this chapter.) You will see even more clearly why becoming aware of and removing your mind chaos is so important for a world of peace and harmony.

PRINCIPLE #2: CORRESPONDENCE: AS ABOVE SO BELOW

AS ABOVE, SO BELOW; AS BELOW, SO ABOVE. – The Kybalion.

There is always a correspondence between everything, and there is always a correspondence between all of the planes of life. In Chapter Seven, Your Home is a Mirror Image of Your Spirit, you learned how your home could affect your energy. This was based largely upon this principle of Correspondence: As within, so without. If something happens in the greater world, you can be sure that it is also happening to the world of the individual. There are many planes of Correspondence, many of which humans are unaware of at this time. (Perhaps you will intelligently reason a new awareness by using this principle.)

The following are three planes to consider:

The laws of Nature (the workings and functioning of earth – A Physical Plane)

The laws of Humans (the microcosm – the small world – A Mental Plane)

The laws of the Universe (the macrocosm – Spirit – A Spiritual Plane)

These planes are, in reality, all of one Life. The planes listed above correspond to each other, if you know one, you know the others. Man (microcosm) is created in the image of God. He is created in the likeness of the universe (the macrocosm) - The principle of Correspondence.

By understanding this principle, you can solve many hidden secrets of nature and understand that which would be unknowable to you. You can apply this principle to the material, mental, and spiritual planes. This is a mental tool, which you can use to move obstacles which hide from your view. You can look at what is known to you and reason what would be unknown (unseen to you). There is a harmony and agreement between all planes. There is a correspondence between all planes.

Example: If someone is sick of body, you can bring fresh air, (flowers, healthy foods, healthy sounds and scents) into the room. When you use this law, you create and set the outside correspondence to reflect health, and know that the intended correspondence of health is perfect whole and complete for healing to take place on the inside of the body.

You can use the power of prayer (Mental Plane). When you visualize the patient, perfect, whole and complete and see them up and about, living their life in a healthy way, you are working with the law of correspondence and moving energies in the Pool of Creative Mind Stuff to align with your powerful mentality.

Feng shui cures or adjustments work primarily with the principle of correspondence, as without, so within.

PRINCIPLE # 3: VIBRATION: EVERYTHING VIBRATES

NOTHING RESTS; EVERYTHING MOVES; EVERYTHING VIBRATES. – The Kybalion.

Have you ever heard that change is the only constant? Everything is in motion. The differences between different manifestations of solid matter, energy, mind and spirit result mainly from the varying rates of their vibration. The higher the vibration, the higher its position on the vibration scale. Too high a vibration – something may look like it is at rest (like a fast spinning wheel or hummingbird wings) or too slow a vibration – something may look at rest (like a stone.)

Everything vibrates. The difference between matter, light energy, your mind, and your spirit is the result of different rates and dimensions of vibration. Science has proven that there is no such thing as matter. Matter is filled with many molecules, atoms, and particles, all of which vibrate at different rates. Matter is energy, or a force, that is at a lower rate of vibration than spirit. When you pass on, your life vibration lives and merges with like vibrations.

Your mental state depends on your vibration. You can control your mental vibration with practice, intention and attention (the Face Your Self Exercise #2 at the end of this chapter will show you how). If you want to change or transmute your mental state from a slow, depressed, sad vibration to a lighter, happier vibration you can do this with your intention and will – your will is a mental tool. Place your attention upon the mental state you desire. You can also change the mental vibration of others by bringing them down to a sluggish vibration or up to a positive, joyful vibration. Some people do this without even knowing that they are affecting negatively or positively others around them. Be aware how you feel when you are with certain people. Do they bring you down or up? Use your will to protect your mental state but do not get to where you try to stop or control your vibration – stay loose.

Understanding this principle, you have a major tool for changing your life, staying poised and centered and being in control of your life and breath.

Example: Let us say that you just received a telephone call from someone who you love, yet who drains your energy. They tell you things that you really do not want to hear nor need to hear – but they tell you that they have no one else to talk to. Why? Because they have sent everyone else running away! They go on and on, and you, out of love and compassion, listen. They give details about their illnesses, how work is not working for them, how their friends all went to the movies and didn't call them, how so-and-so did them harm. You hang up with a heavy heart. You are drained. You have tried many times to make this person happy but their own clutter will not allow it to happen. Make use of the law of vibration. Play some light-hearted music, open the windows and allow the fresh air and sunshine to bring your vibration back into balance. Ring some happy bells and even wear them around your neck, burn a scented candle, or take a walk. You cannot allow the caller's toxic vibration to permanently affect you.

Note: It is sad when someone we love is cluttered and does not face their own self as the possible cause of their misery. All you can do is what you can do. Do not allow your own vibrant life force to suffer. You are not being selfish or uncaring.

PRINCIPLE # 4: POLARITY: EVERYTHING HAS ITS PAIR OF OPPOSITES

EYERYTHING IS DUAL; EVERY THING HAS POLES; EVERYTHING HAS ITS PAIR OF OPPOSITES; LIKE AND UNLIKE ARE THE SAME; OPPOSITES ARE IDENTICAL IN NATURE, BUT DIFFERENT IN DEGREE; EXTREMES MEET; ALL TRUTHS ARE BUT HALF-TRUTHS; ALL PARADOXES MAY BE RECONCILED.
- The Kybalion.

Everything has its other side. There are two sides to everything. So everything is and isn't at the same time. (There are two sides to a coin, there are two sides to a story, all truths are half-truths, point/counterpoint). Therefore, opposites are identical in nature but different in their degree.

Heat and cold are really the same, they only differ in a matter of degree (a form or rate of vibration.)

> Light – Dark
> Large – Small
> Hard – Soft
> Black – White
> Sharp – Dull
> Noise – Quiet
> Positive – Negative
> High – Low
> Happy – Sad

This same principle operates on the mental plane as:
Love – Hate
Like – Dislike
It is possible to change the vibrations of hate to the vibrations of love by using your own mind and your will. Be aware that good and evil are poles of the same thing. Transmuting evil into good is an application of the Principle of Polarity or Mental Alchemy.

Your subconscious (your passions, failures, weaknesses) is the other side of your conscious (your thinking, feeling, willing, memory, reason, intellect). Learn to know and accept both sides of you to understand the whole you which is Divine.

Use the tool of Polarity to help you balance extreme emotions, sensations or experiences. When you experience an extreme emotion, sensation or event, (such as hate), think of its opposite pole. This will allow you to take some of the power away from that emotion or sensation and bring yourself and/or the situation into balance.

Think of the yin/yang symbol – when something becomes so yang that it cannot be *any yanger* it becomes yin. When you get to the highest part of the day at high noon – boom – the next second the sun starts to set. If you find yourself so low and depressed – boom – you pick yourself up and start climbing the mountain again. Another example of being aware of the cycles or circular motion of polarity is love and hate. Imagine an argument where you and another were so angry at each other that you could not be any angrier. What usually happens next? Both parties make up and make love again.

Example: Many marriages and business partnerships work out because each person brings a perspective that is often opposite from each other. These opposites actually make a whole (the right and left brain personalities). When you are aware of the duality of all things, and enhance your understanding of life experiences, you will be able to become a great mediator.

PRINCIPLE # 5: RHYTHM: THERE IS A TIME FOR EVERYTHING

Everything flows, out and in: everything has its tides; all things rise and fall; the pendulum swing manifests in everything; the measure of the swing to the right is the measure of the swing to the left, rhythm compensates.
- The Kybalion.

You breathe in, you breathe out. You are born to this world, you die to this world. The river runs upstream, then the river runs downstream. The tides flow in and the tides flow out. Everything has its equal and opposite reaction. There is an advance and a retreat, a rising and a sinking (of your chest when you breathe, the sun and the moon), creation and destruction, the rise and fall of nations, the rise and fall of your mental state. It is like a pendulum. There is a rhythm between all pairs of opposites or poles (the rhythm is closely related to the principle of polarity).

By using this principle, you can get from one pole to another. You cannot stop or cancel this law of rhythm, but you can escape its effects.

Example: You can do this by applying the mental law of neutralization where you do not connect with an extreme pole.

It is a rainy, gloomy day – do you go with that mood?
It is a Monday – do you get depressed?
You are to be married - are you overjoyed?
You are to be divorced – are you depressed?

Polarize yourself (by using your mental will) at a point on the swing where you want to rest, then neutralize the rhythmic swing (which would carry you to the other pole). Let's say you are depressed that it is a Monday and you were very happy over the weekend. How can you use the law of naturalization to neutralize this swing? Center yourself – realize the rhythm of the week – all of it is neither good or bad – breathe in a relaxed way, and face your day in a grounded, positive way. When you live from your center you do not experience manic highs or lows.

PRINCIPLE # 6: CAUSE AND EFFECT: KARMA

EVERY CAUSE HAS ITS EFFECT; EVERY EFFECT HAS ITS CAUSE, EVERYTHING HAPPENS ACCORDING TO LAW, CHANCE IS BUT A NAME FOR LAW NOT RECOGNIZED; THERE ARE MANY PLANES OF CAUSATION BUT NOTHING ESCAPES THE LAW. – The Kybalion.

This principle has to do with magnetism, or attraction. A saying exemplifying this is, When the student is ready, the teacher will come. Your mind can be a strong magnetic attractor (of course its opposite is also true – it can also repel).

Masses of people are carried along- obedient to their environmental politics, religions, mass community thinking and to the wills and desires of others. The power of suggestion and other outward causes move these people like pawns where they think that they have control over their own lives, but they don't.. Are you a pawn? How do you know? Do you create your moods, character, qualities and powers? Do you intentionally choose, design, and clean up your land, home and workspace or the environments around you? Or do you just accept that things are the way they are and let unseen forces move you along? You can be a player in the game of life instead of being played, by being aware of the laws of cause and effect.

There are many planes of cause and effect (causation) – the higher planes dominate the lower planes. We all need to obey the causation of the higher planes (such as gravity or universal light, sound and color), but you can help to RULE on your own plane. This ruling is not to be used as a manipulation for power and greed.

A THOUGHT TO REMEMBER:

Nothing rises higher than its own source (therefore, if you are thinking as a low energy you will live as a low energy) and nothing is ever manifested in an effect that is not in the cause.

"Life and mind can never evolve from blind energy or force.
There is always a cause.
Nothing is evolved unless it is involved." - The Kybalion.

Another way to say this is," Whatsoever a man sowed, that shall he also reap."

This law of cause and effect governs the elemental principles of fire, water, air, earth. You will learn to recognize these elemental natures within you in this chapter's second Face Your Self Exercise.

This principle reflects evolution and development – the law of Karma. Life is like a school. Some of us are in kindergarten and some of us are born with Masters Degrees and some of us die still in Kindergarten. Karma is a way to describe the life we are born into and the lessons that we are meant to learn in this life and from past lives. You are born with your karma of past lives and will die with the karma you have created in this lifetime and that of past lives that you have not faced. You do not have to accept this as such - ponder this for yourself – think, reason, and live your life and come to your own conclusions.

MINI EXERCISE:

Name five effects in your life right now (what you are experiencing presently). Then see if you can find and name the root cause that set that effect in motion to begin with.

Once you understand this law, you realize that there is no such thing as chance. When people say something happened by chance, they do not recognize or perceive what cause was existing to create the effect that they are experiencing. I invite you to look at your life and be honest with yourself. See if you can find the root cause of a current life situation. I have clients who say that their relationships are not working. Often the root cause of the situation is that they do not love themselves or they are not being honest with themselves about their role.

Example: By going to school and taking courses, you are creating a cause, which will have an effect on the path of the rest of your life. If you do not study, that cause will also have its effect.

PRINCIPLE # 7: GENDER: EVERYTHING IS MASCULINE/FEMININE

GENDER IS IN EVERYTHING; EVERYTHING HAS ITS MASCULINE AND FEMININE PRINCIPLES, GENDER MANIFESTS ON ALL PLANES. – The Kybalion.

Gender in this sense means relating to generation or creation, not sexual attributes. This law is true not only on the physical plane, but on the mental and spiritual planes as well.

Whenever anything is created, produced or manifested on any plane, the principle of gender exists. The Masculine Gender is always in the direction of giving out or expressing - using your will. The Feminine Gender is always in the direction of receiving impressions – new thoughts, concepts and ideas. Imagination is a feminine dimension of the Principle of Gender. Taking action is a masculine dimension of the Principle of Gender.

It is important that you balance these two forces of Masculine and Feminine Genders. Without the Feminine, the Masculine is apt to act without restraint, order, or reason, resulting in chaos. If you polarize yourself with only the Feminine, you will find yourself reflecting all the time, dreaming and not actually doing anything, which will result in your stagnation. When you have both the masculine and feminine genders present and working in balance within you, you will get thoughtful action that will breed success.

To the pure, all things are pure; to the base, all things are base. This law is not about lust, perversion or degraded teachings. - The Kybalion.

Example: When you come up with a good idea and talk about it (the feminine polarity of gender) nothing really happens – but the idea is the starting place of creation. Next you start to do research, make telephone calls and set up meetings with investors or ways to manufacture what you want to create. You look at places to rent and start the business – you make sacrifices to make it happen (the masculine polarity of gender). You need both – the creative (feminine) and the causation (masculine) to make it happen.

MINI EXERCISE:

Practice and Meditate Upon the Following:

Be conscious of all the words you speak, day in and day out, so that you understand what you are creating. It is better not to speak than to speak a harmful word. (Mentalism)

Any word can be divided within itself. When you speak one way but feel another, your words (your creation signals) become confused and create a fog. (Polarity) It is important to speak with clear intention to crystallize your words – that means your mind, body and spirit must be in alignment. Be responsible for your creation of your life situation.

Sometimes it is preferable to admit your negative and lower self motives. This implies an attitude of truthfulness, humility, courage, and faith. Your hidden lower self dwells in wishful thinking, pride, fear of exposing what is not perfect, laziness and lack of faith. (Rhythm) Better to be truthful than to lie to yourself.

There is a direct linkage between the power of your words and your self-value. (Correspondence)

The words that are spoken out loud and the words that are not heard outside your ear are equally powerful. In fact, your recurring thoughts (silent words) can have roots, and be far stronger than the everyday chatter of your spoken word. A thought can be challenged, debated and corrected to help you Achieve Your TRUE Potential. (Gender)

Every personality is an expression of a different kind of energy – a different kind of element. Feelings have different types of energy, as do all mental, physical, and spiritual levels. To feel and recognize the power and energy of the words you use is very important. (Vibration)

Only when you begin to clearly look at the chain and connection between your words and your experiences will you gain a deep understanding and security that you are indeed part of the creative process. (Cause and Effect)

When you experience a creation that is undesirable and limiting, you must look and challenge the word responsible for this state. (Mentalism)

When you do not give, you cannot receive. Giving and receiving are one. Taking is giving (you give the opportunity to someone else to give and help) if it comes with sincerity and thankfulness, rather than grabbing or cheating. (Mentalism, Correspondence, Vibration, Polarity, Rhythm, Cause and Effect, Gender)

The Echo

Where Am I?

Where Am I?

I am here.

I am here.

I love you.

I love you.

FACE YOUR SELF EXERCISES

You are a Divine Being walking among other Divine Beings. You have the ability to engage in highly creative activities. The work of Face Your Self is meant to be self-empowering and self-inspiring. It will put you in contact with divinity and assist you to live your life consistent with cosmic laws and serve mankind and the natural world. It is important for you to gather and focus your energies on your mental and physical planes as well as the astral and etheric planes in order for you to materialize your dreams and purposes.

Your words are a creative agent. They are a point of explosion of psychic nuclear power. Your words create movement and a chain reaction of one link logically affecting and affecting the next (Cause and Effect). Each word has feeling, attitude, will and intentionality behind it (Polarity and Vibration). Your words are the sum total of your beliefs, and any time you speak, you speak that belief, whether you are conscious of it or not (Mentalism). Your words influence and create your world (Correspondence). When you change the polarity of your words, the rhythm of your life will become natural and you will feel complete and balanced (Gender).

EXERCISE #1:
CREATION: THE POWER OF YOUR WORDS

You can intentionally create when your words and thoughts carry clear intent.

OBJECTIVE:

You will be empowered by the intentional use of your words and thoughts.

You will develop a deeper understanding of the seven principles noted in this appendix through using your words.

WHAT YOU WILL NEED:

Your Magic Notebook
A pen or pencil

EXERCISE:

1. Sit in your quiet space, and write out an affirmation about your life right now.

Some examples are:

I am a success right here and now.
All good is always coming to me.
I am healthy and strong.

I am a friend to all I meet.
I have many friends who love me.

2. Take that affirmation and make it into a personal mantra for one week.

- Say it to yourself while you are brushing your teeth, while you are driving your car and before you sit down to eat.
- Say it to yourself whenever you find a little doubt in your heart.
- Say it to yourself whenever you are faced with uncertainty.
- If any doubt comes up – look at that doubt – delve into that doubt and find the root of that doubt. Reread this book if you feel it may help you.

EXERCISE # 2:

UNDERSTAND YOUR SELF THROUGH THE NATURAL ELEMENTS

The reality is that you are a natural being existing and living in an ocean of cycles, dimensions and vibrations of magnetism, light, sound, color, and geometric structure.

Studying the four elements in nature (Air, Water, Fire, Earth) is parallel in alignment to Principle # 2: Correspondence. By understanding the nature of the four elements (how they act and behave), you will better understand yourself (how you act and behave). The Native Americans created their medicine wheel based upon the four elements and directions of North, East, South, and West.

Balancing the four elements in your mind, body and spirit, as pure energy, brings you astral equilibrium and further psychological understanding of your self.

Air has a mental activity and can be used for creating and developing new ideas.

Water has a strong relationship to your emotions and can be used for purification.

Fire has a spiritual dimension. It affects your life force and can be used for inspiration.

Earth relates to our physical self and can be connected to wisdom and power.

The following is a chart which outlines the positive and negative aspects of the four elements: Fire, Air, Water, and Earth.

A THOUGHT TO REMEMBER:

Everything has a duality - even the elements.

Look to see how they relate to your emotions and wellbeing, and help you Face Your Self.

ELEMENTS

Fire: (inspiration/spiritual)
Jealously, hatred, unproductiveness, anger, vindictiveness, irascibility
Activity, enthusiasm, firmness, courage, daring

Air: (new ideas)
Frivolity, boasting, squandering, gossiping, lust
Joy, dexterity, kindness, optimism, diligence

Water: (purification)
Indifference, laziness, frigidity, compliance, shyness, instability
Modesty, compassion, tranquility, tenderness, forgiveness

Earth: (wisdom)
Laziness, melancholy, irregularity, dullness
Respect, endurance, conscientiousness, sobriety, punctuality, thoroughness, responsibility

Objective:
You will better understand how the elements are expressing in your mind, body and spirit, and ultimately be able to use them to achieve lasting balance.

What you will need:
Your Magic Notebook
A pen or pencil

EXERCISE:

1. List as many of your ugly character traits that you can think of: failures, habits, passions, intentions, etc. Be as hard and as merciless as you can – the more you can think of the better for you. Do this for a week or two and do not proceed until after this

period. This is very important work to do if you want to achieve equilibrium – without it you will not progress. You must know your dark side.

To aid you in this process:

   In quiet meditation go back to the times of past situations and reflect on how you behaved in each instance. Make a note about your faults or frailties.
Assign each of your faults to one of the above elements.

2. After doing this for at least one week, make three columns in your magic notebook:
   Column # 1: Your biggest failures – those which influence you strongest and which happen with the slightest opportunity.
   Column # 2: Those faults ,which happen less frequently.
   Column # 3: Those faults that happen every now and then.

3. Repeat the above steps 1 and 2 with your good qualities.

4. Next, take two pages in your notebook and write White or Yin on the top of one page where you will list your higher vibrational characteristics and Black or Yang on the top of the other page where you will list your lower vibrational qualities.

Use these pages as psycho-mirrors to remember and be clear on knowing your good or bad qualities. These mirrors will aid you in easily recognizing which element is prevailing in you. Through awareness of any imbalances, you can consciously bring your thought and actions into balance using the elements and their positive qualities. This is necessary for you to attain balance and for your further development.

In working and learning from the natural elements, it is recommended that you spend time with nature. Surround yourself with natural fabrics and home goods. Surround yourself with natural people. Eat natural foods and exercise your body in a natural way. Your best teacher is Nature. With Nature, you can know all of the wisdom of the ages (the law of correspondence) - learn from Nature. Nature is your best teacher (Introduction to this book). Unless you know something for yourself – you know nothing. Spend time with Nature to be healthy, wealthy and wise.

A THOUGHT TO REMEMBER:

Nature can seem nasty at times – but it is not – all is in right order. Look at a rock or a tree and see perfection in the reality of its truthfulness.

Imagination is more important than knowledge. I never came upon my discoveries through the process of rational thinking. Albert Einstein

WITHIN YOU WITHOUT YOU

Songwriter: George Harrison

We were talking-about the space between us all
And the people-who hide themselves behind a wall of illusion
Never glimpse the truth-then it's far too late-when they pass away.
We were talking-about the love we all could share-when we find it
To try our best to hold it there-with our love
With our love-we could save the world-if they only knew.
Try to realize it's all within yourself
No-one else can make you change
And to see you're really only very small,
And life flows ON within you and without you.
We were talking-about the love that's gone so cold and the people,
Who gain the world and lose their soul-
They don't know-they can't see-are you one of them?
When you've seen beyond yourself-then you may find, peace of mind,
Is waiting there-
And the time will come when you see
we're all one, and life flows on within you and without you.

May you be guided by the truth of your heart, may you see beauty reflected back to you wherever you look, and may all want to rest their head in the good of your arms.

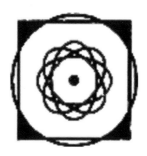